C000244477

ISSUES IN POLITICAL THEORY

Political Theory has undergone a remarkable development in recent years. From a state in which it was once declared dead, it has come to occupy a central place in the study of Politics. Both political ideas and the wide-ranging arguments to which they give rise are now treated in a rigorous, analytical, fashion, and political theorists have contributed to disciplines as diverse as economics, sociology and law. These developments have made the subject more challenging and exciting, but they have also added to the difficulties of students and others coming to the subject for the first time. Much of the burgeoning literature in specialist books and journals is readily intelligible only to those who are already well-versed in the subject.

Issues in Political Theory is a series conceived in response to this situation. It consists of a number of detailed and comprehensive studies of issues central to Political Theory which take account of the latest developments in scholarly debate. While making original contributions to the subject, books in the series are written especially for those who are new to Political Theory. Each volume aims to introduce its readers to the intricacies of a fundamental political issue and to help them find their way through the detailed, and often complicated, argument that issue has attracted.

PETER JONES
ALBERT WEALE

ISSUES IN POLITICAL THEORY

Series editors: PETER JONES and ALBERT WEALE

Published
David Beetham: **The Legitimation of Power**
Tom Campbell: **Justice** (2nd edn)
John Horton: **Political Obligation**
Peter Jones: **Rights**
Albert Weale: **Democracy**

Forthcoming
Raymond Plant: **Equality**
Hillel Steiner: **Utilitarianism**

Justice

Second Edition

Tom Campbell

© Tom D. Campbell 1988, 2001

All rights reserved. No reproduction, copy or transmission of
this publication may be made without written permission.

No paragraph of this publication may be reproduced, copied or
transmitted save with written permission or in accordance with
the provisions of the Copyright, Designs and Patents Act 1988,
or under the terms of any licence permitting limited copying
issued by the Copyright Licensing Agency, 90 Tottenham Court
Road, London W1P 0LP.

Any person who does any unauthorised act in relation to this
publication may be liable to criminal prosecution and civil
claims for damages.

The author has asserted his right to be identified as the author of
this work in accordance with the Copyright, Designs and Patents
Act 1988.

First edition 1988
Reprinted 3 times
Second edition 2001

 Published by
MACMILLAN PRESS LTD
Houndmills, Basingstoke, Hampshire RG21 6XS
and London
Companies and representatives
throughout the world

ISBN 0–333–91421–X hardcover
ISBN 0–333–91422–8 paperback

A catalogue record for this book is available
from the British Library.

This book is printed on paper suitable for recycling and
made from fully managed and sustained forest sources.

10 9 8 7 6 5 4 3 2 1
10 09 08 07 06 05 04 03 02 01

Printed in China

 Published in the United States of America by
ST. MARTIN'S PRESS, LLC
Scholarly and Reference Division
175 Fifth Avenue, New York, N.Y. 10010

ISBN 0–312–23619–0 hardcover
ISBN 0–312–23620–4 paperback

To Molly, who doesn't listen patiently

Contents

Preface and Acknowledgements

The material for this book has been gathered over many years' teaching and research, mainly in the University of Glasgow, in the Departments of Politics, Moral Philosophy, and Jurisprudence, and more recently in the Faculty of Law at The Australian National University. My debts to colleagues and students at these institutions are too numerous to mention.

While the author's preference for a desert-based analysis of justice will be evident to the reader, the book surveys a wide range of contemporary theories, including those which are deeply critical of the very idea of justice. Considerable attention is given to the practical applications of these theories in specific areas of political and legal interest as well as to the ideological associations of competing theories. A thematic concern of the book is to demonstrate how traditional analyses of justice can be reconfigured so as to address current social and political problems.

The aim of the second edition is to clarify and extend the original text and give more detailed attention to libertarianism, communitarianism and feminism. There are now two introductory chapters and a new concluding chapter. Bruce Ackerman's discussion of neutrality has been absorbed into other chapters. New chapters deal with the work of Robert Nozick, whose contribution has proved remarkably enduring, Iris Marion Young, a feminist who takes justice seriously, and Jürgen Habermas, whose recent work is having a major impact on political theories of law and justice.

Canberra, December 1999   *Tom Campbell*

1 What is Justice?

Justice is one of those core moral and political terms which claim universal importance and feature centrally in all social and political theories. Indeed, for many theorists it is the prime and overarching concept of public life, although it is increasingly overshadowed by the global attention being accorded to human rights, a phenomenon which is discussed in the concluding chapter of this work. This almost universal popularity breeds a diversity of analyses and applications of justice which can bewilder and discourage those who seek precision and clarity in their approach to political issues. Disagreement abounds over what it means to call a situation just or unjust, what sort of actions are just or unjust and how we should go about settling these controversial matters. This book seeks to provide a helpful map of this contentious territory, exploring and testing those claims to universal value which the language of justice evokes and suggesting how we might arrive at our own views on what justice is about and what sort of situations are just or unjust.

In this chapter I deal with the largely conceptual question of what is distinctive about the discourse of justice. First, I note the range of social and political contexts in which justice features and draw attention to the ideological associations of different approaches to justice. Then I offer a preliminary analysis of justice in terms of merit, which involves a combination of the notions of equality and desert, and dissociate this analysis from the common assumption that justice is by definition necessarily the prime social and political value. Finally, I explore the extent to which all issues of justice are about distribution, concluding that justice can usefully be tied to distribution in a broad sense which goes beyond the allocation of economic and political benefits and burdens and includes non-comparative, retributive and rectificatory principles as well.

In Chapter 2, I take these issues further in relation to the more substantive question: what is just? There I raise general issues about how, if at all, we can go about arriving at correct answers to such questions and contrast the liberal tradition, which relates justice to universal individual rights and the limitations these place on government power, with the recently formulated communitarian response to liberalism that situates the discourse of justice more in the ongoing social and political life of actual communities.

Chapter 3 relates the analysis of justice to the idea of rights in general and human rights in particular. This paves the way for a consideration of the rights-oriented libertarian theory of Robert Nozick, as the first of a number of influential and important theories of justice which I use to illustrate the range of conceptual and substantive views of justice together with their applications to specific areas of political and social concern. These theories represent only samples of what might be covered in a book on justice but they represent the main competing analyses on offer in contemporary political theory.

Arguments about justice and injustice feature centrally in current political debates concerning law, social policy and economic organisation. Inequalities of income and employment opportunities, disparities in property ownership, deprivations which arise from unemployment, disablement, illness and old age, uncompensated injuries sustained through accident or as a result of the criminal behaviour of others and the sufferings of the victims of class, race, gender and state oppression – all these, and much more, are routinely denounced as not simply wrong, but unjust. Ultimately any theory of justice should formulate the criteria we should use to identify what sort of situations are properly described as just or unjust, thus answering the question 'what is just?' Our first and preliminary task is to figure out what the language of justice is about. This involves identifying the values and assumptions which feature distinctively in the discourse of justice generally and enable us to distinguish the discourse of justice from that of other social and political values, such as efficiency, autonomy, equality, dignity, humanity and love.

The roots of justice

The extensive variety, internal complexity and long history of the ideas which are associated with the notion of justice make many different perceptions of justice seem – at least initially – equally plausible. This is well illustrated by the common beliefs that justice is primarily a negative, conservative, minimal, purely public but, within its sphere, overriding virtue, beliefs which are all illuminating in their way but can be highly misleading and contentious.

Those who hold that it is essentially a negative virtue hold that justice is largely concerned with how people should *not* treat each other. There is some basis for the belief that it is the sense of *in*justice or grievance that is at the core of our ideas about justice and explains its powerful emotive force. Justice is normally the language of complaint, and sometimes of revenge. It is in resented deprivation and the consciousness of having been wronged that much justice talk is rooted. Justice is therefore often analysed as a negative virtue whose demands can be met simply by doing nothing beyond refraining from injuring others. According to one contemporary theorist, 'the grammar of justice is intimately connected with the invocation of justice when we object to wrong' and hence to feelings of indignation and abhorrence (Wolgast, 1987, p.xii). On this view, justice, in so far as it is a positive or action-requiring virtue, is about righting wrongs through punishment, ensuring compensation for victims, or in some other way responding appropriately to the perpetration of injustice. This explains why theories of justice throughout the centuries tend to reflect the perceived injustices of the time, be they related to property, gender, race or power.

Associated with the negative view of justice as essentially having to do with injustice is the assumption that justice is a purely conservative value. The idea of injustice is closely associated with reactions of disappointment to unfulfilled expectations. Hence justice, at least in its negative expressions, can have strong conservative implications in that it seeks to sustain the status quo in society against destructive and disorderly intrusions. Thus, justice is often taken to require keeping within the rules of established social relationships, treating everyone in accordance with the expectations that have been legitimated by customary arrangements, conventions and laws, and putting right any deviations from accepted social norms.

However, most worked-out views as to what constitutes injustice involve a more substantial vision of justice with a positive element that requires action which goes beyond putting right the wrongs that have been done and includes promoting an ideal of just human relationships as part of a harmonious and healthy society. Reformist political programmes, which highlight novel grievances or extend traditional expectations to other social groups, standardly appeal to a community's sense of justice and injustice. Established social rules and laws are not immune to the critique of injustice. There are reformist as well as conservative notions of justice and there are positive (or active) as well as negative (or passive) notions of justice, which commit their users to bring about admirable social arrangements.

Other conceptual associations of justice are founded on the fact that justice is a standard ingredient of the language of legitimacy. Political regimes use their role in furthering the cause of justice as a central basis for the justification of their right to rule, while the perpetration and protection of injustice by governments is a common justification for civil disobedience and political revolution. In this context justice, as distinct from benevolence or utility, often represents the minimal requirements for the vindication of political power. This fits its perceived importance in the hierarchy of values. Nevertheless justice is also used to express perfectionist ideals about the best forms of human relationships in the most utopian of societies which no actual state can be expected to achieve. The concepts of full equality of opportunity and fair rewards for socially beneficial effort are examples of aspirational ideals of justice. States which are way beyond the threshold of legitimacy may still fall short in terms of justice and the concept of justice has applications far beyond identifying the threshold of political legitimacy. There are maximalist as well as minimalist notions of justice, as is well illustrated by the socialist maxim 'from each according to their ability, to each according to their needs' (see Chapter 8).

A strong case can also be made for the assumption that justice is primarily a public or political virtue in that it concerns the conduct and objectives of states, officials and public bodies rather than purely economic or domestic matters, which constitute the private sphere. Hence the association of justice with law and public policy. Indeed, justice is normally considered to be *the* legal virtue and largely out of place in personal relationships. And yet, the relevance of justice is not confined to narrowly political matters. Families, friendship groups and voluntary associations as well as courts and governments can be just and unjust, although this may not be central to their objectives. Further, it is a matter for investigation whether justice in the small group has any bearing on justice in the state, as it is whether justice in the law is the same sort of thing as justice in the society as a whole, but it is clear that justice has significant applications in all these areas. There are social as well as political notions of justice. Indeed, criticism of restricting the discourse of justice to the 'public' sphere is a frequent theme of socialist and feminist theorists.

Another common assumption is that justice is peremptory, or, in technical philosophical jargon, deontological, or 'right in itself' irrespective of its consequences. Indeed, justice is often seen as a particularly forceful deontic or imperative norm that does not permit of delay, deviation or compromise. Justice, it is often asserted, must be done and be done in full before any other objectives or values can be implemented. This assumption of the primacy and imperiousness of justice sometimes goes with the view that it is possible to be precise about what justice requires in a way that is not feasible with other more expansive and intangible virtues. The peremptory character of justice fits easily with the notion of justice as a minimal and negative virtue according to which justice is maintained as long as people do not injure others in specified ways. More positive and open-ended approaches to justice accommodate to the view that justice is simply one virtue amongst others, and one which may have to give way to what are, on occasions, more pressing and important values, such as liberty or loyalty, particularly outside the spheres of law and politics. Yet even these more diffuse analyses of justice do not do away with its deontic form.

Many other perspectives on justice reveal assumptions which are in tension or outright conflict with each other. Justice may be viewed as an individual or as a group matter. It may be tied to law or dissociated from all coercive relationships. It may be viewed as the expression or as the antithesis of love and concern. It may be associated with decision-making in accordance with general principles, or with careful consideration of the 'merits' of each particular case. This kaleidoscope of diverse images presents a confusing and often incoherent picture of justice. In this chapter I examine this bewildering landscape in order to make the discourse of justice more intelligible and useful for the purposes of contemporary political analysis and choice. To this end, first I note the ideological associations of different theories of justice and then commend a relatively neutral analysis of the concept of justice in terms of equality and desert, but reject the common view that justice is always the prime social and political value. Finally, I explore the contention that justice has primarily a distributive focus.

Justice and ideology

Behind and beyond the differing glimpses of justice outlined above stand competing political and social ideologies, different world-views which combine basic value commitments with a set of assumptions about human nature and society. Ideologies, such as liberalism, socialism and feminism, have a major effect on what it is that justice is thought to be about and why it is or is not significant. Justice takes on different guises in different political ideologies and these ideologies adapt the notion of justice so as to fit more readily into their preferred outlook.

Justice may also be seen as ideological in a more specific and derogatory sense, popularised by Marx, according to which it offers a phoney vision of an ideal situation of equality and fairness which actually masks and perpetrates oppressive power relationships. It is part of the Marxist theory of exploitation that the class with eco-nomic power in a particular type of society is sustained in power partly by the 'false consciousness' of those classes who mistakenly accept the ideals of the ruling class as representing the interests of all classes. Thus justice, in a capitalist system, is the ideology of the ruling class in the sense that it represent the interests of capitalists and falsely purports to legitimate existing social and economic relationships as being objectively in the interests of all classes. A similar association between ideas of justice and the phenomenon of male dominance is found in many feminist theories of justice.

While there is no doubt that all moral and political concepts are part of the culture and rhetoric which sustain existing power rela-tionships, I have already noted that the language of justice is fre-quently used to criticise existing power relationships, making it implausible to argue that justice always disguises legitimation of the status quo, although there is no doubt that it frequently does so. However, all operative theories of justice are ideological in the weak sense that they are embedded in a particular world-view. Thus, it is illuminating to compare libertarian, welfare liberal and communit-arian ideologies of justice, even if it turns out that they are not all equally self-serving.

Libertarian justice stresses individual rights as the irreducible basis for social organisation, with justice being a matter of each individual getting that to which they are entitled by virtue of their exercise of these rights. This is the approach adopted by Robert Nozick (see Chapter 3). In content such rights cluster around the idea of the autonomy and independence of each individual and the premise that all individuals may choose to do what they like as long as they do not infringe the rights of others. For libertarians, justice is a normative structure within which individuals can pursue their own goals without infringing the rights of others. It is limited, precise and stringent. Libertarian justice has more to do with freedom than equality, for although there is a strong presupposition of formal equality whereby persons are equal with respect to their equal possession of identical rights, there is no suggestion that the exercise of these equal rights will or should result in anything like an actual equality of social and economic positions, indeed the opposite is assumed.

The ideology of welfare liberalism, of which John Rawls may be taken as a mild example (see Chapter 5), also gives central place to individual rights, but is more concerned with justice as a matter of the general distribution of benefits and burdens in a society in which outcomes as much as process are important variables. Here 'welfare' refers to the totality of the happiness and well-being of all persons and particularly to the alleviation of the sufferings of the poor and disadvantaged. In this ideology justice is focused on the distribution of welfare but is quite open-ended with respect to what form that distribution should take or to what range of social and economic benefits and burdens to which it applies. It is individualistic with respect to its commitment to the value of each distinct person but holistic in the way it seeks to go about achieving justice through the management of a society to produce a fair overall distribution of goods and evils within a system of equal basic rights.

In this respect welfare liberalism has affinities to the moral theory of utilitarianism, according to which the ultimate moral standard is maximal utility, so that moral decisions come down to calculating what makes for the greatest happiness of the greatest number, which in practice means prioritising the relief of suffering. Equality of distribution has to be seen in the context of maximising the realisation of everyone's desires, with equality of distribution coming in as one way of producing the quantitatively best outcome. If distributions are considered just in so far as they are effective in reducing suffering, welfare liberalism merges with what might be called liberal socialism. However, as we shall see, Rawls is concerned to distance himself from a purely utilitarian philosophy.

It should be noted that utilitarianism, as a moral theory stressing the significance of the consequences of human actions and

organisations, can underpin ideologies with very different outcomes
in which the stress on equality, beyond the assertion that each
individual counts for one in the calculus of utility, is not seen as
having egalitarian implications. Instead, the emphasis is placed on
individual liberty in contexts where there are protected opportunities for unfettered exchange between individuals as the principal
mechanism for attaining the greatest happiness of the greatest number. We may see this form of utilitarianism at work in economic
theories of justice, such as Richard Posner's (see Chapter 6), and
various forms of political ideology which are sometimes referred to
as 'economic rationalism'. In this guise, utilitarianism features as an
alternative to Nozick's scheme of rights as the justification for
libertarian views on the limited role of the state.

Both libertarianism and Rawls's welfare liberalism rest on strong
assertions of individual independence and autonomy as the bedrock
of justice. In this they may be contrasted with a range of ideologies
that stress the priority of society, community or state over the
conception of individuals as units which are detachable from their
cultural context. 'Communitarian' is a convenient and currently
popular label to identify positions which seek to get away from
the stark individualism of individual rights and regard all values
as embedded in a particular social or community culture, the understanding being that all cultures, even individualistic ones, construct
a set of values and expectations within which all human interaction
takes place. 'Justice', on this communitarian view, refers to the
proper functioning of a particular type of society in accordance
with its own values and world-view.

As a viewpoint, communitarianism is distinguished by its rejection of the more extreme forms of individualism according to which
societies are simply organisations to promote the interests of individuals whose values and significance are established independently
of the society of which they are a part. Communitarianism becomes
more ideological in a narrow political sense when it adopts either
the form of a traditional conservative commitment to sustaining
existing social relationships, or the form of a proactive movement
committed to the creation of an ideal of genuine community. Proactive forms of ideological communitarianism may take various
guises, including visions of a socialist utopia in which justice is
done in that there is actual substantive equality brought about
by seeing to it that people have what they need to be full and
equal members of their society, or a feminist ideal in which gender

oppression is eliminated and cooperative and caring values dominate.

These and other contrasting ideological approaches to justice are all reflected in the particular theories discussed in this book. Thus Nozick and, on some interpretations, Dworkin are readily identifiable as libertarian. Rawls is a modified welfare liberal. Posner is an economic utilitarian. Marx is a type of communitarian. Young may be seen as a feminist with both liberal and communitarian elements. These ideological divisions are important for the understanding and interpretation of theories of justice, but they are not the prime focus of this book. Rather the object is to offer analytical expositions and philosophical critiques of the principal contending theories which have most relevance to the contemporary world.

It is not denied that political divergencies often underlie the juxtaposed ideas of justice as negative or positive, conservative or reformist, minimalist or maximalist. And it is acknowledged that conceptual analysis of key political concepts, such as justice, cannot be ultimately insulated from ideological disagreement. Nevertheless, there is much to be gained by way of clarity and understanding for a philosophical discussion which initially puts to one side overt ideological disagreement and seeks to work on the concepts, distinctions and presuppositions involved in different theories of justice. When, in due course, we come to take a position on ideological issues, we can then aspire to make choices which are lucid and informed. Approached in this way philosophical discussions of such concepts as justice may reveal that conceptual frameworks may often be detached from their ideological origins and deployed in new ways within different ideological frameworks. This opens up the range of choices available to us as we struggle with the ultimately personal matter of articulating our own moral and political outlook.

A meritorian analysis

Any account of justice must be able to take account of the immense variety and complexity of its meanings, applications and ideological associations, and seek to uncover such unity as may underlie its different political manifestations without minimising the extent of significant disagreement. In the absence of the naive belief that there is a 'true' or 'correct' meaning of 'justice', we must proceed by elucidating the actual deployment of the language of justice in all its variety to the point where stipulative choices have to be made in order to arrive at a clear and coherent set of conceptual distinctions which point up the nature of the political questions which are at issue. There may be no one correct analysis of justice but there are certainly more or less useful ones.

In these circumstances it is tempting to fall back on the technique of outlining an exceedingly vague and catch-all analysis which captures all the varied uses of justice as the term is actually used and then to move rapidly on and distinguish the varying concep-tions of justice which embody the differing and competing moral views which coexist within the catch-all umbrella concept. The *concept* is then taken to provide the 'meaning' of justice, while the *conceptions* enunciate the evaluative criteria variously deployed to determine that certain types of situation are just or unjust. Thus the concept of justice may be analysed as a set of principles for assessing social and political institutions, while conceptions of justice repres-ent differing views on the proper content of these principles.

Rawls, for instance, sees justice as a set of principles for 'assigning rights and duties in the basic institutions of society' and defining 'the appropriate distribution of the benefits and burdens of social co-operation' (1971, p.4). In this context, the concept of justice means 'a proper balance between competing claims', while a con-ception of justice is 'a set of related principles for identifying the relevant considerations which determine this balance' (p.10).

Alternatively, since Rawls's starting-point does not take in all the uses to which the language of justice has been put, we might, in preference, adopt the more traditional approach according to which the concept of justice is defined as 'giving to each his [or her] due', with rival conceptions of justice indicating what is to count as a person's due in accordance with differing moral outlooks. Thus Miller (1976) holds that 'the just state of affairs is that in which each individual has exactly those benefits and burdens which are due to him' (p.20) and goes on to say that 'the important questions about justice emerge when we try to settle what a person's "due" actually means' (p.24).

According to either view, it may be assumed that analyses of the concept of justice tell us what justice is all about in a detached and philosophical manner, while analyses of the differing conceptions of justice state what justice is in concrete terms and so enter the disputed arena of contentious and ideological political debate. In this way, utilising the concept/conceptions distinction is a common and to some extent an illuminating and unavoidable strategy, but it has certain drawbacks, which, as we shall see, are exacerbated by current assumptions about the primacy of justice as a political value.

In particular, there is a danger that the concept of justice is rendered too broad and its distinctive moral territory is obscured. This happens when the concept/conceptions distinction becomes disengaged from the actual uses of the language of justice in the debates from which the conventional analyses take their initial material and impetus. This is particularly so at the 'concept' level which often fails to capture the distinctive content of the consciousness of justice in contrast to other ideals, such as humanity or the pursuit of happiness. Indeed any analysis which sets out to capture the full range of uses to which the language of justice is put may turn out to be unmanageably open-ended, taking in the entire compendium of fundamental political concepts. This characteristic of over-extendedness, which tends to be the fate of all political terms with essentially favourable emotive connotations, is a common and unfortunate result of the deployment of the concept/conceptions distinction.

In order to clarify the nature of political disagreements, it is helpful to develop a set of concepts which are as distinct and precise as possible. It is therefore important, when analysing the concept of justice, not to cast its net too wide, so that justice becomes indistinguishable from the sum of social and political values. This can be done without ignoring the full range of justice discourse as it is applied in different spheres, provided that, in each sphere, we distinguish broad or loose uses from those which seek to use 'justice' in its particular connotations. Here it is best to follow Aristotle in Book V of his *Nicomachean Ethics* where, having distinguished between justice as the 'complete virtue' and justice as 'a part of virtue', he goes on to concentrate on the latter.

Further, the concept/conceptions distinction can be misleading if based on the assumption that there is a clear line of demarcation between a morally neutral, if highly general, concept of justice on the one hand and specific conceptions which embody substantive moral interpretations of the general concept on the other hand. This strategy does not allow for the possibility that the concept of justice itself represents a distinguishable moral point of view which puts limitations on what can reasonably count as a conception of justice. Thus, serious consideration has to be given to the possibility, for instance, that justice is an inherently legalistic or liberal or masculine concept. On the other hand, there is a danger of arriving at a restrictive analysis of the concept of justice which excludes rival political or philosophical views on an arbitrary basis. Avoidance of excessive generality in the pursuit of a relatively value-neutral concept of justice as a partial political virtue may be achieved by paying close attention to the uses of the language of justice which enable us to pick out those instances where 'justice' is used in a sense which is clearly intended to distinguish it from other values. We must be aware, however, that the linguistic usages to which we appeal in order to establish a very specific concept of justice may be tendentious or dated, reflecting the experience and bias of the philosopher and their community rather than the alleged neutrality of ordinary and typical discourse. Analyses of the concept of justice which dictate its specific meaning may often be no more than devices for putting one set of values beyond the scope of critical evaluation.

For these reasons I adopt in this book a two-level analysis of theories of justice. At the first level, those who are generally regarded amongst English-speaking philosophers as important and original theorists of justice in recent times are presented in their own terms and in accordance with their own assumptions about the meaning and scope of justice. None have been excluded on the grounds that their theories are not really about justice but about something else which is mistakenly called justice, although such brutal treatment might have philosophical justification in some cases. At a second level, however, the theories presented are subjected to criticism from the point of view of a particular and controversial analysis of justice as a specific rather than an all-encompassing social and political value.

The specific analysis I have adopted at the second level is a combination of what I call equalitarian and meritorian elements. By 'equalitarian' I mean involving a commitment to a substantive idea of equality which approximates to what is standardly referred to as egalitarianism, according to which every person ought to enjoy essentially the same or equivalent circumstances, but in this case is a presumption which may be overridden by considerations of desert or merit. I call this presumption 'prior equality' to indicate that it is the starting-point from which departures must be justified. By a 'meritorian' analysis of justice I mean one which accommodates considerations of individual worthiness as a necessary and prime factor in the determination of what is just. It follows that there is a necessary connection between justice and desert, first in the broad sense that justice in all its aspects has to do with treating persons as being of equal worth in the sense that their experiences and actions as responsible sentient creatures have the same intrinsic importance, and second in a narrower sense that such treatment permits and requires dealing with people differently in accordance with their deserts, that is, what is due to them in virtue of their conduct. Using the concept/conceptions distinction, the desert (or perhaps the equalitarian–meritorian) analysis is that the concept of justice assumes prior equality as the initial benchmark and requires that departures from this benchmark reflect the deserts of those involved, while differing conceptions of justice have to do with what counts as desert. This develops into the general contention that a state of affairs is just if and only if it is one which accurately reflects the equal worth and unequal worthiness of sentient and responsible persons.

Prioritising justice

The apparently traditionalist analysis of justice in terms of equality and desert is rendered unexpectedly open in its implications when it is dissociated from the common assumption that justice is necessarily the prime social value, even if only in matters of distribution. When conjoined with the now almost standard premise that justice is the prime value of sound social institutions, conceptions of justice become antagonists for ideological supremacy in a manner which distorts rather than clarifies the distinctiveness of justice-relevant considerations. If justice is defined as the priority political value, then whatever is adopted as a political priority automatically becomes dignified with the title of justice. On the other hand, if we take the view that the moral significance of justice in relation to other values is external to its analysis, and remains a matter for independent moral assessment – so that justice is not axiomatically given any special privileges in the competition for political primacy – then we can adopt a more dispassionate approach to the question of what justice is about. From this ideologically less pressured position it is plausible to say that the equalitarian–meritorian idea of justice captures most accurately the import of the language of justice in its distinctive uses, emphasising both equality and desert without committing us to the idea that either substantive equality or treatment in accordance with desert is an overriding social value.

However, to deny the political primacy of justice runs counter to the consensus of most contemporary theorists of justice in the liberal tradition. Justice is generally held to be second only to economic prosperity as the prime value of contemporary social and political organisation. Hence, the significance of arguments about justice as an 'essentially contested' concept which many different ideological positions wish to claim as their own and interpret in their own way. The popularity of justice as a political concept is reflected in Rawls's view that 'justice is the first virtue of social institutions, as truth is of systems of thought' (1971, p.3). In other words, whatever other moral values a society may seek to realise, it must first achieve justice. Although this position has been vigorously disputed by some recent theorists, notably Sandel (1982), who pioneered the 'communitarian' label, it is generally held that, at least in distributive matters, 'justice is a very important, perhaps the most important virtue displayed by a society' (Sadurski, 1985, p.12). Few take the line – which is canvassed in this book and has become more accepted since the publication of the first edition in 1988 – that not only is justice only one distributive consideration amongst others, but it is a factor which is not necessarily of the highest moral significance in politics. Once we give up the dogma that justice is constituted by the first and overriding principles of social and political organisation, then it may be possible to agree on a more reflective and specific working concept of justice which takes its place alongside overlapping and competing ideals such as liberty, utility and humanity. In general, however, it has to be accepted that for the vast majority of theorists justice is held to be the central and commanding concept of current mainstream normative political philosophy.

The priority of justice has become so much a common philosophical premise that it has for many theorists the feel of an analytic truth, but this is clearly a mistake. If 'justice' is *defined* as the overall standard of social rightness, then logically no other value can stand prior to justice since all relevant values are subsumed under its umbrella. But if justice is anything less than the sum or proper balance of all social values, its priority cannot simply be assumed, even in distributive matters. Judgements of priority are substantive moral opinions and the priority of justice as a particular value, once brought into the light of day, may be open to serious doubt. It is possible arbitrarily to define justice as the prime social value and then to go on and fill in its content with whatsoever is thought to be morally most important in social distribution, and perhaps also in the aggregation of benefits and burdens. But this dogmatic approach has the effect of undermining our efforts at conceptual clarification by removing the constraints imposed by the informal logic of the language of justice in actual political debate, thereby rendering dangerously misleading any subsequent appeals to our 'intuitions' about what we think is 'just' or 'unjust', for such intuitions are rooted in our operative rather than in our stipulative normative concepts. If, instead, we keep an open mind about the primacy of justice, it is possible to take a more relaxed and philosophical approach to the conceptual analysis of justice, for we will not, in arriving at this analysis, be committing ourselves at the same time to any particular political priorities. It is, for instance, possible to take the moral and political position that considerations of humanity, that is, concern for the suffering of human beings, should routinely take precedence over justice, that is, the requirement that treatment be in accordance with desert.

The non-prioritising equalitarian–meritorian analysis of justice sketched above is intended to provide a manageable standpoint for relating and criticising theories of justice. This analysis does not, however, serve either as the philosophical conclusion of this book or as its main organising principle. My objective is, rather, to identify the issues generally encompassed within the discourses of justice and survey the central competing theories of justice illustrated by reference to practical political disagreements.

Beyond distribution

Wider and less controversial than the meritorian analysis of justice is the common contention that the distinctive role of justice as a political value is that it concerns the evaluation of how benefits and burdens are distributed between individuals and social groups.

If we go back, for the moment, to the broad contention that justice is a matter of ensuring that each person receives that which they are due, a number of subdivisions of justice may be identified. Thus, the distinction between righting wrongs by punishment or compensation on the one hand and ensuring fair distributions of

benefits and burdens between social groups, races, classes or genders on the other is the core of the standard distinction between
corrective or remedial justice on the one hand and social or distributive justice on the other. While righting wrongs may be seen as
simply one part of ensuring fair distributions, it is common to
view these two types of justice as quite disparate and discontinuous,
the former having to do mainly with the law and the latter with
social policy, particularly taxation and welfare. It is part of the
objective of this introductory chapter to indicate that, on the
meritorian analysis of justice, there may be a deep conceptual connection between corrective and distributive justice.

The illustrative analyses of the concept of justice which have been
mentioned so far presuppose that justice, in all its aspects, has to do
with states of affairs which involve persons, or at least sentient
beings. Justice does not arise in our treatment of inanimate things,
and possibly not in our treatment of animals. Thus Raphael contends that 'justice and injustice, impartiality and partiality, arise
only in our treatment of human beings' (1970, p.177). Precisely
what it is about persons that makes them appropriate subjects for
justice is unclear. It may be their capacity for feeling pleasure and
pain; it may be their possession of reason and/or their capacity for
making choices and acting accordingly. It is part of a theory of
justice to identify the characteristics of human beings which are
logically presupposed by these conceptual limitations on the applicability of justice and make it clear why justice applies only to our
treatment of persons.

A useful starting-point here is the influential analysis of justice
provided by the Scottish Enlightenment philosopher David Hume
(1739). For Hume justice is a conventional device for preserving
social order by settling disputes between individuals who are making incompatible claims on relatively abundant but nevertheless
scarce resources. This means, in Hume's case, that justice is primarily concerned with a system of property, but his view can be more
generally stated in terms of the thesis that justice has to do with the
distribution of benefits and burdens, and in particular the distribution of scarce resources. Thus injustice may be regarded as a feature
of situations in which one person or group of persons wrongly
receives less or more than other persons or groups. This makes
justice essentially a matter of contested unfavourable comparisons
concerning the allocation of desirable and undesirable objects and
experiences in a society or group.

If we accept this view, we can then proceed to distinguish different types of justice according to the nature of the valued and disvalued things whose distribution is in question, whether they be economic (economic justice), political (political justice), educational (educational justice) or punitive (criminal justice), and then consider the nature of the 'justicising' (that is 'just-making') factors in each sphere of distributive concern.

This distributional definition of justice may be considered unduly restrictive in its exclusion of all aggregative or quantititive factors. Surely, it is argued, it matters how much there is to distribute as well as how the distribution is made. Indeed, for Hume, the significance of justice is the social utility of having a settled system of property rules. Perhaps for this reason, Rawls, who takes a basically distributive view of justice, argues that justice does involve the maximising of benefits so long as those worse off are advantaged to some degree. Others take a similar line, either in a weaker form, to the effect that maximising benefits is not in itself unjust, or in a stronger form, in which justice positively requires maximisation of benefits, always provided that certain distributive considerations are also taken into account.

The move to incorporate aggregation into the domain of justice can be seen as an example of the tendency to broaden the concept of justice so that it may take in all socially desirable objectives. Rawls himself, as we shall see, is somewhat cavalier with respect to the distinctive meaning of justice, and it is unsurprising therefore that the *prima facie* moral desirability of maximising goods and minimising evils should be brought into his overall scheme of justice. It is regrettable that this over-inclusive approach weakens a contrast which is one of the fixed points of most analyses of justice, namely the qualitative difference between considerations of justice and the principle of utility (that is, the principle that it is always right to maximise goods and minimise evils). One of the standard objections to utilitarianism is that it leads to distributions which are substantively unjust in that it permits sacrificing the interests of some individuals to promote the well-being of others if the latter gain more than the former lose. This fixed-point contrast between justice and utility is greatly weakened when aggregative considerations are introduced into the concept of justice. Rawls's line is not, however, fatal to the contrast between utility and justice, since the essence of utilitarianism is the claim that utility is the *sole* moral criterion, both of aggregation and distribution, and any view which limits the role of utility is, to that extent, non-utilitarian. Nevertheless it would seem better to claim that increasing the quantum of utility without reference to its distribution is not contrary to justice rather than to say that maximising utility is part of the justice ideal.

A more radical dispute about justice and distribution concerns the claim that it is fundamentally misleading to link justice to any distributive goal whatsoever. Thus Hayek (1976, pp.62–100) denies that the distribution of benefits and burdens is the consequence of a distributive process, and argues that the whole notion of social or distributive justice is therefore meaningless. No person or group, he contends, has made a general distribution of wealth or any other desirable or undesirable thing. It is therefore mistaken to speak of a distribution as being unjust, for only the actions of persons can be unjust. This, in turn, means that it is nonsense to speak of redistribution, since there never was in the first place any distribution which could serve as the basis for a revised distribution. He then goes on to argue that the attempt to impose patterns is inherently destructive of liberty. Thus, in a society where there is a free market in commodities, so that the overall outcome of economic activity is not the product of conscious choice but the unintended consequence of the innumerable discrete choices of individuals, there can be no use for the idea of redistributive justice and the attempt to impose a distribution is destructive of the freedom of the individual within that society.

Hayek's approach fails to make the important distinction between states of affairs which are consciously and deliberately brought about and those which *can* be intentionally altered, whatever their origin. There is an uncontroversial and choice-neutral sense of 'distribution' in which it refers simply to the quantity of any given variable belonging to a number of distinct individual entities or persons. And, where there is any possibility of a distribution which affects human welfare being changed by human action, then there may be reason to assess that state of affairs in terms of justice and injustice, or indeed in terms of balancing one liberty against another, so that appropriate remedial action may be attempted. Whether or not the original distribution is the intended result of human action is immaterial, unless we wish to go on and raise the separate question of who, if anyone, is responsible for its occurrence. Hayek is not, of course, unaware of this distinction. His position is rather that, in a liberal society, no one has the duty to promote any particular distribution, if only because this cannot be done without constant interference with individual liberty to an extent which would destroy the free market. This is an ideological position which gives priority to certain forms of liberty over justice and does not in itself render the idea of distributive justice meaningless in situations capable of being changed by political intervention. Furthermore it sometimes makes perfect sense to speak of situations as just or unjust when it is not within anyone's power even to change them. Value judgements do not always have to be directed at action in each instance of their use. They may also be used to assess the desirability of unalterable situations. Certainly it is possible to hold the pessimistic view that, in an imperfect world, justice is an ideal norm which is capable only of very limited implementation.

Nevertheless the idea that justice is essentially concerned with sustaining a particular pattern of distribution in desired goods and undesired ills does seem too constricting in so far as it ignores those theories which regard justice as having to do with acting in accordance with one's rights or entitlements. Thus, as I discuss in Chapter 3, Nozick (1974, Part II), argues that a person's possessions or 'holdings' are just if they are the result of legitimate actions, that is, actions which are in accordance with rules of ownership, transfer and the rectification of illegitimate transfers, whatever the distributive pattern which results. Without dropping the term 'distributive justice', Nozick favours what he calls a 'historical' rather than an 'end-state' approach to justice in which justice is a matter of how people came to possess their holdings, rather than a matter of measuring holdings against some characteristics of the holders – such as their needs or their moral merits – which would enable us to think in terms of a particular pattern as the end-state of the distributive process in which holdings are matched with the present characteristics of the individuals concerned.

It is relatively easy to brush aside as overly dogmatic the refusal to countenance the possibility of end-state views of justice which Nozick, like Hayek, rejects for what appear to be primarily ideological reasons, such as hostility to the welfare state. It is certainly possible for societies to strive to attain patterned distributions, even if they are largely unsuccessful and sometimes coercive in the pursuit of their chosen goals. It is less easy to rule out historical or entitlement theories as possible theories of justice on the grounds that they do not directly relate to distribution as a preconceived objective. However, there is no formal difficulty here since distributions, considered simply as patterns, may be characterised by variables which incorporate reference to past events, as when the relevant distributive characteristics are such historical facts as the occurrence of a promise or the receipt of a gift. Indeed this approach overlaps with some standard specifications of patterned end-states, particularly those which draw on the relative deserts of the holders of goods. To distribute according to merit and demerit is an inherently backward-looking exercise. Distributive definitions of justice require only that existing patterns may be altered in the direction establishing favoured patterns and need make no demand that these patterns be ahistorical in their variables.

Nevertheless, it may be true that the distributive paradigm does exclude important aspects of justice. Thus, as we will see in Chapter 9, Iris Marion Young considers that an overemphasis on distributive issues masks the significance of class, race and gender oppression as exemplars of injustice. Even if we stick with the view that justice in all its manifestations has to do with questions of distribution it may still be useful to distinguish something called 'distributive justice' from other types of justice, even though these other types have an essential connection with distributive matters. Thus, in a distinction which goes back to Book V of Aristotle's *Nicomachean Ethics,* we may contrast 'distributive justice' and 'corrective justice'. Distributive justice, in this narrow sense, refers to the distribution of benefits to social groups while corrective justice, in a broad sense, concerns punishments, compensation for injuries and unfair exchange (sometimes referred to as commutative justice). In recent times this distinction has been developed into a contrast between 'social justice' which has to do with 'the distribution of benefits and burdens throughout a society' and 'legal justice' which concerns 'punishment of wrongdoing and the compensation of injury through the creation and enforcement of a public set of rules' (Miller, 1976, p.22).

In Chapter 2, I argue that this distinction is highly misleading as a general account of the relationship between law and justice, if only because law is a key instrument in the determination of the overall distribution of benefits and burdens in a society. But it is often useful to give separate attention to those distributive issues which arise in situations where one individual has wronged or harmed another, and these issues do tend to be dealt with by distinct areas of law. The general characteristic of these situations is that some corrective procedure is in order, perhaps because of a specific demerit of an offending individual (as in the area of criminal law), or because of specific harm caused through the fault of another person which calls for compensation or redress (the law of tort or delict), or because of some unfairness or other impropriety which has arisen in the processes of exchange or other voluntary agreements in society (the law of contract). All these situations presuppose a specific interaction between individuals and the demand that something like the status quo, as it existed before that interaction, be restored. This is a limited matter of seeing justice done either between individuals or to individuals, and, perhaps for this reason, 'it seems proper to call this a form of individual, not of social justice' (Honoré, 1970, p.65) even if both involve a degree of redistribution of benefits and burdens.

It must be emphasised that the thesis that there is a close relationship between justice and distribution of benefits and burdens, so that the distinctiveness of justice relates at least primarily to its relevance to distributive matters, is disputed by those who concentrate their attention on issues of social, economic and political power, particularly when power is seen as a form of oppressive relationship. Thus Marx and Young are both more concerned with freedom from economic, social and political domination than they are with the distribution of goods or offices. Such theorists may seek to shift attention away from the distribution of economic benefits and burdens towards oppressive social, economic and political relationships and argue that justice (or rather injustice) is a matter of oppression rather than distribution. Of course, this may be only to say that the most important distributions are distributions of power but this in itself is an important corrective to the outlook of those who work with a narrow consumer view of the sort of distributions which justice is about.

It should be noted that all these conceptual points about justice and its sub divisions may be taken on board without endorsing the view that justice is always the prime social value, or even always a value at all. We must leave room in our discussions of justice for views which express grave doubts about justice as an ideal. Quite apart from cynical sceptics like Thrasymachus in Plato's *Republic* who hold that justice is nothing but the interests of the stronger, and the more optimistic critiques of Marx to the effect that justice is a bourgeois value for which a truly communist society will have no use, there are those who regard justice as expressing norms which are too masculine, too individualistic, too formal, or too cold and impersonal. We will see that such criticisms can often be met by radically revising our conceptual inheritance or downgrading the priority of justice rather than by simply accepting or rejecting the critiques.

With all these reservations, it remains illuminating to say that justice has to do with the distribution amongst persons of benefits and burdens, these being loosely defined so as to cover any desirable or undesirable thing or experience. We can then move on to ask whether simply *any* morally relevant distributive consideration is to be considered as an element in justice or whether only some types of moral consideration are 'justicising' or just-making factors. This takes us into the matter of how we should go about determining not so much what justice is about, but what it is that is just and unjust.

2 What is Just?

This chapter takes us nearer to those fundamental philosophical questions about justice which concern our knowledge of substantive justice and injustice. Its focus is less on the concept of justice and more on questions about the proper criteria for determining whether something is or is not just or unjust, a substantive matter that is directly addressed in most theories of justice.

I begin by giving more content to the ideas of equality and desert, the two concepts which feature centrally in the meritorian account of justice. This analysis is then applied to the standard but puzzling distinction between two distinct categories of justice, legal and social, which enables further exploration of the idea of equality, particularly the maxim that we ought to treat equals equally. I then raise some general epistemological issues about how we might go about acquiring 'knowledge' of substantive justice. In this epistemological context, equality features in the guise of impartiality, that is, the even-handed consideration of all distributive claims, which is a frequently favoured method of determining what is just. Finally, I give further consideration to communitarian approaches to justice, principally with respect to the epistemology of communitaranism which challenges our ability to step outside our cultural context and make universal or cosmopolitan claims about what is and is not just. For the communitarian, impartiality, for instance, can function successfully as a way of determining what is just only within a particular tradition and is problematic as a way of evaluating the values of other cultures and groups. This discussion paves the way for understanding the communitarian critiques of liberal theories of justice which feature later in the book (see, for instance, the criticisms of Rawls presented in Chapter 5) and offer a challenge to the very possibility of giving anything more than a personal or subjective answer to the question 'what is just?'

Equality and desert

At the first, permissive, level of analysis, which is identified in Chapter 1 as involving an eclectic and broad-brush approach to the idea of justice, perhaps the most promising specification of the concept of justice beyond the idea of distributing benefits and burdens is that justice is the embodiment of the ancient principle, discussed in Book I of Plato's *Republic* and given its classic formulation in the *Institutes* of Justinian, that 'justice is the set and constant purpose to give every man his due'.

For some theorists this formula has the advantage of flexibility in that it leaves entirely open what is to count as a person's due, and it also has the advantage of capturing the idea that justice is a requirement rather than an optional extra. Other things being equal people ought to receive that which is due to them as a matter of right, not of grace and favour. And, since much social regulation may be regarded as being directed to ensuring that people receive their dues through specifying the mutual obligations of members of a society, this may explain the legal connotations of justice. So, the formula 'to each according to his or her due' appears to take in both the forcefulness and legalism of justice discourse.

However, we have already noted that neither the moral priority nor the legal monopoly of justice can be taken for granted, so that the extent and nature of the imperative force of 'due' should not be exaggerated. There are in life many minor injustices whose rectification may be very much an optional extra. Certainly it is not the case that justice by definition requires legal expression and protection. Justice features as a standard for judging distributions within families, educational establishments and economic units, in ways which are by and large outside the ambit of the law. Thus, although the use of legal mechanisms to ensure that people receive that which is their due is for some theorists a paradigm of what justice is about, it must be a mistake to give a restrictive interpretation of 'due' in this context.

A more serious difficulty with this starting-point is that, if we focus on the specific meaning of justice, the formula 'to each his or her due' appears too broad. For, given that it is possible to count almost anything as a person's 'due', it allows for the concept of justice to accommodate discriminatory distributions in accordance with social class, race, sex or many other properties whose distributive use is in general the antithesis of justice. Many would argue that these criteria have no proper part in any conceivable theory of justice. This objection may reflect no more than a misunderstanding of the nature of the analysis of the concept of justice which, it should be remembered, is intended to indicate the general scope of controversies about what is just, rather than to establish how these controversies ought to be resolved in terms of particular conceptions of justice. If it is said to be unjust to allocate goods according to race, class or birth, then this may be taken as presupposing the thesis that justice (as opposed to liberty or efficiency for instance) has to do with the determination of what is due to persons. A theory of the concept of justice aims to distinguish the just from the non-just, not to take a view on what is just as distinct from unjust.

However, this response ignores the possibility that justice concerns a limited range of morally relevant distributive criteria. Moreover, it seems highly likely that this is so, since there are morally significant criteria, such as maximising happiness, which have distributive implications but are clearly not criteria of justice. Economic necessity may require that extraordinarily high salaries be paid to a few people with essential skills, or that bribes be given to those who have it in their power to inflict serious social harm through their control of vital natural resources. The question of whether or not it is right to distribute goods for such reasons is largely a matter of utility rather than justice and is conceptually different from such issues as what is a fair rate for the job, or to what extent punishment is just. To meet these difficulties 'due' has to be given a more precise meaning.

Such reflections generate suggestions for limiting the range of possible criteria for a just distribution. For instance, Miller (1976, p.20) includes only those which refer to 'personal characteristics and circumstances'. On this basis he goes on to identify three independent 'interpretations of justice which may be summarized in the three principles: to each according to his rights; to each according to his deserts; to each according to his needs' (p.27). This does seem to emphasise that justice has to do with the individual's treatment. However, unless these three types of consideration can be given some further illuminating theoretical connection, it appears a rather arbitrary list of relevant personal characteristics and circumstances, particularly as the criterion of need features centrally in other moral concepts, such as beneficence or humanity.

Another more limited but more coherent suggestion, which is applied only to what he calls 'social justice', is made by Honoré

(1970) who puts forward two propositions about justice. First, 'all men considered merely as men and apart from their conduct or choice have a claim to an equal share in all those things, here called advantages, which are generally desired and are in fact conducive to well-being'. The second proposition is that 'there are a limited number of principles of discrimination and that the claim of men to an equal share in all advantages can fairly be modified, restricted or limited by only two main factors. These are the choice of the claimant or the citizen on the one hand and his conduct on the other' (p.63).

Honoré's second proposition has the advantage of explaining why justice is contrasted not only with utility but also with distributions which are the outcome of good luck or ill fortune. Further, the particular relevance of conduct and choice to justice could be explained by their role in the assessment of desert which gives precedence to Miller's principle of desert over his alternative principles of rights and needs. This would mean that all forms of justice have to do with requiting people in terms of their personal responsibility as moral agents.

However, the application of these criteria follows on from Honoré's first proposition which makes it clear that any distinctions that are made between individuals must presuppose a position of initial or, as I shall call it, 'prior' equality. On one reading of the relationship between justice and equality, equality is taken to mean no more than the requirement that every person should receive that which is their due, which is in turn interpreted to mean no more than the formal principle that like cases should be treated alike. This is sometimes called the principle of formal justice, since it involves the application of whatever criteria of distribution are being used in a consistent manner, irrespective of the content or substantive merits of the criteria in question. The justification of the criteria, as distinct from their accurate implementation, is then regarded as a matter of substantive or material justice to be determined by the exercise of further moral judgement. Formal justice of this sort places few limitations on the inequality of the outcomes arising from the application of whatever principles are consistently applied.

Evidently, Honoré's idea of what I call prior equality goes beyond pure formal justice to an assertion that in some respects human beings are equal and should therefore receive equal treatment until such time as relevant reasons are given for treating them differently. However, it would seem that justice in its totality cannot be identified with a simple idea of literal equality in which after everything has been taken into account all human beings are placed in the *same* situation as regards the desirables and undesirables of life. Such egalitarian interpretations of equality are routinely contrasted with justice, presumably because justice is in part concerned with distinguishing between persons and groups and justifying their differential treatment. Egalitarianism is at most one possible substantive view of justice and cannot therefore be regarded as essential to the concept of justice itself. However, it is a plausible and attractive reading of the idea of prior equality that departures from egalitarian distributions require justification. Indeed, many proposals for social reform put forward in the name of justice do call for a move towards more equal material conditions from human beings on the grounds that the differences in the material conditions from human life are far too great. This may be because differences between individuals, such as their different merits, are seldom as substantial as the differences in benefits and burdens which typically occur in actual societies. In this case Honoré's analysis of justice may be said to express the specific moral viewpoint, championed by Bruce Ackerman in his influential book *Social Justice in the Liberal State* (1980), that unequal life situations must be justified, so that every theory of justice must seek to explain or justify the basic presumption of the equality of persons as well as demonstrate legitimate grounds for differential treatment.

The assumption of prior equality does require justification through the identification of some characteristics that all persons possess which can plausibly be claimed to be what gives them intrinsic significance or importance. Thus, when J. S. Mill attributed to Bentham the imperative 'everybody to count for one, nobody to count for more than one' (Mill, 1863, p.58), this was based on the belief that one person's pleasure is as important as everyone else's. Your pleasure is as important as mine and my desires are of equal moral significance to those of any other person. In this case, the principle of equal worth is founded on the equality of human beings as centres of pleasure or desire satisfaction.

The idea that equal consideration, in the sense of the acknowledgement of equal worth, is built into the concept of justice is an ancient and attractive one. As a principle it appears to carry with it major substantive implications, since it rules out the total neglect of one person or group of persons: all must be given equal weight, for all are of equal worth. In reality these implications are not considerable unless certain assumptions are made about what sort of factor ought to be taken into account and given equal weight, to whomsoever they apply. It is, therefore, common to write into the idea of equal worth a substantive notion of what factors are to be taken into account when determining the import of the idea of equal worth. For the utilitarian this is the capacity for experiencing pleasure and pain. For others, such as Immanuel Kant, it is the ability to think, choose and be held responsible for one's actions. The principle of equal worth thus becomes the principle that people should have equal consideration as persons, so defined.

Some such idea of the equal worth of all humans is probably presupposed by the concept of justice, but as a principle it does not in itself encapsulate the distinctive concerns of justice. The principle of equal worth may well be fundamental to the moral point of view in its entirety. Certainly it is a presupposition of classical utilitarianism as well as Kantian autonomy theory. It is possible, therefore, that what distinguishes justice as a moral consideration is that it proposes reasons which justify treatment that results in inequality. Again, however, this is not something which is unique to justice, for any moral consideration may justify unequal treatment. A theory of justice must, therefore, be able to identify and connect the reasons for differential treatment which have distinctively to do with justice. It seems doubtful that this can be done without adopting something like the meritorian thesis that justice has to do with the unequal worthiness of human beings and how this should be reflected in our treatment of each other. It may also be that the determination of what counts as equal worth for the purposes of justice involves some reference to those properties of human beings that makes it reasonable for us to praise and blame them. In other words, justice presupposes that persons have equal worth as responsible agents. This makes for a close connection between the ideas of equal worth and unequal worthiness. However, there is a danger that this underplays equality of experience, in particular the idea that the happiness of everyone matters equally. It is, therefore, safer to assume that equal worth is based on a number of factors which include sentience or self-awareness, the capacity for feeling pleasure and pain and the characteristics which enable human beings to make considered choices, particularly moral choices.

The meritorian view that justice is to do with the equal worth and unequal worthiness of human beings is hardly a morally neutral analysis of the concept of justice, but then perhaps justice is not a morally neutral concept but represents a type of substantive moral approach. The meritorian analysis does leave open a vast range of issues within its moral parameters, for it still has to be decided which features of human beings are fundamental to their status as responsible agents, what is to count as merit and demerit, and what implications individual differences in the dimension of desert have for our treatment of each other. It leaves open, also, whether justice, so construed, is always of overriding, or even major, significance in determining what is morally right. Human beings are not only responsible moral agents, they are also, for instance, sentient beings with important experiences of pleasure and pain, something which lies at the base of egalitarian demands which may not be well formulated in the distinctive language of justice. Any account of what justice is about must take note that common humanity, or even generous beneficence, may sometimes be in conflict with, and more important than, the claims of justice, as my analysis of equal worth suggests.

The substance of formal justice

Although Honoré's analysis of social justice can be used to bring out, through the ideas of desert and individual responsibility, under-lying features of social justice which indicate its affinity with legal justice, we have noted that Honoré himself maintains a distinction between what he calls 'social' and 'individual' justice, which indic-ates that he goes along with the standard view that the two are importantly distinct. Indeed most modern theories of justice have little to say about justice in law despite the fact that justice might appear to be *the* legal virtue. The distribution of the benefits and burdens of social cooperation is thought to be one type of concern, the attribution of liability and punishment quite another, hence the sharp distinction between social or distributive justice on the one hand and individual or legal justice on the other.

In so far as they have something to contribute to the integration of so-called social and legal justice, contemporary theorists of just-ice tend to deploy the distinction between formal and material justice, equating the former with law and the latter with morality or politics. Law, it is said, has to do with the fair and accurate application of rules, that is, in the terminology of Perelman (1963, p.11), with 'abstract' as opposed to the 'concrete' justice which concerns the content of such rules. The same basic distinction is given a number of different labels in the literature. Sidgwick (1901, p.273) contrasts the 'customary' justice, which upholds established conventions, with 'ideal' justice, which has to do with 'an ideal system of rules of distribution which ought to exist, but perhaps has never existed'. Here I shall use the terms 'formal' justice for treatment in accordance with existing authoritative rules and 'material' (or sometimes 'substantive') justice for those criteria of justice which are pertinent to the assessment of the rules themselves.

Formal justice often seems to have an almost arbitrary connection with material justice, and is usually treated as a side issue to be mentioned briefly before proceeding to the substantive moral issues which are roughly equated with the sphere of social justice. This separation in turn neatly coincides with the sharp line drawn by legal positivists between what the law is and what the law ought to be. Legal theory is then taken to be about the identification of which rules are to count as valid laws and the idea of 'natural justice' is taken to refer only to certain technical matters of procedure which have no significant connection with the justice of the rules' content (see Hart, 1961, pp.202ff.). It is then up to moral and political philosophers to argue about the justice of the content of rules and whether these should be founded on merit, need or some other criterion.

This division of labour leaves unexplained the close historical and conceptual ties between law and justice. If legal justice is purely formal and therefore no more than an accurate implementation of legal rules, then it would appear that there is no closer link between law and justice than there is between justice and rule-governed bureaucratic administration. A purely formal sense of justice would seem to have insufficient moral import to explain the association of law and justice and the strength of feeling to which legal injustices give rise. A closer analysis of the ideas associated with formal justice, particularly its relation to the principles' conformity to what is known as the 'rule of law', reveals a more profound conceptual connection between the formal and the material aspects of justice discourse and so helps to overcome the sharp distinction that is so often drawn between legal and social justice.

Exploration of these issues calls for a more detailed consideration of the idea and significance of formal justice. If formal justice is defined simply as the accurate implementation of preexisting rules, then its importance seems to derive from the significance of the rules themselves. If the rule is justified, then it follows that its application is justified, and this is so – at least *prima facie* – in every instance to which the rule has application. In the case of some rules (such as the rule of the road, or other complex sets of rules relating to closely interacting cooperative behaviour), something close to complete conformity may be required to achieve their purposes, and consistent rule-following is then of particular instrumental importance. In other cases, such as rules prohibiting homicide, which do not have a similar 'threshold' effect, the value of the rule is realised in every conformity to it, so that its significance in each instance is not directly dependent on the rule being consistently and generally adhered to in other instances. However, with both types of rule, the moral significance of formal justice is derived from the content of the rules in question and the objectives which they have been designed to achieve.

These examples suggest that the consistent application of rules is not a matter of justice, formal or otherwise, unless the rules are rules of justice. Certainly we do not speak of formal justice in connection with the application of every type of rule. Maladministration of the rules of a game is not generally described as unjust (although here the associated concept of fairness may apply) and it is certainly not 'unjust', although it may be inefficient, to be inconsistent in the use of the rules of language or computer programming. We might, therefore, define formal justice more restrictively as the consistent application of the rules of justice. This would have the advantage of a clear connection between justice in its formal and material aspects.

However, the reduction of formal to material justice in this way does not account for all the assumptions made about formal justice. The idea of formal justice is often applied to the application of any rules which have a bearing on the locations of benefits and burdens, whether or not these arise from considerations of justice in the substantive sense. Thus in the case of an arbitrary rule that redheads in the workforce be paid an extra day's wages each week, it is felt to be formally unjust if some redheads do not receive the unmerited and discriminatory benefit while yet other redheads do receive the benefit. The idea is that the inconsistent application of benefit-or burden-allocating rules is not a mere technical inefficiency or logical inconsistency, but an actual type of injustice which is quite distinct from the type of benefit or burden in question and from the reasons for having the rules in the first place. What is at stake, it is argued, is simply a matter of the justice of treating like cases alike.

There would indeed appear to be deeply rooted instinctive re-actions of resentment which are aroused by 'unequal' treatment in such a purely formal sense. This instinct is manifested at a very early age by siblings who are treated differently by their parents. In the adult world it is evident in arguments about comparability in wage rates, where the demand for greater remuneration is based primarily on what is paid for similar work by other groups. In general it would seem that it is regarded as unjust to confer a benefit or burden on one or more members of a group without doing so on all other members of the group, and that this applies even when the rule in question is regarded as materially unjustified and even unjust.

It may be, however, that, whatever the emotional reactions to imperfect rule implementation might be, there is no real injustice in the incompleteness of the application of unjustified rules in that all such judgements, if they are to be sustained, depend on the assump-tion that the rule in question is defensible. It is certainly sometimes hard to see the justice of applying an unjust rule merely because it has been applied to others. If we have imprisoned one morally innocent man it can scarcely be regarded as unjust not to imprison all innocent men. The demands for such purely formal justice may be effective in the pursuit of benefits against authorities who have favoured other groups conventionally regarded as similar, but this is because of the *ad hominem* force of such arguments, since the authorities in question are likely to be committed to the justifiability of the rules they have already deployed and this can be used to extract concessions from them.

Whether or not mere formal 'injustice', independently of the content of the rules, constitutes a genuine grievance is a matter of rather fine moral intuition. Certainly it does not seem a substantial enough consideration to explain the significance of law for the pursuit of justice. The missing ingredients in the concept of mere formal justice may be tied up in the associated ideal of the rule of law according to which it is held that political power ought to be channelled through a system of general rules which are impartially applied by an independent authority according to standard proced-ures which guarantee such matters as a fair hearing for those who are liable to benefit or suffer as a consequence of the application of these rules.

Unfortunately for our purposes the rule of law is a very mixed bag of requirements, not all of which appear to have a direct bearing on questions of justice. The arbitrary uses of political power may of course produce injustice, as when unmerited harms are inflicted on individuals at the behest of the power-holders, but even greater injustices may be perpetrated by the efficient application of unjust rules.

There are, however, some elements of the ideal of the rule of law which are relatively independent of the substance of rules and which do appear to have a connection with justice. These elements are to be found in the so-called 'principles of legality', which are identified by Fuller in relation to his eight ways of 'failing to make law', an activity which he described as 'subjecting human conduct to the governance of rules' (Fuller, 1969, p.46). In accordance with well-established principles of the rule of law, Fuller argued that successful law-making requires that rules be general, publicised, prospective, understandable, non-contradictory, possible to conform to, relatively constant and consistently applied (see pp.3ff.). He further argues that a total failure in any one of these respects does not result merely in a bad system of law but produces something which is not properly called a legal system at all, the reason being that it cannot effectively govern human conduct. If, for instance, the rules in question are totally unknown to the citizens of a polity, then they cannot be used to control their behaviour. On the other hand, the full realisation of all these conditions is an aspiration or ideal to which no actual legal system can completely attain.

What distinguishes Fuller's thesis is that, while allowing that the morality of the content of the law is something that raises issues which are 'external' to the law, he insists that there is an 'internal' morality embedded in the idea of law as he has defined it. He reaches this view by noting that in the case of each type of legal 'inefficiency' there is an associated form of moral outrage. Retrospective laws, for instance, do not merely fail to change behaviour, they are also felt to be grossly unfair. Unclear laws are 'brutally absurd', contradictory laws are 'repugnant', while laws requiring the impossible are brutal as well as pointless. The citizens of Fuller's inefficient law-maker, King Rex, are not only ungoverned, they are also indignant, for they have had to suffer both the disorder of the kingdom and the injustice of being penalised according to unpredictable decisions and rules to which they were powerless to conform.

Fuller has, in general, failed to convince his audience that there is a logically necessary connection between efficiency and morality in law. In the abstract, the morality of the means must be judged by reference to the morality of the ends in question and law would seem to be no exception to this rule. The fact that evil and corrupt regimes utilise clear, consistent and prospective rules in itself seems to add nothing to their morality, any more than efficiency in theft adds to the moral quality of that enterprise.

Nevertheless there would appear to be at least a contingent connection between Fuller's model of law and aspects of moral value which come within the ambit or the rule of law. For instance, where the rules concerned satisfy Fuller's standards it is in principle possible for citizens to change their behaviour so as to avoid the penal consequences of disobedience. This may count for little if such behaviour involves them in what they regard as grossly immoral or undesirable conduct, but the fact that citizens have a choice to make in relation to the rules and their consequences is in some sense a recognition of their status as responsible agents. No doubt Fuller overstates this point, but it has some force:

'To embark on the enterprise of subjecting human conduct to the governance of rules involves of necessity a commitment to the view that man is, or can become, a responsible agent, capable of understanding, following rules and answerable for his defaults.

Every departure from the law's inner morality is an affront to man's dignity as a responsible agent. To judge his actions by unpublished and retrospective laws, or to order him to do the impossible is to convey to him your indifference to his powers of self-determination.' (1969, p.162)

Other normal, but by no means necessary, features of modern legal systems are similarly responsibility-oriented. Some of the standards of so-called 'due process' or 'natural justice' fit neatly into this category. Thus the requirements of due notice to any charges, the opportunity to be heard and cross-question witnesses and have evidence duly considered in open court can be seen as, in part at least, elementary extensions of the treatment of people as responsible beings: 'what makes law an appropriate method of social control is not that it is more efficient than other more manipulative or coercive methods, but that it embodies a proper respect for the citizen as a rational agent' (Duff, 1986, p.97). Not only do such procedures promote accuracy in the application of rules, they also embody a commitment to vindicating the propriety of the procedures to the vulnerable individual: 'rules of procedure do not guarantee that decisions will be just. Rather they constitute necessary, or near necessary, conditions of the decision-making process being a process with which a man could be expected to identify' (Lucas, 1980, p.97). Moreover a fair hearing along these lines is clearly a matter which is fundamentally involved in the sort of justice that is expected in our courts of law.

These considerations connect in turn with the idea that impartiality is an aspect of the justice which applies in relative independence of the content of rules. This ideal may be unpacked in a multitude of ways, many of which we have already analysed as part of formal justice. For instance, the notion that only those factors explicitly contained in publicly expressed rules should be taken into account in the application of rules is part of what it is to judge impartially, as are the other ingredients of 'natural justice' which have just been mentioned. But there are additional aspects in the idea of judicial impartiality which go beyond the notion of accurate and publicly justified rule application and relate more to the use of significant judicial discretion in areas where rules run out or require extensive interpretation. Here the judge who has no personal connection with the parties in court, and who is not regarded as partisan in relation to matters of civil dispute but will nevertheless take a detailed interest in the matters at hand, is preferred. Just as having general rules can be seen as an attempt to transcend individual prejudice or bias, so there is a notion that judges should sustain impartiality in their even-handed dealing with those matters which are not precisely determined by the applicable rules.

Although the ideal of the impartial judge is by no means an analytical requirement of a legal system, this, along with the associated rules of natural justice, is so closely associated with the modern idea of the proper conduct of law as to embody the sort of justice that is expected of the law. Once this is appreciated then it becomes possible to articulate the common element between this enhanced idea of formal justice, on the one hand, and material or substantive justice, on the other hand, since both have to do with different aspects of the treating of people as responsible agents.

On this account, the justice with which law is concerned is continuous in kind with the justice of distributions which are not primarily the concern of courts of law, for both 'legal' and 'social' justice have to do with the treatment of persons as responsible agents. More abstract accounts of formal justice, according to which justice is no more than a matter of logical consistency, especially when conjoined with a theory of material justice which discounts considerations of desert, are more likely to end up with a strong and inexplicable disjunction between our ideas of legal and social justice.

Knowledge of justice

So far, we have picked our way through competing analyses of justice in a pragmatic way, having an ear for the discourse of justice, seeking a measure of clarity and precision and keeping an eye on the sort of practical issues that we expect a theory of justice to confront. I have indicated my preference for a meritorian analysis which combines an assumption of prior equality with justified departures from that equality on grounds of differential desert. This preference, it is claimed, fits well with the actual discourse of justice and serves to clarify and illuminate the distinctive features of justice as a political value.

The matter of how we are to go about deciding substantive questions as to what justice actually requires is more problematic because it involves us in adopting a view as to how evaluative questions in general can and ought to be settled. This raises issues about the objectivity of moral judgement and the legitimacy of political decision-making systems of much broader application and concern than to justice alone. Yet every theory of justice must develop or utilise a meta-moral theory which indicates if and how we can know what is just and a normative political philosophy which indicates how, in the light of such a meta-moral theory, disagreements about what is just ought to be settled. The moral philosophy questions have to be addressed by any theory of justice which seeks to provide guidance as to what is just. The political philosophy questions have to be addressed by any theory of justice which uses justice as a measure of the rightness or acceptability of laws and the ways in which they are administered.

There are particular problems for theories which assume a sceptical meta-moral theory, to the effect that there are no objective standards of truth and falsity or moral rightness to constrain our choice of criteria of substantive justice, and seek to legitimate a preference for a particular way of settling evaluative disputes about mandatory social requirements, such as law. Thus, if it is suggested that, in the absence of objective moral criteria which can be used to determine what is just, disputes about justice ought to be settled by elected representatives in legislative assemblies or by courts administering bills of rights, reasons have to be provided for accepting these political decision-making processes which do not themselves assume controversial moral judgements. This is a difficult intellectual feat to accomplish and theories of justice involving moral scepticism are prone to the internal inconsistency of both affirming and denying that there are moral truths. Most theories of justice, therefore, seek to develop or utilise some theory of knowledge or epistemology that can be used to support such value judgements as are required to support their suggestions as to how, as individuals and citizens, we ought to go about deciding what is just.

Such an enterprise runs counter to the outlook of much postmodern philosophy which is distrustful of grand theories and ambitious truth claims. In fact, when 'justice' is presented as a basic building block of our moral universe there is much legitimate scepticism that what we are dealing with is a rhetoric which can be examined and deconstructed but should not be taken at face value. Thus, I have already cast doubt on the idea that justice is always the prime social good or supreme political value. Other philosophers question whether there is any real substance behind the rhetoric of the language of justice and some argue that the discourse of justice is as likely to be utilised for oppressive and inegalitarian purposes as it is to further liberation and equality. Further, it is a characteristically postmodern view that there is no one conception of justice which is arguably superior to all others, which makes for considerable scepticism as to the usefulness of continuing the discourse of justice at all. Nevertheless, in its 'deconstruction' of grand theories, postmodern thought is chacteristically hostile to existing power relations, at once detached and ironical and yet also committed to the interests of vulnerable people. In this vein, Drucilla Cornell *et al.* note the ambivalent value posture of deconstructive thought: 'deconstruction has been associated with cynicism towards the very idea of justice . . . even its critics recognize that deconstruction is, in some way, aligned with the marginalized' (1992, p.ix).

More generally, opinions as to what is substantively just or unjust have been long regarded in certain philosophical traditions as essentially undecidable on the grounds that there is no way to establish objectively what are ultimately matters of individual preference. As a fundamental moral value, justice, on the non-cognitivist view in moral philosophy according to which moral judgements are expressions of feeling rather than statements of fact or reason, relates to our practical attitudes, desires and commitments and not to our knowledge or cognitive beliefs.

Even if we do not adopt the radical sceptics' position, their approaches are helpful in sharpening our critical approach to theories of justice, particularly theories which attempt to provide overarching theories or aspire to political neutrality. And if we do go along with even moderately sceptical positions, thought must be given to what, if anything, can take their functional place in discourse which attempts to establish a pattern of acceptable ongoing social and political relationships. This may take the form of promoting a more directly democratic form of government, or a quiet acquiescence in any tolerable status quo, or, perhaps, a nihilistic rejection of the issues as meaningless and without point.

Objections to common-sense beliefs about justice and other fundamental values are often expressed in terms of relativism. Value judgements, including those about justice, are all asserted to be relative to the person or group whose values they are. There are at least three radically different ways of interpreting this claim. The first is the rather weak and uncontroversial thesis that right and wrong vary with circumstances, so that it may be right to steal when you are starving, but not otherwise. Second is the more daring thesis that it is just for one person or group to act in one way but equally just for another person or group, with respect to essentially the same situation, to act in another and incompatible manner. In other words, relativism means that justice and injustice vary according to whose conduct is being assessed. It is just for a Christian to act in one way, but equally it is just for a Muslim to act in a quite different way so that justice varies from person to person as it varies between situation and situation. On this first view of circumstantial relativism, it may be just for a nomadic tribe to abandon old and sick persons but it is not just for this to happen in a settled agrarian society. In the second form of relativism, it is equally just for a society with one tradition to practise female child circumcision or child marriage as it is for another society with a different tradition to prohibit it. Both views are compatible with objectivist or cognitivist epistemologies which hold that we can know what is just and unjust. They are relativist only because they claim that the substance of justice varies with the persons and cultures involved. This is to say much more than that there are different beliefs about what is just in different societies; it is to claim that these beliefs, even if in conflict with one another, may all be correct. In this they differ from the third sense of 'relativism' according to which so-called moral 'truths' are relative to the beliefs and feelings of those who hold them, a position which is better described as 'subjectivism'.

Objective relativism of the second sort is puzzling to those who hold to the view that judgements of moral right and wrong are universalisable in that what is right for one person in one situation must, according to the logic of moral discourse, be right for everyone in the same situation. Those who hold to the doctrine of universalisability tend not to accept that mere differences of personality or culture are relevant to the determination for what is morally right and wrong. As Martha Nussbaum argues in her defence of cosmopolitan values, if child female circumcision and child marriage are wrong for one child in one society they are wrong for all children in all societies (Nussbaum, 1999). In practice, of course, such sweeping universality of moral right and wrong is not required by the doctrine of universalisability, for there may be many morally relevant differences between the situations in which individuals find themselves which affect their rights and duties. Poverty, danger and capacity to change things are three illustrative variables which can properly affect judgements of justice even on the strictest version of universalisability. Even in the case of female child circumcision, it is possible to conceive of the practice being justified on the basis of the medical condition of certain children. Nevertheless, there is a tendency for those who adhere to the doctrine of universalisability to claim that in certain basic moral matters, universalisability does mean universality: it is always wrong for anybody to kill, to steal, to lie or to discriminate on racial grounds.

Issues of moral objectivity and relativism more generally cannot be directly addressed in this book, but we should note the specific epistemological challenges which relate particularly to the question of what is just. These concern the aspects of justice which relate to its alleged (1) foundational status, (2) anti-utilitarianism, and (3) acontextualism or universality. Finally I draw attention to the dual role of such standards as impartiality and equality in both the epistemology and the substance of the question: what is just?

First, because justice is often held to concern the identification of basic or fundamental values, it is particularly prone to be associated with epistemologies of self-evidence, which hold to certain alleged undeniable truths, such as the right to life or the (correlative) duty not to kill. Having obtained our consent to these self-evident moral insights, the theories then proceed to deduce practical conclusions from these simple abstract propositions which either confirm or challenge our everyday moral views as to what is just and unjust. This approach has the epistemological advantage of not requiring to establish the attainability of moral truth generally but only with respect to the few simple truths of justice. The problems for such epistemologies arise in the process of specifying the implications of the self-evident truths, a process which tends to raise the suspicion that agreement at the level of abstract general rights masks moral disagreement behind a façade of common language. The standard criticism of moral epistemologies of self-evidence is that such undeniable truths as can be agreed upon have the characteristics of empty verbal formulae or tautologies of the sort which obtain agreement to the proposition that we ought not to murder on the basis of the unstated definition of murder as morally unjustified homicide.

The second point about the specific epistemological challenges presented by justice is that justice is routinely used as a basis for the criticism of utilitarianism, thus making it difficult for theories of justice to draw upon the epistemologies associated with this major tradition within moral and political philosophy. Utilitarianism reduces moral issues to questions about what maximises human happiness (or preference satisfaction) and minimises human pain (or preference frustration), and argues that these are uncontroversial goals. This means that most moral issues involve answering empirical questions about the consequences of adopting this or that rule or making this or that decision. Since empirical questions, such as determining the causes of pleasure and pain, are not thought to have the same epistemological problems as evaluative questions, utilitarian theories of justice do have the advantage of minimising epistemological problems, but they seem generally unsuited to explain our intuitions about the injustice of such practices as making minorities suffer for the benefit of majorities or punishing innocent persons who are believed to be guilty in order to deter potential criminals. Indeed, it would appear that considerations of justice have most force and relevance precisely in situations where utilitarian reasoning is producing morally unacceptable results.

The third general point about the particular epistemologies of justice is the difficulty of drawing on those moral epistemologies which stress the contextuality of moral evaluation and argue that moral rightness is to be discerned within the specific particularities of everyday human relationships, which cannot be reduced to the simple formulas of moral rules, so that we have to rely on the contextualised judgement of the habitually virtuous person seeking to do the right thing in situations of endless complexity and nuance. This outlook does not go easily with a claim to universal moral truths. An implication of such theories is that we should withdraw as much moral decision-making as we can from the public sphere in which there must be, if only for reasons of efficiency, considerable dependence on the administration of agreed rules. In consequence such epistemologically attractive theories of contextualised moral truth seem inappropriate to those aspects of justice which relate to the workings of public institutions.

Finally, with respect to the epistemology of justice, it is interesting to note that some general criteria which are standardly used to analyse justice and formulate answers to the question of what is just also feature in the epistemologies of justice. For instance, the ideal of judicial impartiality, which we have noted as an aspect of the rule of law, is also deployed as a technique for determining what is to count as materially just. The opinion of the impartial and well-informed judge, in one form or another, is a standard base for what are said to be materially just decisions, including decisions about the proper content of distributive rules. As we shall see, variations on this theme of impartiality abound in epistemological investigations into the acceptable bases of judgements of material justice, which suggests that there may be further fundamental affinities between the bases of formal and material justice.

This significant and deep connection between formal and material justice can be seen in analyses of the idea of judicial impartiality which goes beyond formal interpretations of the principle that like cases should be treated alike, to the more substantive claim that this principle itself rests on the belief that, in some sense of 'equality', all human beings are 'equal'. Again, it is fascinating to note that the idea of equality is brought to the fore in many theories as the basis on which disagreements about justice (and other matters) ought to be settled. Thus equal participation in debate about what is justice, associated with equal decision-making power through electorally equal voting procedures, is often presented as the best way to obtain the correct answer as to the substantive content of just equality and difference. Of course, institutionalised impartiality or equal input to decision-making processes may be seen as alternatives to moral epistemology which substitutes political pragmatism for moral truth, but, as we will see, many theories which draw on impartiality and procedural equality do present these concepts as epistemologic-ally reliable means for answering our question: what is just?

The communitarian critique of liberal justice

Whether or not we can have knowledge of what is just is a philosophical issue which cuts across the ideological divides. Thus utilitarian epistemologies, which concentrate on the empirical paths to knowledge of what causes pleasure and pain, can feature in libertarian, welfare liberal or socialist systems of thought. However, liberal and libertarian approaches which focus on individual rights tend to draw on self-evident insights into what is right and wrong to derive moral imperatives such as 'do not kill' and 'tell the truth'. I explore several variations of this approach to moral epistemology in several of the chapters which follow, but this chapter concludes with the epistemological critique presented by communitarians who, amongst others, cast doubt on our capacity to transcend our inher-ited social values through moral intuition, specialist reasoning or impartial dialogue.

'Communitarianism' is a recently coined term which usefully covers a range of views that run counter to the assumptions of liberal individualism without being too closely associated with a specific political alternative. Most of the communitarian critique of liberalism is a matter of straightforward rejection of its moral individualism which, it is argued, overstresses personal freedom and underplays social responsibility. Liberalism, the moral critique runs, concentrates too much on autonomy and independence and not enough on reciprocity, loyalty and solidarity. It mistakenly analyses valued social ends in terms of the sum of the goods chosen by individuals and fails to take adequate account of the public goods which are a shared part of community life that cannot be disaggreg-ated into individual parcels. These are responses which would be common to aspects of such diverse anti-individualistic theories as Marxism, feminism, and traditionalist, organic and hierarchical social theories.

Underlying this moral disagreement is a profound ontological point about the emptiness of the idea of the individual once abstracted from the social context which gives that individual life a concrete reality, a reality which is constituted by the network of social relationships within which every individual finds their identity and meaning. Thus Sandel (1982) argues that persons are in part constituted by the purposes, beliefs and attitudes that they have as members of a community which provides them with the relationships through which they come to have an individual identity and a meaningful existence. There is no such thing as an 'unencumbered self' in which individual identity is separable from social identity. This central critical point is deployed in their criticism of Rawls and in the general assessment of the liberal theories discussed in this book.

There is also an epistemological side to communitarianism which is directly relevant to the theme of this chapter. The communitarian position is that each community has its own concept and conceptions of justice and that we cannot stand outside these cultural constructs and arrive at a trans-societal theory of justice which stands above and judges the beliefs and attitudes of particular cultural communities. Ideas and standards of justice are embedded in culturally specific groups and collectivities with a communal and organic life of their own within which their particular discourse of justice makes sense. For the communtarian, the question is not 'what is just?' but 'whose justice are we talking about?'

This epistemological communitarianism is forcefully stated in MacIntyre (1981) which contends that abstract impersonal standards have no meaning outside the confines of social practices, that is,

'any coherent and complex form of socially established cooperative human activity through which goods internal to that form of activity are realized in the course of trying to achieve those standards of excellence which are appropriate to, and partially definitive of, that form of activity, with the result that human powers to achieve excellence, and human conceptions of the ends and goods involved, are systematically extended.' (p.175)

Practices coalesce in different cultural traditions which give significance and importance to the practices which contribute to their social reality. This cultural background provides a necessary basis for

meaningful moral discourse. More recently MacIntyre has reaf-
firmed that thinkers 'are only to be understood properly when
placed in the context of traditions' (MacIntyre, 1988, p.8) but he
has acknowledged that, when traditions break down, there is a
period of epistemological crisis when traditions may import previously foreign elements to form a new cultural system, and 'the
rival claims to truth of contending traditions of enquiry depend for
their vindication upon the adequacy and the explanatory power of
the histories which the resources of each of those traditions in
conflict enable their adherents to write' (1988, p.403). However,
this is more a concession to the reality of cultural change than any
acceptance of the cosmopolitan or universalist view that external
criticism of other social systems is intelligible and justifiable.

A mild form of communitarian epistemology is to be found in
Michael Walzer's idea that there are 'spheres of justice'. He points
out that it is often assumed that we must respond in terms of one
overarching reply that gathers together a set of substantive principles which can be drawn upon to determine what is just in any and
all circumstances. We have already noted that this may be questioned with respect to the cultural variations which undermine
many claims to the universality of principles of justice. It is also
salutary to confront the more radical claim that, even within the
same culture, there are disparate conceptions of justice which apply
in different areas of social, economic and political life. This
approach suggests that we may be able to identify more limited
but more powerful principles which are to be drawn neither from
intuitions of self-evident truths nor from calculations of utility, but
are embedded in the social conventions of reasonableness rooted in
specific areas of social practice.

The idea that there are different spheres of justice which ought to
be kept distinct is persuasively argued by Walzer (1983), whose
work exemplifies some of the 'communitarian' themes which feature
throughout the book in the criticism of liberal theories of justice.
Walzer's thesis is that justice has to do with the distribution of
goods and that different considerations apply according to the
type of goods in question, so that it is wrong to look for one
criterion (or set of criteria) which covers the distribution of such
disparate goals as social security, money, offices, work, leisure,
education, love, religion and political power. He argues that the
tendency to erect a comprehensive and unitary set of principles of
justice reinforces the politically and morally unfortunate practice of

cumulating the inequalities which may arise legitimately in the distribution of particular species of good. Through the encouragement of the assumption that the good reasons for having inequalities in one sphere are also good reasons for inequalities in all spheres, the resultant distributions of wealth, political power and educational opportunity, for example, tend to coalesce around the same individuals and groups. This produces the phenomenon of 'dominance' in which some people are at the beck and call of others in all significant aspects of life. Such dominance is an evil which can be avoided by making the different spheres autonomous so that there will be in each society a variety of distinct inequalities in different spheres, a state of affairs which he describes as 'complex' equality.

Notwithstanding the attractions of this thesis, it is a part of the second (critical) level of presentation adopted here that a theory of justice should be able to identify common features which explain how we are able to speak of justice and injustice in such diverse spheres as taxation, liability in tort and equality of opportunity in education. Indeed it can be seen as a major weakness of much contemporary philosophy of justice that it has so little to contribute to our understanding of the relationship between justice in the three principal spheres in which current issues of justice arise: law, welfare and remuneration for work. In particular, although many analyses of social justice do at least seek to bring together considerations of justice in the welfare and employment spheres, they are often at a loss to explain how justice in these areas relates to justice in the administration of law, thus fostering the conceptually and politically unhappy idea that legal justice and social justice are quite distinct phenomena.

Walzer's undoubted insights can be accommodated by allowing that the specification of what counts as just may well vary from sphere to sphere – so that, for instance, a just distribution of political offices need not be on the same basis as a just distribution of educational facilities – while leaving for further consideration whether or not there are common assumptions behind the specific criteria of justice used and what degree of overlap there is between the determinants of justice in each sphere. Walzer overstates his case with his implausible contention that there are distinct 'social meanings' associated with each type of social good which contain their own autonomous distributive considerations, so that, for instance, 'need' is relevant to the provision of health care but not to the distribution of political authority. This contention, which is convincing in some contexts but is of dubious generality, is highly dependent on the priority assumption which we have questioned, namely that whatever are the prime grounds for distribution in a sphere are considerations of 'justice', so that all decisively good reasons for particular social arrangements are misleadingly deemed to be requirements of justice.

Thus Walzer's particular case against desert as the general criterion of justice is that there are sometimes other morally acceptable grounds for distributing such goods as political office or sexual love (1983, pp.23–5). This ignores the possibility that these other grounds relate to moral justification of the allocations in question which have nothing to do with justice in its distinctive sense. Thus we may rightly select people for political office for reasons other than doing justice to the rival political candidates for office. In general, Walzer's efforts to erect boundaries between different spheres appears to be motivated more by his desire to have a conceptual basis for resisting 'dominance' than by a concern for justice as such. Injustice is a particular evil which needs explication independently of the distinct problem of the tyranny which results from cumulative injustices.

Walzer's contribution illustrates the difficulties which can arise from combining a generalised concept of justice with the working assumption of the primacy of justice. It also demonstrates the problems of distinguishing between approaches to justice on a consistent basis. Different theorists address themselves to rather different issues. Some concentrate on the general analysis of the idea of justice and its role in political debate and decision-making, others are more taken up with the specific criteria of justice – that is, the nature of the standards that are used in determining the justice or injustice of social arrangements and choices. Still others are primarily interested in the epistemological question of how we can make rational decisions about what criteria of justice to adopt and how to apply them in practice.

Despite these divergent emphases, and the other difficulties to which I have drawn attention, I assume that, ideally, every theory of justice should seek to establish an outline of the overall concept of justice, clarify the meaning and application of certain preferred criteria or conceptions of justice and give some indication of how we are to go about assessing the acceptability and significance of such criteria. In the context of a particular theoretical approach, each subsequent chapter raises questions about the conceptual analysis of justice, considers the normative criteria of justice employed and examines the proferred methodology for settling disputes about what is just and unjust. The intention is to help the reader to grasp the central features of each theoretical approach to justice and gain some appreciation of its practical import. This scheme of presentation is designed to encourage comparisons between theories, even where they differ radically in their emphases. At the same time some general criticisms of each theory will be offered in terms of its conceptual plausibility, its substantive moral content and its epistemological foundations.

3 Justice as Entitlement: Nozick and Property

The violation of rights is often cited as a standard example of injustice. It is unsurprising, therefore, that attempts are made to analyse justice purely in terms of rights. Justice is then a matter of respecting rights and providing remedies for their infringement or violation. In accordance with the logic of the concept of justice articulated in Chapter 2, 'to each his or her due' is interpreted as meaning 'to each his or her rights', with differing conceptions of justice giving varying content to the rights in question.

This powerful thesis, which is adopted by Robert Nozick, whose theory of justice is the main focus of this chapter, appears to capture some of the most important aspects of justice discourse identified in the previous chapters. It fits the major significance which is normally attributed to justice, in that to assert something as a right is to assert that it may properly be insisted upon and is no mere optional extra or merely desirable goal. Rights, like justice, are – in Nozick's term – matters of entitlement. They do not depend on the grace and favour of others. Rights generate obligations on the part of others, obligations which are in some sense owed to and can be required by the right-holder.

Viewing justice as a matter of rights also points up the emphasis on the interests of the individual which is a feature of justice discourse. For although collectives may be ascribed rights, the rights which justice theorists have in mind are primarily those which protect individuals against the singly lesser but cumulatively greater interests of large numbers of other people. In the words of Ronald Dworkin, a rights theorist whose work is discussed in the next chapter, rights are 'trumps', in that they cannot be set aside at the behest of majorities or policies aimed at the overall good of society. The rights he has in mind are those individual rights, such as freedom of speech and equality before the law, which are given special constitutional protection in many jurisdictions, but the same logic, although perhaps in a weaker form, may be applied to rights in general. Consequently, 'justice as entitlements' or 'justice as rights' fits well with the generally anti-utilitarian flavour of justice.

The idea that individuals have rights captures also the belief that the possession of rights enhances the dignity of the right-holder (see Feinberg, 1970b, pp.243–57), and so exemplifies the idea of respect for persons which is often said to lie at the core of what it is to treat people justly. This contention is often thought to rest on a restrictive analysis of rights which confines the term to one type of right, namely rights which give the right-holder the opportunity to control the action of others, if he or she opts to do so. However, the wider analysis of rights as rule-protected interests, which makes such optional powers a contingent feature of rights (that is, a feature which characterises some rights but not others), also enables us to see in the language of rights a commitment to the equal worth of every individual and the consequent priority of certain individual interests over considerations of the general good.

The idea of justice as rights also accords with the legal associations of justice, and offers a ready explanation as to why courts of law are regarded as courts of justice. Rights have to do with the implementation of societal rules or other authoritative standards, such as are embodied in laws. Similarly, the rights theory of justice can explain the connection between justice, remedies and punishments, and makes it clear why the demands of justice so often involve calls for the establishment of laws whose enforcement can be overseen by courts of law rather than left to the discretion of bureaucratic organisations.

On the other hand, it can be argued that rights have a narrower scope than justice. Rights seem most at home in limited areas where individual interests are protected by definitive rules capable of being adjudicated in courts of law. This may be important for the rectification of injustices done to individuals but it does not seem to have the same foothold where matters of wider collective or 'social' justice are concerned. Unjustified economic inequalities, the absence of educational opportunity and discrimination in employment are all grave social injustices but they are not objectives whose attainment can always readily be effectively pursued by means of legally enforceable entitlements. To take in these wider issues we have to have recourse to some idea of background 'moral' rights whose nature and content are highly controversial and often obscure.

Moral rights are, in general, regarded as standards or values which determine the proper content of rules which affect the welfare and interests of individuals. If this means no more than that they are the rights we ought to have, then the concept is clear enough but the values it encompasses are obviously far wider than justice alone, for the full range of social and political values are relevant to the determination of 'positive' rights (that is, the rights which are embodied in actual laws and social conventions). If, however, it is argued that there are pre-legal and pre-social 'natural' rights which all men and women have independent of the authoritative rules of their society, then it may be that the distinctive properties of these rights will help us to identify what is just and unjust. Unfortunately the nature and reality of such mysterious entities as moral rights are hard to establish, a difficulty which is encountered by Nozick's entitlement theory.

Moreover, the stress which the tradition of rights places on the freedom of the individual may be seen as a real hindrance to the achievement of the sort of egalitarian and welfare-oriented society which some see as a prime goal of justice. It may be that many rights give individuals unreasonable powers of veto over important social objectives whose justification is their contribution to justice. With its emphasis on individual choice and the liberty of the individual the theory of justice as rights often turns out to be an ideologically partisan theory in which liberty is favoured disproportionately over equality.

Rights and formal justice

Given the difficulties confronting the justice as moral rights thesis, it is common to retreat to a more limited objective and argue that rights are particularly germane to the analysis of *formal* justice, which may be defined as treating people in accordance with their existing socially recognised positive rights (see Chapter 2). Questions of material justice are then treated separately by means other than an appeal to rights. This has the advantage of demonstrating the distinctiveness of the language of rights. The appeal to rights is seen as an appeal to established rules or conventions which settle the matter in hand without the need to consider all other morally relevant, factors. If rights are conventional entitlements which block further debate in relation to the issues at stake, this enables us, for instance, to make a clear distinction between 'right' and 'rights', and we can then go on to identify justice with the latter.

This response substantially diminishes the claimed connection between rights and justice since it now excludes from justice material questions about the content of rights-conferring rules. It becomes a particularly weak thesis if the arguments outlined earlier concerning the moral unimportance of so-called pure formal justice are taken into account, since, as we have seen, formal justice, so conceived, places no real limitations on the possible content of rules and, in abstraction from such content, is of questionable moral significance.

However, since in ordinary and technical legal terminology not all rules or norms embody rights, it may be that those rules which do confer rights *are* constrained with respect to their content, and that this constraint is a pointer to what justice is about. In other words, there may be a distinctive rationale for rights-conferring rules which is the real nub of the justice as rights thesis. For instance, if, following the thicker analysis of formal justice and the rule of law outlined in the previous chapter, the rights approach is extended to take in the idea of the equal worth of persons as a basis of the justification for ensuring that a society is governed by a system of rules, then the justice as rights thesis acquires rather more substance, although it still does not give a great deal of guidance as to the content of the rules in question. We could say, however, that rights, and therefore justice, involve a commitment to recognising the equal worth of persons.

The idea of equal worth can itself be developed in the light of theories of rights which seek to state what it is about persons that make them potential bearers or subjects of rights. Thus, if rights are defined, in accordance with the 'will' theory of rights, as normative powers of control over the behaviour of others, powers which the right-holder may exercise or not at his or her discretion (see Hart, 1973, pp.171–201), then the rights thesis could be interpreted as saying that individuals should have such powers, and that justice is done when these are established and upheld by law or social convention. The discretionary powers involved in claiming and waiving rights may be justified as expressions of individual autonomy or as devices for protecting individual interests, and formal justice is then seen as giving effect to these morally desirable powers.

If, furthermore, we take the will theory of rights to include the proposition that human beings have, or ought to have, rights in

virtue of their capacities as rational agents, then we have the begin-
nings of a pre-legal conception of moral rights of some substance.
Such a position, which goes back at least as far as Kant, is exhibited
by Gewirth's thesis that persons have rights to the necessary conditions for human action (see Gewirth, 1978, chapter 2). This view,
when combined with certain truisms about the nature of action and
its empirical prerequisites, carries significant import for the content
of rights and hence, on the general approach under consideration,
for the nature of material as well as formal justice. Moreover it has
the advantage of bringing together the two types of justice – formal
and material – in an explanatory way since both involve respecting
individuals as autonomous choosers.

The will theory, and the associated idea of rights as the preconditions on human agency, are, however, overly restrictive analyses of
rights, for rights are routinely predicated on subjects, such as young
children and mentally handicapped people, who lack the capacity
for rational choice and autonomous action (see MacCormick, 1977,
pp.189–207). Moreover, when subsumed into the justice as rights
thesis, the will theory does not account for the formal justice of rules
which do not instantiate or protect powers or options. It is normally
assumed that formal justice arises in relation to the application of
any rules which have a bearing on the welfare or interests of persons, whether or not the rules confer powers or 'options'. This gives
rise to the broader theory of rights according to which a right is a
normatively protected interest (see Campbell, 1983, pp.92–102).

Because the interest theory of rights is more open-ended, it is
better suited than the will theory to provide an analysis of rights
which makes it plausible to claim that formal justice normally arises
in the application of all, or at least most, societal rules, for such
rules normally have some bearing on human interests. Its weakness
is that it is rather too broad to distinguish rules which confer rights
from those which do not, for almost any rule can be conceived of as
protecting a multiplicity of interests. However, the interest theory of
rights has the advantage of greater ideological neutrality, in that it
does not assume that the protection of individual choice has a
greater claim to the status of a right than, for instance, the relief
of suffering.

It would seem, therefore, that, although theories of rights may
help us to some extent in filling out the bare notion of the equal
worth of individuals, the more plausible of the rights theories on
offer are too broad to provide an analysis which takes us beyond the

mere outline of a rationale for having a system of formal justice, namely that it helps to protect and further human interests. If we wish to progress to a theory which can have a more substantial account of material justice it is necessary to have more specific guidance as to the nature and content of the so-called 'moral' rights which, it is claimed, provide standards for the assessment of the justice of the content of rules.

Justice as human rights

In order to extend the 'justice as rights' hypothesis from formal to material justice, we may resort to the distinction between the general idea of moral rights and that sub-category of those moral rights which are deemed to be 'natural' or 'human' rights. The identification of the distinctive nature of such rights is a difficult and controversial task. Indeed, lack of agreement about what constitutes a human right breeds doubt about the very concept of human rights. Most attempts at analysing human rights start out from the general position that human rights are a sub-category of moral rights which are universal (in that they apply to all persons everywhere and at all times), inalienable (in that they can be neither taken nor given away) and of overriding importance (so that they take precedence over all other considerations).

The problem of identifying more than a very few 'negative' rights – that is, rights *not* to be treated in certain ways – which meet these criteria is also great. Perhaps only the right not to be tortured is completely universal and inalienable, and even that may be doubted. For this reason the criteria are often watered down in various respects, particularly if it is thought desirable to include the 'social' and 'economic' rights, such as the right to education or health care, within the list of human rights. These rights are 'positive' in the sense that they are rights to be treated in certain ways, call for positive action on the part of others and usually depend on the deployment of scarce resources whose availability cannot be guaranteed everywhere and at all times. Unless formulated in an intolerably vague way, such rights cannot plausibly be claimed to be completely universal and entirely independent of particular economic circumstances, although much the same can be said about civil and political rights which cannot be secured in reality without significant resources.

However, if it is possible to arrive at an acceptable definition of human rights, material justice can then be defined in terms of securing such basic or human rights, and/or providing remedies for their infringement or violation. This has the advantage of making justice only one among the many considerations which may lead us to enact positive entitlements and, given the significance attached to human rights, it does much to explain the importance which many attach to the pursuit of justice.

In general the justice as human rights thesis generates more acute forms of the attractions and difficulties of regarding justice as having to do with rights of any sort. Particularly promising is its account of the conflict between justice and utility since human rights cannot, because they are defined as overriding rights, be sacrificed to the general happiness. A weakness of the human rights approach lies in its retreat from a positivist interpretation of rights according to which rights are defined in terms of existing societal or legal rules. Justice as human rights is, therefore, unable adequately to account for the legal flavour of justice. Of course, there is a long history of attempts to translate human rights into legal form, but in general they lend themselves more to political rhetoric than to legal formulation and adjudication. The language of human rights expresses ideals and aspirations which need to be honed down into specific entitlements before the rights they are said to embody have any connection with formal justice and the rule of law, which require the accurate implementation of preexisting rules.

The criticism that human rights, conceived along the lines of the traditional analyses, are non-justiciable may be thought to run counter to the experience of those jurisdictions which have operative conventions or bills of rights to which appeal can be made through courts against any action or inaction which is seriously detrimental to individuals, even if these are in accordance with the ordinary legislated law of the land. Does not the experience of the European Court of Human Rights, or of the Supreme Court of the United States of America, illustrate the viability of giving the force of positive law to the idea of human rights?

Certainly the notion of rights which have a special constitutional status in that they cannot be overturned, even by the otherwise lawful actions of governments, has become a reality which many political observers welcome as a way of providing some check on the failures and excesses even of democratic governments in matters which can readily be thought of in terms of injustice. If human rights are then defined as fundamental rights, that is, rights with special constitutional protection, then the idea of human rights does seem to have legal application. This is only achieved however by a patently positivistic analysis of human rights according to which they are equated with rules laid down by human decision, in this case through the enactment of the appropriate constitutional provisions. Human rights then become constitutionally entrenched rules, often administered by specialist courts, rather than simply a type of moral right of a sort to which appeal can be made to justify the setting up of such human rights conventions and special courts in the first place. It requires to be demonstrated, therefore, that in making their decisions human rights adjudicators are applying preexisting and specific notions of pre-legal human rights. It may be that all that is going on is the creation of a new system of rules and precedents of a rather indeterminate nature which permit the extensive exercise of discretionary powers by an elite group of lawyers who are constrained only by political considerations and a highly unspecific tradition of human rights discourse as this is embodied in brief and ambiguous lists of human rights. The existence and application of bills of rights, and their constitutional equivalents, does not in itself prove the reality of the human rights in the moral form on which they are alleged to be based (see Campbell *et al.*, 1986, chapters 1 and 2).

Those who would present a view of justice in terms of human rights have to provide a coherent account of these rights and the way we determine what they are. Furthermore they have to indicate that violation of these rights is properly regarded as a matter of injustice, for there may be some things, such as torture, which we ought never to inflict on each other, but which are wrong not because of their injustice but for some other moral reason, such as their inhumanity. It may be that general theories of rights can help here, although, on close inspection, they throw up the very types of moral disagreement which we are seeking to resolve. In particular, the standard conflicts between liberty (as exemplified in the will theory of rights) and egalitarianism (which has more affinity with the interest theory) may have to be resolved before it is possible to identify either the form or the content of the rights to which special constitutional protection is to be given. At this level of debate the rights approach often appears to have little to offer beyond an appeal to dogmatic self-evidence or unchallengeable moral intuitions. Yet, there are no reasonably specific rights-conferring rules capable of obtaining the agreement of dispassionate and informed persons, even within the same culture, so that it is doubtful whether the idea that there are moral rights (let alone that special sub-category of moral rights called *human* rights) is at all helpful in fixing our criteria of material justice. To settle controversial matters by an appeal to moral rights, human or otherwise, may be to do no more than pit one set of prejudices against another.

Given the epistemological blind alley into which rights discourse often leads us, it may be that we should give up the idea of moral rights except in the 'manifesto' sense which refers to the rights which we believe ought to exist in a morally adequate society. This would be to abandon as unhelpful the notion of human rights, except in so far as it refers to the idea of giving special constitutional status to some rights as a device for the protection of important human interests. Whether such rights are thought to have a particularly close connection with the concept of justice would then become a matter for subsequent analysis.

These are the sort of challenges to which rights theories respond in many different ways. For instance, Gewirth (1978), as we have seen, develops a Kantian basis for rights in terms of autonomy, while Finnis (1980) follows the natural law tradition of Aristotle and Aquinas. Another example is dealt with in the next chapter where I consider a particularly significant contribution to theories of rights as a basis for justice that has been made by Ronald Dworkin who, in *Taking Rights Seriously*, presents a sustained effort to bridge the gap between the notions of moral and positive rights in a manner which, if successful, would provide a basis for presenting an attractive form of the 'justice as rights' thesis. This chapter deals with the less legally oriented approach of Nozick who builds on the tradition of self-evident moral rights derived from the philosophy of John Locke which is taken up and applied in the Declaration of Independence that led to the foundation of the United States.

Ownership and entitlement

Discussing the contribution of Robert Nozick before that of John Rawls is slightly out of chronological order, since Nozick's *Anarchy, State and Utopia* (1974) was published three years after Rawls's *A Theory of Justice* (1971). Indeed Nozick's book may be regarded as a lively response to Rawls's more substantial work with which he deals explicitly. Nevertheless, Nozick's influential but somewhat idiosyncratic book has the advantage of presenting simple conclusions from a limited individualistic methodology, which makes it an accessible yet challenging introduction to my selection of specific theories of justice and in many ways clears the way for the more sustained theory elaborated by Rawls.

The entitlement theory of justice expounded by Nozick in *Anarchy, State and Utopia* is better known for its radical conclusions than for its unusual methodology. More than anything else its rampant *laissez-faire*, minimal-state libertarianism marks the book out as a classic of the 1970s, so much in tune with the new right politics of Margaret Thatcher and Ronald Reagan, and so incomprehensible to those who considered the welfare state as a progressive and permanent feature of the modern world. Yet, there is as much of interest in the method as in the conclusions of a book which revives an Enlightenment project of deducing political consequences from self-evident rights, using the eighteenth-century device of 'conjectural history', which reconstructs a possible history in order to explain and commend a political philosophy, in this case a form of libertarian semi-anarchism.

Moreover, we have already noted, in Chapter 1, Nozick's use of Hayek's critique of all attempts to distribute benefits and burdens in accordance with a set pattern, on the grounds that such programmes involve unacceptable intrusions on individual autonomy and are doomed to failure through the lack of reliable information about societies and economies. In this and other ways, *Anarchy, State and Utopia* can be seen as a riposte to Rawls's welfare liberalism, although they have in common a fundamental individualistic approach which makes them both targets of the communitarian critique which we looked at in the Chapter 2. Nozick's rampant individualism, in particular, is the antithesis of communitarianism.

In philosophical terms, Nozick and Rawls share considerable debt to the Enlightenment, particularly to Immanuel Kant and his insistence that human beings, as rational agents, must be treated as ends in themselves and never merely as means to securing benefit to some other person. Both also give a central role to the idea that consent is a fundamental concept of political philosophy, although it plays rather different roles in their theories. However, in contrast to Rawls, Nozick does not seek to defend the arbitrary starting-point from which his conjectural history commences.

Indeed, he may be said to have renounced its findings as incomplete, or simply wrong (see Nozick, 1989, p.292). Nevertheless, as a powerful if oversimplified expression of a political theory of justice which reflects current ideological orthodoxy in most western democracies, particularly the United States, it is worthy of careful study.

The gist of Nozick's position is that, prior to or independently of the existence of social and political systems, individuals have rights to property, life and liberty. These 'natural' rights are entitlements to be left alone, uncoerced in any manner which violates these rights. Since the only form of state which could have emerged without violating these rights is a state which is confined to defending them, such a minimal or 'night-watchman' state is the most that can be justified. This means that any attempt by the state to redistribute benefits is a form of theft and is therefore illegitimate. All other services which fall outside the scope of the minimal state can be provided by voluntary associations and commercial relationships, such as insurance schemes. Welfare provision on the basis of need is a matter for freely given charity. Finally, limiting state power to the protection of basic rights opens the way for multiple utopian ways of life as organised with the free consent of different associations of individuals who have the same or complementary conceptions of the good life. Justice is a matter of not violating rights, of enforcing voluntary agreements and rectifying such violations of rights as do occur. All this is a matter of entitlement which is not dependent on any calculation of the advantages or drawbacks of respecting and enforcing rights or the prospect of equalising in any way the distribution of benefits and burdens.

Nozick's theory of justice is constructed out of his theory of rights. His theory of rights rests on an unshakeable conviction that there are some things that we ought not to do to other people, no matter how beneficial the consequences might be for ourselves, for others, or even for the persons themselves. He illustrates this in relation to 'the forcible redistribution of bodily parts' (Nozick, 1974, p.206). No one, he claims, can rightly be required to donate even a non-vital organ to another person, even if that person's life depends upon it. This, he believes, demonstrates that we own our own bodies in the strong sense that we have an absolute right to control what happens to our bodies and no one is entitled to interfere with our bodies without our consent (provided we have not violated any equivalent rights of other people).

This right illustrates the principal features of the entitlement theory, for (1) the right is not dependent on its recognition by any human institution or culture – the right is natural or moral, (2) the right does not depend on the deserts, needs or usefulness of the right-holder – the right is absolute, (3) the right cannot be over-ridden by any consideration of general welfare or benefit to other persons – the right is inviolable, (4) the right correlates with the duty of others not to interfere with that which the person has a right to – the right is in this sense negative (positive rights arise only by voluntary agreement), (5) the right-holder may waive their right by consent to others doing what would otherwise be a violation of that right – the rights are alienable, and (6) the right is a 'side constraint' which limits the conduct of others rather than an end to be pursued by the right-holder or by those others.

These features also apply to further rights which are unpacked from the idea or the right to ownership of one's body. First it is interpreted as covering the right to life, and, more controversially, to the right to liberty in the sense of bodily movement. Further this is taken to mean that a person is entitled to do whatever they like with their body and their life (provided that they do not violate the body, life or liberty of other people) including acquiring ownership of things other than other people through the exercise of bodily capacities. This last step depends heavily on Locke's contention that people have a right to that with which they 'mix their labour', a process whereby a person's ownership of their body is extended to the ownership of material things which they appropriate (unless someone else has appropriated it first). This entitlement does not mean that the person is morally correct in doing any action which does not violate the rights of another, but it does mean that no one else may rightly interfere with what they are doing without first gaining their consent.

By keeping his list of basic rights short with the listed rights closely connected with each other and taking them to be purely negative rights, Nozick is able to sustain the claim that his basic rights cannot be overridden even by each other since there is no situation in which refraining from violating one such basic right involves violating another one, as would be the case if respecting rights involved taking action to protect and enhance the interests of others.

Nozick's way of obtaining our agreement to his theory is in part to present vivid examples of the 'side constraints' we accept as paramount in everyday life. We do not accept that it is right to kill one person in order to save ten people, or to enslave one person in order to please others. He then seeks to relate these moral intuitions to the general claim that the property-based liberties he identifies as basic rights are connected with the idea of meaningful existence. Human beings, he claims, are active, creative creatures able to set themselves goals and pursue plans of action. This is what makes them capable of meaningful lives and sustains the claim that they have a right to self-ownership and the life, liberty and further possessions that may be acquired by the exercise of these rights without violating the same rights of others.

This model of meaningful creativity is a familiar and interesting view of the significance of human existence, but it is not one that is specific enough to warrant the particular claims he makes with regard to the content and nature of basic rights. In particular, it is compatible with basic rights involving positive duties correlative to the protected interests to ensure that people have the wherewithal to live meaningful lives, and could readily be held to require a much wider range of rights directed towards the reduction of suffering and assuring equally meaningful lives. Further, it seems unduly dog-matic to give such a moral monopoly to meaningfulness. Everything here seems to depend on which moral intuitions we start with. Nozick generalises recklessly from examples which generate outrage at unwarranted infringement of bodily integrity and the free exercise of meaningful creativity. Other examples would lead to equally strong outrage at the unwarranted infliction of pain on innocent people.

Nozick's justice

The analysis of justice which flows from the assertion of a selected core of natural rights is straightforward. Everything depends on the entitlements that are constituted by natural rights as Nozick con-ceives of them. Justice is about property, or 'holdings', as he refers to possessions. Justice is then broken down into the acquisition of holdings, the transfer of holdings and the rectification of past injustices. Justice in the acquisition of holdings is about how people come to own that which was previously unowned. In brief, Nozick holds that whatever unowned thing a person appropriates and works becomes their property provided the appropriation does not leave others worse off. Justice in transfer is about voluntary exchange. Justice in rectification is about reversing unjust acquisitions and transfers.

Both the idea of acquiring property by 'mixing' labour with material objects and the proviso of leaving enough for others derive from Locke. In Locke's analysis there is a background assumption that God gave the material world to human beings for their benefit and the argument that mixing labour is (at least sometimes) a way of increasing the value of the objects in question. Nozick relies on neither of these factors – which have both utilitarian and theological flavour – and does not make clear how he wishes to spell out Locke's 'mixing' analogy in an intelligible way. We could have here the beginning of an argument from desert, on the basis that those who labour productively have a greater claim to that which they have laboured on than others, but this would take us only so far as rewarding those who work, say on the land, to the extent that they increase its value and perhaps as far as their work benefits other people. This does not have the libertarian consequences of an absolute property right that Nozick desires. If the purpose of having private property is to benefit humankind by making the land productive, then the matter of who owns what, and what rights owners have over their property, must be subordinate to the wider objective, something that runs counter to Nozick's analysis.

It would appear also that Nozick has let a Trojan Horse into his theory by accepting even a weakened version of the Lockean proviso (which is, that there be 'enough and as good' left for others) since this proviso must be justified by some reference to the overall consequences of permitting this or that property acquisition, such as not leaving others to starve or able to lead meaningful lives. This brings in a background purpose for having a system of property including rules of acquisition, a purpose which can then be used to determine whether or not Nozick's rule of acquisition is the right one. Why not, for instance, limit acquisition to that amount of land or good that a person or family are able to work on together, or which is sufficient to keep them in comfort, and no more?

Justice in transfer relates to voluntary exchanges of holdings justly acquired. Voluntariness is an essential ingredient of all just transfers. Indeed everything which follows from a consensual transfer of justly acquired goods is just. In a now famous example Nozick supports his position by pointing to the 'justice' of the way in which the sporting superstar, Wilt Chamberlain, became exceedingly wealthy through the more than voluntary enthusiasm with which his fans bought tickets to see him play. Chamberlain's talents are his own and his play is his own labour, and the transfers are consensual, so the unequal outcome is just, for 'whatever arises from a just situation by just steps is itself just' (1974, p.151). The intuitive appeal of this position is undermined by Nozick's acceptance that a voluntary act includes one that a person is forced to take by circumstances of nature rather than by unwarranted coercion by other human beings (1974, p.262). This means that he includes as 'voluntary' many choices which people do not want to make but must make in order to survive. It is not therefore free and willing consent that matters, but whether the 'coercion' applied by other people is or is not warranted, and this depends, on Nozick's view, on whether or not it involves a threat to violate a preexisting right. Voluntariness therefore plays a subordinate role to his basic property right of bodily ownership and the implied right to whatever that body labours on.

If the liberal voluntariness principle is not the be-all and end-all of political philosophy, then it seems proper that we at least modify Nozick's position to require that transfers are voluntary in a stronger sense than he permits, that is, that they are made with adequate knowledge of the nature of the goods and the consequences of the transfers in a situation in which genuine alternatives are open to them (see Paul, 1982; and Cohen, 1978). This would, however, destroy the purity and simplicity of the theory.

Finally, justice in rectification involves putting right the wrongs which occur as a result of acquisition without the mixing of labour, or through involuntary transfers. Again, this is an immediately attractive and intuitively sound approach which fits with important matters that are generally thought to be an essential part of justice. Rectificatory justice is normally taken to include punishment as well as transfer of money and holdings which have been wrongly acquired, hence the close connection between justice and law and the association of justice and desert. Nozick's justice in rectification is attractive in relation to simple examples of returning stolen property or handing back land that has been taken by force or fraud. There may be great difficulties in putting this into effect when the holding has been destroyed or damaged or the wrong done is to human life and liberty rather than material possessions, however a substitution of retributive punishment for transfer of holdings might be brought in to fill this contingent gap.

No doubt the matter is simplified by the limited ways in which property may be unjustly acquired and transferred but there are immense counterbalancing complexities which arise once we try to put such an approach into systematic practice. In the actual world there can scarcely be any property that has not been acquired without a degree of Nozickean injustice and it seems ridiculous because impossible to go back to the beginning and work out the original rightful owners of holdings and discount all involuntary transfers. If there is any overarching rationale for having a system of property and rules of acquisition it would surely count against the instability and uncertainty which would arise from efforts to put right the past in such a wholesale way. However, this is perhaps a problem which will be encountered by any theory of justice with a rectificatory element.

The implications of Nozick's three aspects of justice for the idea of justice as a whole are very significant. Justice as entitlement seems incompatible with the common assumption that justice is about distribution, not in a historical sense relating to how a particular distribution of holdings came about, but about what pattern of distribution is the best one. Should holdings be distributed literally equally (to everyone the same amount)? Or should they be distributed in proportion to the merit of those involved, or their needs, or some other characteristic, such as their capacities or how much other people like or love them? It is a major feature of Nozick's theory that the pursuit of all such patterns is a violation of rights since it inevitably involves taking away goods from some and redistributing them to other people in order to establish the pattern and this must involve injustice or taking away those things which have been justly acquired. Justice is not about establishing a pattern, it is about how whatever pattern or lack of one there happens to be came about. The fact that Wilt Chamberlain has much more than other people, much more than he merits or needs, is irrelevant to the justice of his holdings.

Nozick is here drawing on the familiar fact that in all human societies some people, by dint or work, skill, cunning, luck or self-control, end up with more than others, and the widespread assumption that there is nothing intrinsically wrong with this. Moreover, any effort to rectify such a situation and establish a pattern which is either equal or in line with some approved set of criteria involves a deprivation of liberty, an element of coercion which takes away that which people have used their liberty to acquire or have received through the voluntary actions of others. Not only does a measure of inequality seem perfectly natural but the effort to counter such inequality as emerges naturally seems oppressive. It follows, for Nozick, that all 'end-state' theories, theories which seek to achieve a specified distributional outcome, are unacceptable violations of natural justice. In one stroke he seems to have undermined some basic principles of the welfare state in which progressive taxation for the sake of remedying gross inequalities and providing basic services to those who need them are taken for granted as part of social justice. The force of his position can be seen in typical objections to the patterned provision of welfare, such as the unfair penalisation of savings and state support of those who are voluntarily idle.

Of course, not all patterns have these defects. In particular, a pattern which is based on desert or merit can count savings as meritorious and view voluntary idleness as undeserving. Desert in general can be seen as historical rather than end-state since it depends on past conduct, albeit usually much wider in scope than Nozick allows. Moreover it is at least conceivable that members of a society could voluntarily adopt a system whereby a pattern is achieved in part through such devices as progressive taxation. There are clearly practical difficulties in achieving both these goals given the problems of assessing merit, obtaining agreement as to the best pattern of distribution and bringing about these desired outcomes. These difficulties may be sufficiently major to justify Nozick's hostility to end-state justice, particularly if it is regarded as the overriding moral goal of a society. Hayek, as we have seen, argues forcibly to this effect (see p.18). It cannot be said, however, that Nozick has succeeded in demonstrating the injustice of all attempts to move, through progressive taxation and other devices, towards a pattern which would reflect distribution in accordance with desert, or some other favoured criterion. At most we can accept that establishing patterns is not the whole of justice and that any moves in this direction must be tempered by the liberty deficits which may arise in their implementation and the need to demonstrate the grounds for allowing such deficits. However, in a world in which some have wealth far beyond what they can use to significantly improve their well-being and many more suffer through deprivation of the necessities of life, this is not too hard to achieve.

Further, in actual societies it is clear that the capacity of some to generate more holdings than others is crucially dependent on the society in which they live, the activities of those who have gone before them, the social class and family and gender and race into which they were born and the good or ill fortune of health, location and time. These essentially communitarian points undermine the intuitive force of Nozick's examples which derive from our revulsion at the compulsory reallocation of bodily parts or the forced labour of slaves. To appreciate Nozick's response to such objections, it is necessary to take a look at the role of conjectural history in his overall theory and the significance he attaches to showing what sort of state could emerge in accordance with his libertarian principles of justice.

Conjectural history and the minimal state

The device whereby social theorists of the eighteenth century sought to fill in the large gaps in their knowledge of the development of human societies by constructing a story of what could have happened, or is likely to have happened, in the light of their knowledge of human nature and the general workings of human societies is called 'conjectural history'. Its main purpose was to give an explanation for the historical stages with which they were familiar. Hence there were innumerable attempts to paint a picture of how modern property systems and associated forms of government must have developed from the time when human beings lived by hunting in small groups through the stages of pastoral, agricultural and urban mercantile civilisations.

Such accounts frequently had a justificatory aspect in that they were designed to show the propriety of existing arrangements as reasonable responses to prior and continuing human conditions. Nozick deploys conjectural history in this basically justificatory manner to argue that, given the natural rights of bodily ownership, life and liberty, only a minimal state could have arisen without violating the principles of justice in acquisition and transfer.

Starting with the Enlightenment notion of the state of nature, a situation before government and perhaps before any structured social relationships, Nozick works forward, not to the traditional and fanciful idea of a social contract which sets up society and/or government, but to show how a minimal state could emerge justly without any large-scale unanimous agreement between all potential citizens. While theorists such as Hobbes made the justification of a strong state easier by drawing a bleak picture of the state of nature as a dangerous, violent and poverty-stricken condition, Nozick gives us a pleasant enough account of the state of nature as a condition of some peace and basic prosperity if only because people do have the benefit of their knowledge of natural rights which leads them to respect the property of others and favour voluntary transfers.

The difficulties that would result from the uncooperative and unjust conduct of some members of the society can be rectified by local voluntary agreements between individuals and groups to protect their justly acquired property, lives and liberty. Thus, we can envisage mutual protection agencies in which significant numbers of individuals join forces to protect their natural rights. It would be reasonable for such agencies to develop a system of division of labour and to pay some of their number to provide the necessary protection and rectificatory procedures (Nozick, 1974, pp.11–16).

Problems are then envisaged to occur between competing protective agencies in overlapping geographical areas. Some agencies will flourish because they are more successful than others in providing good protection for lesser cost than their rivals. Nozick accepts that some of these conflicts must lead to fighting with a dominant agency arising as a result of the superior use of force against other successful protective agencies competing for the same business. However, he thinks that this will be seen as wasteful, and presumably also unjust, and so such conflicts will come to be settled by setting up courts to adjudicate competing claims and develop rules which can be followed for their competition, so that we have a number of private agencies and a common judicial system.

This system is not, in Nozick's view, strictly a state since no one is forced to join and anyone may continue to enforce their own rights as an independent operator. States emerge only when the independent individuals are required to join under one overall protective agency for a territory. He argues that such individuals could be rightly forced to join because, as independents, they would be continually favouring their own interests when these conflict with those of others. Lacking the impartiality of courts dealing with the cases of other parties, independent operators are routinely unjust, therefore it is a matter of rectificatory justice that they can be required to submit to the ruling of the courts which have emerged as a result of a voluntary process.

A similar argument justifies the use of force against those who would resist the judgments of the courts and the operations of the dominant protection agencies working under the agreement of those courts. Those who do not conform voluntarily may be regard as systematically partial to their own interests and therefore prone to injustice. Thus we have a situation in which we have a state, albeit a minimal one, confined to the application of a limited range of natural rights. Moreover this state is not the result of any fanciful social contract. Nor is it the result of any unjust act on the part of those who have now the right to use force. This minimal state and nothing more can be conjectured as having resulted from morally permissible steps, moral permissibility being determined by Nozick's entitlement theory of justice.

If this imaginary history can be established as a counter-factual possibility, then we have powerful supporting reasons against welfare states seeking to impose any form of end-state pattern on their subjects. To engage in such redistribution would be to exercise a power which could not have been acquired justly. Those whose liberty and property are affected would then have a claim in rectificatory justice against the state. As it is Nozick does allow that the minimal state has the duty to provide protective services to all those in its territory irrespective of whether or not they can afford to pay for these services. This apparently redistributive policy is justified, however, by the fact that they have been (rightly) coerced to join the state, or at least to compensate them for not being allowed to leave the state. Moreover, Nozick seems to accept that the same protective services would be used to protect everyone irrespective of the level of contribution they make to the protective agencies' income, an interesting concession in the direction of egalitarianism.

All this seems a clever but not very convincing myth which may succeed in providing a justification of a minimal state by his own method, although it should be said that there are more straightforward consequentialist reasons for vindicating a system of mandatory rules and an associated enforcement agency for the protection of basic interests, reasons of efficiency, fairness and flexibility, as outlined in Hart (1961, chapter 5), which lists some of the benefits which arise from emerging systems of law as societies develop into complex and changing systems.

For Nozick, however, his own approach matters because it is crucial to his further claim that nothing more than a minimal state can be justified. Efficiency and fairness in themselves could generate all sorts of state functions, including the duty to see to the general well-being of the members of a society. Nozick is able to block these moves by arguing that no amount of good consequences can override the sort of inviolable negative rights which provide the sole moral basis for social and political arrangements. This retains the coherence of his theory, perhaps at the expense of casting further doubt on his claim that there are no other rights or no other values which must be taken into account in any adequate theory of justice.

Nozick's restricted vision

It is possible to argue that the importance of Nozick's account of justice as entitlement lies in its libertarian conclusions rather than the arguments which are deployed to support this ideology. Certainly, it is widely held that his arguments are incomplete and inconclusive. Nevertheless there is a power to many of his points which demands careful response and measured argument. It may well be that some version of an entitlement theory, which makes rights central and defines them in a narrow and forceful way as something more than mere aspirations, is a necessary part of any palatable theory of justice. Nor can the dangers to liberty which he and Hayek see in the redistributive state be lightly rejected.

His theory certainly requires a broader conception of desert which takes into account variations in capacity to take advantage of opportunities to acquire and exchange goods. He also requires a firmer basis for his rather arbitrary selection of self-ownership as so all-pervasive and exclusive in the theory of justice and to make room for other moral intuitions such as those about the resultant inequalities of his scheme. When these complicating factors are taken into account there emerges a clash between the desert and the liberty aspects of the theory. Indeed, one advantage of his approach is the way in which it can be used to highlight this divergence, which may be conceptualised as a clash within justice, or between justice and liberty, or between freedom and equality, which needs to be systematically acknowledged. Even so, it is hard not to conclude that, despite the flavour of desert in his theory of just acquisition, Nozick's theory is more about liberty than it is about justice. Moreover, his vision of liberty is itself rather narrow since it ignores the consequences, even for meaningful creativity, of initial disparities of wealth and talent.

Nozick's theory of justice as entitlement demonstrates the difficulty of finding a foundation for the assertion of basic rights in a strong form, a difficulty which, as we will see, multiplies as a wider range of rights is added to those few which Nozick recognises, something which most adherents to the human rights tradition would wish to do.

4 Justice as Rights: Dworkin and Minorities

Nozick's entitlement theory of justice is only one of several recent attempts to ground justice in rights. John Rawls and Ronald Dworkin provide us with alternative and more sustained theories which give a central role in justice theory to the concept of rights. Just as Nozick's book comes chronologically slightly after Rawls's main work but is logically prior in its less developed philosophical foundations, so it makes sense to deal with Dworkin's more legally oriented theory of justice before tackling the broader political theory developed with such sophistication by Rawls.

Dworkin echoes Nozick's commitment to fundamental rights in a form that overrides all other considerations. In Dworkin's famous phrase, rights are trumps. Where a basic right applies nothing can stand in its way. However, he differs from Nozick with respect both to the content of rights and their derivation. Dworkin's substantive emphasis is on equality rather than liberty, 'equal concern and respect' being his grounding moral principle. Further, Dworkin locates the articulation of rights more in actual rather than hypothetical history. In particular the history of law, at least in certain jurisdictions, is taken as a manifestation which gives concrete form to the basic principles of justice. Moreover, Dworkin seeks to commend giving institutional instantiation to the idea of fundamental rights as prior to all other sources of legitimate government by endorsing the constitutional devices of bills of rights and judicial review of legislation which is such a significant factor in the political system of the United States.

Dworkin may be viewed as a legal rather than a political theorist for much of his work is taken up with the proper method of interpreting legal texts, but his overall position is a social and political philosophy which ultimately subordinates law to moral scrutiny. While, in his theory, constitutional courts should play a major role in developing the moral insights which lead to improve interpretations of fundamental rights, this is a form of reasoning which he invites all citizens to join in and can in principle be detached from the particular constitutional system that he recommends.

Dworkin's rights

That Dworkin has not generally been regarded as primarily a theorist of justice is an indication of the extent to which considerations of so-called social justice have become detached from legal contexts but, as his recent writings make clear, he is as much concerned with wide issues of social justice as with the specific nature of legal justice. While it is primarily of rights that Dworkin writes, his analysis of rights is carried out firmly within the assumption that justice is a matter of determining what rights persons have and ensuring that they are treated in accordance with these rights. Not only does he contend that 'it is a matter of injustice when judges make mistakes about legal rights' (Dworkin, 1978, p.130), he also insists that 'the institution of rights rests on the conviction that the invasion of a relatively important right ... is a grave injustice' (1978, p.199). This is because, in his view, rights bear on the dignity and equality of persons, factors which are, for Dworkin, the very foundations of justice. Thus, in the Dworkinian scheme of things, justice and rights go together so that, for instance, the question of whether or not a practice such as positive discrimination is unjust is treated as a question about whether or not the practice violates the rights of those affected by it (see 1978, pp.22, 198 and 231). He is therefore firmly committed to a rights theory of justice, although he would accept that this is simply one interpretation of a concept with a long and varied history (see Dworkin, 1986, pp.73–6), albeit one which fits the main paradigms of our time.

Dworkin divides political theories, including theories of justice, into three groups. The first consists of teleological theories which are ultimately based on goals (states of affairs that may be advanced or preserved by political acts). Utilitarianism is one such theory. The other two theories are deontological ones in that they rest on convictions about the rightness or wrongness of acts in themselves, independently of their further consequences. Of these deontological theories, the first is rights-based and the second duty-based. In this context he says that a person has 'a *right* to a particular political act, within a political theory, if the failure to provide that act, when he calls for it, would be unjustified within that theory even if the goals of the theory would, on the balance, be disserviced by that act' (1978, p.169), while a person has 'a *duty* to act in a particular way, within a political theory, if a political decision constraining such an act is justified within that theory notwithstanding that no goal of the system would be served by that decision' (1978, p.170).

While Dworkin contends that all theories involve goals, rights and duties, he argues that they differ as to which type of norm is fundamental from the point of view of ultimate justifications. Thus goals may be justified because they promote rights or duties, while rights or duties may be justified, in a rule-utilitarian manner, on the grounds that, in the long run, they promote certain goals. Similarly rights may be justified on the basis of their correlative duties, or duties may be justified in terms of their correlative rights. Alternatively, goals, rights or duties may be justified by reference to other more basic goals, rights or duties or, on the other hand, they may stand on their own as being in no need of further justification.

Ultimately, however, justifications must be grounded in one or other type of consideration. Each political theory will not only have its own particular set of goals, rights and duties but 'will give ultimate pride of place to just one of these concepts; it will take some overriding goal, or some set of fundamental rights, or some set of transcendent duties, as fundamental, and show other goals, rights, and duties as subordinate and derivative' (1978, p.171). Thus, all theories, except for 'intuitionist' theories, which present a pluralism of ultimate bases, are either goal-based (like utilitarianism), duty-based (like Kant's categorical imperative theory) or rights-based (like Tom Paine's theory of revolution). Dworkin permits all three types of theory to have a concept of justice in that all three approaches generate positive rights, but he regards the rights-based theories as preferable for the formulation of a conception of justice.

The focus of Dworkin's theory of rights is not directed towards ordinary positive rights. He interprets ordinary positive rights along the lines of the will theory as having to do with actions that the right-holder may or may not 'call for' as he or she chooses, and he assumes that in normal circumstances justice requires implementation of these rights. However, his concern is rather with the 'background' rights which act as the ultimate justifications for ordinary positive rights and also set strict limits on the propriety of any goals that may be endorsed. He allows that not all goals are justified in terms of rights but insists that no pursuit of a goal may be of a form which violates a basic right. Basic rights are thus moral or political rights which generate entitlements: 'if someone has a right to something, then it is wrong for the government to deny it to him even though it would be in the general interest to do so' (1978, p.269).

As is the case with all rights, basic rights act as restraints on behaviour, including goal-seeking behaviour. That is why they are conceived as 'trumps', for they have automatic precedence over or exclude other considerations. This veto power is however a matter of degree in that, while all rights must have some 'exclusionary' force, since they cannot be set aside by every morally relevant consideration (see Raz, 1975, pp.35–48), some rights have greater exclusionary force or trumping power than others. At one extreme on the scale of overridings there are 'absolute rights', which never yield to competing rights or vital goals, while at the other extreme are rights with so little 'weight' that they override scarcely any other rights or goals. Nevertheless every right must have some 'threshold' force which enables it to outweigh other considerations, otherwise it could not function as a right.

With this scheme Dworkin can distinguish between 'background rights, which are rights that provide a justification for political decisions by society in the abstract', and what he calls 'institutional rights, that provide a justification for a decision by some particular and specified political institution'. Background rights are abstract rights which constitute 'the grand rights of political rhetoric' while institutional rights are 'concrete' in that they 'are more precisely defined so as to express more definitely what weight they have against other political aims on particular occasions' (1978, p.93). Abstract rights provide justifications for concrete rights but they carry no immediate remedies, while concrete rights are definitive of what is institutionally due to a person in particular circumstances.

It is a distinguishing feature of Dworkin's analysis of rights that they are not always expressed in rules. Concrete institutional rights are normally formulated in rules which, for Dworkin, means that they can be applied in an 'all-or-nothing' manner. These constitute the paradigmatic legal or positive rights which are the core of normal legal adjudication and which, according to the rule of law, judges should apply in routine courtroom findings. However, Dworkin does not take the standard line of contrasting such positive rights with moral rights and then restricting judges to the adjudication of positive rights, leaving it to legislatures to draw on moral rights for the formulation of legal rules. Rather he argues that the law itself contains 'principles' as well as rules. These principles are distinguished, not by their greater generality or vagueness, but by the fact that, in judicial reasoning, they have a certain 'weight' rather than an 'all-or-nothing' effect, that is, they provide reasons for a particular decision of varying force, but do not definitively dispose of the case in hand. The role of principles in legal reasoning is primarily to decide 'hard' – that is, unclear – cases where there are no unambiguous relevant rules, or where the rules produce results which are unacceptable in terms of certain basic legal principles such as the principle that 'no man should profit from his own wrong' (1978, p.24). These principles embody or imply rights with a more fundamental status in Dworkin's hierarchy of legal norms than ordinary positive rights.

Dworkin's most influential and controversial work is his attempt to demonstrate that the existence of principles within the law undermines the view of legal positivists, such as Hart (1961), that law is a system of rules supplemented by judicial discretion where this is necessary in order to interpret ambiguities in the rules or to fill in gaps where there is no uncontroversially relevant rule by which to decide a particular case. His thesis is that, if we accept legal principles, then judges have a sufficient basis for arriving at a correct legal decision in every case, however 'hard' it may be. Moreover, since these principles are identified with the background moral principles used to justify concrete rights, it follows that legal validity is not a matter of positive enactment alone but involves a moral dimension. This moral dimension, which represents the basic requirements of justice, is expressed in the legal principles which enable judges to decide hard cases without resort to discretionary power.

Dworkin holds to the line that judges determine what the law is, rather than supplement it with their own personal judgements. In determining what principles there are in law and what weight to give them in particular cases judges do, or should, draw on the morality of their society. However, this societal morality is not the moral fashion of the moment, as it might be expressed in an opinion poll, but is to be found in the abstract rights embedded or presupposed in the legislation and political culture of that society in its historical development. The judge is fitted to determine what these principles are because they are discovered by constructing 'a scheme of abstract and concrete principles that provide a coherent justification for all common law precedents and, so far as these are to be justified on principle, constitutional and statutory provisions as well' (1978, pp.116 ff.). This is a style of reasoning familiar to lawyers, who seek to determine the law by considering previous legal decisions in the light of relevant enacted laws which they endeavour to interpret as a coherent whole. Such legal method is, according to Dworkin, extended, where necessary, by a broader appeal to that background political theory which can provide the most coherent justification for the settled law. In this the judge may take account of the general role of law in that society and the current standards of community morality as well as the specifics of past political and legal decisions, for 'political rights are the creatures of both history and morality: what an individual is entitled to have, in civil society, depends upon both the practice and the justice of its political institutions' (1978, p.87).

It cannot be said that Dworkin's strategy for bridging the gap between law and morals, which is insisted upon by the legal positivist, is entirely clear. His objective is to provide a satisfactory delineation of the boundary between legislative and adjudicative decision-making and so preserve the classical doctrine of the separation of powers. He does this by seeking to demonstrate that there is an autonomous mode of judicial decision-making that is compatible with the non-elected status of the judiciary. This thesis rests on the claim that judges are bound by and are able to follow the law rather than create it in every case that comes before them.

To maintain the distinction between legislation and adjudication Dworkin insists on a sharp contrast between decisions based on the rules and principles on the one hand and decisions which involve some reference to goals on the other hand. Legislatures may properly make law in order to further collective goals, such as economic prosperity, as well as to concretise background rights or duties, always provided they do not infringe rights in the pursuit of such goals. Judges, however, may decide cases by reference only to rules and principles. In effect this means that they must make their decisions by reference to rights (for principles as well as rules are expressive of rights), not goals. The right answer in a legal case is, therefore, the decision which treats persons according to their pre-existing rights. While some of these rights will have been enacted by legislatures intent on furthering certain policies, judges may not reason in the light of these policy objectives but must restrict their attention to the concrete rights, and where necessary, the background political or moral rights which have weight in that particular sphere.

Thus standards of justice feature in both adjudication and legislation, but in adjudication justice is the sole consideration, the just decision being the one which gives effect to the rights of the accused or the plaintiffs. In legislation, on the other hand, decisions are made according to a combination of goals and background abstract rights. Only where the latter are involved does justice feature. Thus justice may provide a veto on goal-based legislation which infringes upon background rights. In addition, justice is the sole basis for legislation designed to protect or further abstract rights. In the latter cases, Dworkin argues, rights must be distributed equally, a requirement which does not apply if legislation is a matter of policy, when legislatures may distribute benefits and burdens unevenly if they so choose, provided basic rights are not affected.

It is this connection between rights and equality which provides Dworkin with the underlying moral basis for his theory of rights and thus his analysis of justice. Indeed his ultimate basic right is the right to 'equal consideration and respect' which he distinguishes from actual 'equality of treatment', the term he uses to refer to those situations where each person either receives, or ends up with, the same quantity of the valued commodity that is being distributed. Justice involves the right to treatment as an equal, not the right to equal treatment.

At one level of analysis it appears that the principle of treatment as an equal is part of the very concept of justice, for it is presented as an abstract right which can be satisfied by many different concrete political ideals, including egalitarianism, meritocracy and average utility or Rawlsian fairness. Treatment as an equal requires only that, whatever the details of the system of distribution, government must treat people with equal concern and respect. In particular, government 'must not distribute goods or opportunities unequally on the grounds that some citizens are entitled to more because they are worthy of more concern. It must not constrain liberty on the ground that one citizen's conception of the good life is nobler or superior to another's' (1978, p.273).

This version of the principle of equal worth does not imply that the interests of some citizens may not have to give way to those of others, but it does entail that each citizen's interests will be given the same sympathetic consideration when, for instance, liberty is curtailed in the interests of some collective goal. It also means that the ideals of one person or group should not be imposed on those who do not share them.

To give substance to this 'highly abstract' right Dworkin argues that in the determination of collective goals majority preferences should count, but only where these preferences are based on individuals' aspirations for themselves (their 'personal' preferences) as opposed to their wishes about what should happen to others (their 'external' preferences):

> 'a utilitarian argument that assigns critical weight to the external preferences of members of the community will not be egalitarian in the sense under consideration. It will not respect the right of everyone to be treated with equal concern and respect.' (1978, p.275)

It is because the ordinary democratic process cannot in practice sort out personal from external preferences that the idea of individual political rights is so important, for such rights provide a way of protecting individuals against the external preferences of others, and this:

> 'allows us to enjoy the institutions of political democracy, which enforce overall or unrefined utilitarianism, and yet protect the fundamental right of citizens to equal concern and respect by prohibiting decisions that seem, antecedently, likely to have been reached by virtue of the external components of the preferences democracy reveals.' (1978. p.277)

Hence it is the liberal commitment to equality that is the basis for the protection of individual liberties.

The powerful attraction of Dworkin's approach to rights as the basis for an account of justice lies in the way he relates the formalism of treating persons in accordance with their positive legal rights to the background moral rights which can provide reasons why the accurate implementation of concrete rights is desirable, thus bridging the gap between formal and material justice. He seeks to transcend what he calls a 'rule-book' conception of the rule of law which covers only the idea of strict adherence to legal rules and argues for a 'rights' conception of the rule of law which requires the adjudicator to give due weight to the principles which would justify existing legislative enactments. Moreover the way in which Dworkin connects rights with the concept of the individual as worthy of equal respect ties in with the idea of the moral significance of individual responsibility, the exercise of personal choice and the pursuit of self-determination, all of which give substance to the idea of justice as a distinct and major moral ideal.

The principal weakness of Dworkin's theory is its failure to give a convincing account of the relationship between concrete and background rights. This is partly a matter of the difficulty he has in giving grounds for accepting his thesis that there is a right answer to hard cases of law and that this answer is properly described as discovering and applying the rights of the parties involved. Even if it is conceded that there is a correct answer to every legal dispute, the elaborate form of reasoning required to reach this answer makes it difficult to believe that legal decisions are made only on the basis of something we can recognise as preexisting 'rights'.

In the first place, this contention ignores the substantial role played by appeals to public policy – such as the consequences for governmental objectives like economic efficiency – as the basis for appellate decisions in court. Dworkin has met this difficulty by saying that apparent appeals to policy can always be 'substituted' with arguments of principle. Public policy arguments can readily be rephrased so that they are stated in terms of protecting or furthering the rights of those affected by the policy. This manoeuvre hardly fits in with his contention that goals and hence policies are non-individuated political aims and thus presumably far removed from the idea of individual rights. Indeed, if taken literally, this concession as to the interchangeability of policy and principle undermines all that he has sought to establish about the significance of rights in legal decision-making. All that is left of his thesis is that policies which relate to majority interests are Dworkinian policies while those which relate to minority interests are Dworkinian rights, which seems to make the rights of minorities trump the rights of majorities.

In the second place, it seems a matter of faith for Dworkin to assert that there is an objective way of deciding which decision in hard cases best coheres with the precedents, rules, principles and background political philosophy of a jurisdiction. If the notion of a right answer is merely regulative, in that it does no more than provide an abstract but unattainable goal towards which it is our legal duty to strive, then appeals to rights cannot fulfil their normal function of providing a way of settling disputes by reference to institutional rules or principles, for, ultimately, it simply involves accepting the determinations of persons appointed to make such decisions. Indeed it can be argued that the overt purpose in the formulation of some rules (particularly those which contain references to standards such as 'reasonableness') and many legal principles is to enable the judiciary to deploy general ideas of fairness or desert so that justice may be done in particular cases.

These difficulties are not eased by Dworkin's more recent deployment of the ideas of 'integrity' as an objective of legal reasoning or his proffered analogy between legal and literary textual interpretation (see Dworkin, 1986). In *Law's Empire* (1986) (see also Dworkin, 1996), he develops a rather loosely defined concept of 'integrity' as an important ingredient in legal reasoning that points to the grounding of principle in a holistic but developmental approach to existing legal materials, such as cases and legislation, in a way which is analogous to the writing of a chain novel, in which one author or group of authors takes on the work of previous writers and develops it in a manner which coheres with the story so far and then passes it on to the next authors who are similarly constrained but also creatively free to take the novel into the succeeding chapter. Arguing that law is an essentially interpretive exercise of this sort, in which nothing is determined by the text alone, he holds that courts must strive to construct a coherent body of legal texts. This cannot be done without viewing the law in terms of justifying principles that guide the process of interpretation. It follows that the legal enterprise is one which draws on the fundamental principle of justice that each litigant has to be treated with equal concern and respect. Legal interpretation seeks to express a coherent conception of justice and fairness (1986, p.225). This, of course, opens up the process to unexpected outcomes in which established patterns may be overturned in order that justice may be done to the individuals involved. There remains, therefore, an unresolved tension between the formal justice aspect of requiring that a decision 'fit' the history of prior decisions and the other ingredients of integrity, such as the importance of reaching decisions by fair process and the need to interpret the law in a way which gives apparently overriding significance to principles which the courts believe to embody equal concern and respect. In its weaker form, this means that judges appeal directly to principles of justice to choose between alternative ways in which a decision may be thought to 'fit' in with existing law, so making the decision 'the best that it can be', in roughly the same way as a contributor to the chain novel seeks to write a 'good' chapter and not simply one that makes sense in terms of what has gone before. In a stronger form Dworkin's chain novel approach licenses a direct appeal to principles of justice, thus detaching the development of law from the constraints of precedent and giving legal effect to the moral judgements of judiciaries (see Dworkin, 1996).

It follows from these criticisms that the 'moral' judgements involved in determining rights by reference to principles cannot in practice be subsumed under the methods of formal legal reasoning, so that the gap between formal and material justice, which Dworkin seeks to bridge, inevitably reemerges. Putting the matter in another way, on the Dworkinian approach legal and political reasoning become, at least in the higher courts, indistinguishable, thus undermining the thesis that courts have the last word on rights and legislatures the last word on policies. Background abstract 'rights' dissolve into generalised moral values which cannot function as Dworkinian rights by giving us a relatively objective and politically uncontroversial way of determining entitlements by reference to an authoritative system of norms which can trump other considerations.

Moreover, Dworkin does not give us any reason to accept that law as such contains rights of the sort that he approves of. Writing within the tradition of American jurisprudence and taking it for granted that the political and legal culture of that jurisdiction are of an acceptable democratic and liberal form, he can readily equate his background 'rights' with moral principles of a specific content. It is relatively easy for us to accept the significance of formal justice, or the rule of law, in a system which seeks to render coherent such evidently acceptable meritorian beliefs as the principle that no person may profit by their own wrong. But this does not render more acceptable the coherence of rules and principles which embody the traditions of offensive political cultures. At this point there is a fundamental ambivalence in Dworkin's conception of the moral rights which are 'there' in the law. Sometimes he argues that these rights are the principles which would give a coherent and consistent justification of legal precedents and legislative enactments already posited. At other times he permits an appeal beyond positive rights and evaluations to the basic principle behind all rights, that is, to some explication of the idea that we should treat persons with equal concern and respect.

To meet such criticisms Dworkin would have to argue that the very idea of rights limits the content of principles. In effect he attempts little more than the articulation of the idea of rights as part of a liberal tradition of law and politics. This means that, according to one interpretation, the development of Dworkin's theory requires the Herculean task of seeking the explicit statement of the rights inherent in the American or some other acceptably liberal democratic tradition. This means that the method to discover what rights persons have becomes a task for high-level legal reasoning of the sort he commends.

However, on another interpretation of the Dworkin enterprise we must use the background right of equal concern and respect to work out a basis for deciding which positive rights persons ought to have (and therefore in Dworkin's natural law terminology, actually do have). This is to take the central thrust of Dworkin's theory as licensing appellate courts to decide hard cases by reasoning from fundamental principles to concrete rights, which is precisely what he endorses in his most recent work (Dworkin, 1996). This involves working out the meaning and application of these principles rather than seeking to demonstrate or discover a hidden coherence behind the jumble of statutory provisions, decided cases and historically sanctified political outlooks. At the same time, it would transform Dworkin's approach from a mainly legal to a mainly political philosophy of direct relevance to defining the content of rights independently of past legislative and judicial decisions.

Dworkin's politics

The political dimension of Dworkin's enterprise cannot be carried out by remaining at a level of analysis of 'equal concern and respect' which makes it compatible with a wide range of views on material justice, for we have to be confident that the principle can act as a way of justifying specific decisions where difficult moral choices have to be made. Dworkin attempts the arduous task of putting flesh on the bones of his fundamental principle of justice so that it can fulfil this problematic role. In a long and complex two-part article (Dworkin, 1981) he develops these ideas in relation to what he calls distributional as distinct from political equality. Distributive equality relates to resources other than political power. Political equality is about the distribution of political power. In the first part he dismisses various types of 'equality of welfare' on the general grounds that there is no way of measuring welfare which is at once practicable and acceptable. For instance, 'equality of satisfaction' is intrinsically relative to morally arbitrary or controversial individual tastes and goals while 'equality of success' in achieving preferred objectives is relative to subjective factors, such as individual preferences and ambitions. In other words there are impossible baseline problems in measuring and comparing welfare, whether interpreted as enjoyment, preference or satisfaction, particularly as it is unfair to take into account expensive tastes and unusual ambitions.

An approximation to 'equality of resources', on the other hand, where the individual shares of resources available for private holding are equally distributed, is measurable and manageable through the utilisation of the mechanisms of the market-place in ways which get round the problems of differing tastes and ambitions. In the second part of the article, his basic thesis is that a fair distribution, based on equal concern and respect, will not take into account pure luck, including the distribution of natural endowments, but will allow for the effects of the uses individuals make of their talents and the choices they make in the pursuit of their chosen interests in a liberal economy. In Dworkin's terminology a fair distributive scheme is 'endowment-insensitive' but not 'ambition-sensitive'. This situation is reached through a combination of an imaginary original auction in which all individuals are given equal amounts of currency and can bid for whatever type of scarce resource they wish to the extent that they can afford, and a progressive taxation system which provides compensations and safeguards to an extent that average informed individuals would have insured themselves against had they been given the opportunity to do so at the outset of their entry into society. This insurance cover is taken out in a hypothetical situation of equal risk of such disasters as being born handicapped or suffering later misfortunes.

Such an insurance system does not generate literal equality of resources, for those with scarce and demanded skills who choose to work will find rewards way beyond those guaranteed by any rational insurance system, but it will reflect an acceptable balance which embodies the objective of each individual being treated with the same concern and respect. We will not be compensated because of our expensive tastes or below-average skills but we will be safeguarded against seriously debilitating circumstances and gross lack of ability. All this is worked out in terms of what is considered to be a fair arrangement for a 'number of shipwrecked survivors... washed up on a desert island which has abundant resources and no native population' (1981, p.285). It is assumed that in these circumstances 'no division of resources is an equal division if, once the division is complete, any immigrant would prefer someone else's bundle of resources to his own bundle' (the 'envy test'). This is taken as constituting one way of arriving at a fair outcome, given that each immigrant can argue that 'no one is antecedently entitled to any of the resources, but that they shall instead be dispersed equally among them' (ibid.).

Some of the complexities of this imaginative and convoluted scheme will be considered in the next section, but the important point to note here is the distance we have come from the starting-point of the justice as rights thesis in which we seemed to be promised a way of determining what is just that has some structural similarity to the way in which our actual positive rights are determined in a court of law. Instead we have become enveloped in a controversial exploration of how we determine the basic principles of justice and their practical implications. In other words we are back in the sphere of standard moral and political argument in which the appeal to the rights of individuals settles nothing more specific than, perhaps, a general strategic approach to the issues in question. Such 'rights' are so far removed from the positive rights which feature in determining our day-to-day entitlements that they have no more distinctive role in moral argumentation about what positive rights we ought to have than any other socially relevant moral ideal. In other words the rights thesis, when deployed in relation to material justice, is in danger of losing its distinctive flavour and promised usefulness.

Justice and minorities

The protection of minorities against the moral claims of majorities has long been regarded as a prime test for a theory of justice, for it is to considerations of justice that we look for the grounds on which to limit the political rights of majorities. The issues here relate to the proper limits to the fundamental democratic idea that, in cases of conflict, issues, including legislative matters, be settled by resort to democratic decision procedures which terminate in a vote in which all members of the community may participate, directly or indirectly, and in which that choice which obtains the greatest numerical support should be binding on all. The question arises whether this majoritarian principle implies that there are no limits to what a majority of persons in a polity may decide to impose on unwilling minorities.

Some such limitations are, of course, inherent in the very concept of democracy, since it must be assumed that the majority decision takes place in a constitutional setting in which all have the right to vote and stand for election. This means that democratic majorities cannot remove such political rights from minorities without ceasing to be democratic majorities. By filling out the idea of democracy to include the role of information and communication in making electoral choices 'real', minorities can be guaranteed freedom of speech, freedom of communication in general (hence freedom of the press) and perhaps freedom to demonstrate and protest in order to bring their views to the attention of others. All this can be presented as presupposed by the majoritarian principle. By extension of the same mode of argument, the furtherance of the qualities which are required to make rational choices in a democracy may be included in the ideal of a democracy so that it is possible to argue that some form of educational provision is a democratic right which cannot be taken away by majority fiat.

These democratic restrictions on the rights of majorities can be regarded as a matter of justice if democracy itself is justified on that basis. This may operate at two levels: either the democratic system is based on self-determination rather than, for instance, on utility, and self-determination is seen as a facet of justice, or democratic procedures are in general justified on non-justice grounds but it is contended that it is just that all have an equal opportunity to participate in such procedures.

However, quite apart from these constitutional-based arguments, the question arises as to whether there are other considerations which bear on the limits which may be placed on the substance of the decisions imposed by majorities. That there are, or should be, such limitations is a principal motivation for the enactment of bills of rights and other constitutional curbs on majority powers. Such arrangements can be seen as the dominant background context for Dworkin's discussions of abstract absolute rights. He is evidently concerned to validate the role of the US Supreme Court in adopting a moral reading of the Constitution (see Dworkin, 1996) and is an avowed supporter of the enactment of a bill of rights within the UK (see Dworkin, 1990b).

The question therefore arises whether the principle of equal concern and respect gives us any substantial leverage against majoritarianism by providing a basis for constitutionally protected minority rights beyond those which are logically entailed by the majoritarian principle itself. Dworkin himself has discussed these matters extensively, especially in the context of the politics of discrimination, holding that 'the argument in favour of anti-discrimination statutes, that a minority has a right to equal respect and concern, is an argument of principle' (1978, p.82). Thus, when confronted with the contrast between two racial discrimination cases, one in which 'a black man named Sweatt applied to the University of Texas Law School, but was refused admission because state law provided that only whites could attend' and another in which 'a Jew named DeFunis applied to the University of Washington Law School; he was rejected although his test scores and college grades were such that he would have been admitted if he had been a black or Filipino or ...' (1978, p.223), Dworkin is able to support the Supreme Court decision in favour of Sweatt on the grounds that his exclusion violated Sweatt's constitutional rights, while, at the same time, maintaining that no fundamental right of DeFunis had been infringed.

His argument is that in such cases there is no right to equal treatment because educational places of this type are not something to which every individual has a prior right, so that what matters is whether the persons concerned are being 'treated as equals', that is 'with the same respect and concern as anyone else'. However, while it may be self-evident that Sweatt is not being treated in such a way, the same would appear to be true for DeFunis, whose scholastic achievements are not being given the same weight as those of other persons.

Dworkin's response to such a contention is to point out that, since neither DeFunis, nor anyone else, has the right to a place in a Law School, it is proper for those deciding on entrance policies to have regard to social policy or community goals, such as the desirable racial balance of lawyers who have to serve the different communities within society. This is a matter of policy, not of rights, so DeFunis may be excluded as a consequence of goal-based decision-making.

But is the same not true in the case of Sweatt who also did not have an antecedent right to enter Law School? In this case the answer is different, however, not because there was no policy behind the University of Texas Law School entry criteria (racial harmony might indeed be served by it) but because a fundamental right is violated by the application of its criteria. It is not enough, in Dworkin's view, merely to point out that minority groups feel insulted by discriminatory practices, so that 'If we wish to distinguish *DeFunis* from *Sweatt* or some argument that uses one concept of an insult, we must show that the treatment of the one, but not the other, is in fact unjust' (1978, p.231).

To demonstrate this Dworkin brings in his distinction between personal and external preferences, that is, between preferences which relate solely to individuals' aspirations and desires for themselves, as opposed to their wishes about what they would like to happen to others. Racial segregation policies are based on external preferences to the extent that they involve the majority enacting their wishes for the lives of the members of other racial groups, whereas such considerations do not decisively affect the policy decisions for affirmative action in the absence of which DeFunis would have been admitted.

The distinction between personal and external preferences is a powerful one, if only because it echoes the assumptions of classical utilitarianism and modern welfare economics that rational preferences are preferences based on individual self-interest. However it is doubtful whether it is a powerful enough distinction to achieve such an ambitious objective as the identification of the fundamental rights which prohibit the exploitation of minorities. Rather it serves more as an *ad hoc* device of particular relevance to what is nowadays referred to as 'discrimination', namely the disfavouring of a group on irrelevant grounds where there is an element of dislike or denigration involved. There does seem to be something particularly offensive in a group being disadvantaged as a result of being despised and undervalued, and this is clearly a factor in racial and also in religious and sexual discrimination, which accounts for the element of insult experienced by those who are discriminated against for these reasons. There is thus a basis for saying that, in the distribution of social benefits, we should exclude external preferences, such as whites not wishing blacks, or men not wishing women, to have certain opportunities.

However, while such a device may, in certain political circumstances, open up the prospect of greater equality to such groups and while there may be something to be said morally for discounting this sort of external preference as distasteful or worse, it is hardly exhaustive of the grounds for condemning discrimination and is of dubious relevance to other types of unjustified minority disadvantage.

Thus in discrimination it is the injustice and inhumanity of systematic deprivation in line with racial, religious or sexual differences, as well as the element of insult in the reasons why such inequality is brought about, that are to be condemned. If, for whatever reason, the merits or sufferings of such 'minorities' are not given the same weight as are accorded to the merits and sufferings of the privileged groups, then wrongs have been identified and call for rectification. Thus, if as a result of decision processes which involve nothing more than the self-interested inputs of the 'majorities' certain groups are in fact systematically worse off, as is the case with much 'indirect' discrimination where there is no explicit or even covert use of the basis of the group classification (sex, race or religion) but these groups nevertheless suffer disproportionately, then injustice and perhaps inhumanity are in evidence whether or not external preferences are involved. Dworkin's approach appears to bypass these basic moral insights and highlights another aspect of immorality which is, in most cases, of lesser significance to discriminated groups, to whom the injury is worse than the insult which is so often added to it.

The same points may be made, *a fortiori,* where any individual or group in society suffers as a result of the preferences of the majority, for the fact that majorities take only their own interests into account is, in many respects, grounds for doubting the moral authority of their decisions, the point being that they ought to take into account the welfare of all members of society and to do so in proportion to the needs and merits of each individual. John Stuart Mill's fears concerning the pressure of unenlightened public opinion and the untrammelled political decisions of the enfranchised working classes were not based only on the worry that the progressive elite would be coerced through the application of an inferior morality but also on the grounds that social and political arrangements would be made to suit the uninformed and misguided personal preferences of the majority. Anxieties on this score are not alleviated by excluding external preferences, even if this were a practical alternative

Indeed it is far from clear that external preferences are always irrelevant to social decision-making, particularly when we are in the realm of public goods that cannot be parcelled up into little bits and distributed to individuals as separately valuable items. National defence, adequate policing, architectural preservation, and public goods in general, are more securely sustained and more readily justified by approaches which embody a concern for the welfare of the community as a whole rather than as an aggregation of self-centred preferences. Certainly there is nothing that is insulting and little that is dangerous in permitting external preferences a role in the determination of policy in such matters.

If the distinction between personal and external preferences is not a prime or exhaustive guide to the distinction between policies which infringe rights and those which do not, then it may be that more mileage can be got from Dworkin's model for just distribution of private goods. Would indirect discrimination, for instance, not be excluded by the combination of an equal auction and a hypothetical insurance market?

Due to the complexities and abstractness of Dworkin's more recently formulated decision-making model it is not easy to determine what its actual outcomes would be. This in itself is a major drawback to a theory of justice which is meant to be based on rights, for the advantage of a rights approach should be to set up an authoritative source of guidance as to the entitlements of persons. As far as it is possible to surmise on these matters it would appear that the equal distribution of resource-commanding tokens (whether it be clamshells suggested by Dworkin in his desert island example, or other forms of currency) in combination with the 'perfect' auctioning of all individualisable resources would not produce a distribution skewed against all the minority groups which are at present worse off in existing societies. But since differences in taste and need are not allowed for, and different abilities will inevitably lead to legitimate inequalities through the ensuing processes of economic choices in a market economy, it is clear that other 'inequalities' will emerge which will seem unjustified from other standpoints, such as the merits or needs of those involved.

Dworkin certainly seeks to avoid some merit-based inequalities by using the taxation system to compensate for some (it would appear, extreme) differences of endowment, so that handicapped persons would not be left to starve. And there is no doubt that a properly organised market economy will give higher rewards to some persons who are meritorious because they choose wisely and work hard in proportion to their genetic endowment. However there is little ground for the optimistic view that a society based on Dworkin's ideal of initial equality of resources will approximate to one in which there is a systematic proportionality of resources possessed to the merits and demerits of its citizens, and his approach is undoubtedly ill-adapted to providing for equality of satisfaction of needs. Indeed the correctives of Dworkinian taxation, however progressive, specifically exclude the objective of attaining 'equality of welfare', that is, an equality of satisfactions or 'success' in one's chosen life objectives.

Dworkin has, of course, a host of pertinent arguments against such ideals as 'equality of welfare', most of which are aimed at the impracticality of seeking to ensure equal satisfactions and success, due to the absence of objective and workable measures of 'satisfaction' or 'success'. There is, however, an obvious sense in which equality of resources is a second-best choice for an ideal of justice since it is hard to avoid the feeling that its intuitive plausibility depends on the assumption that equality of resources gives an equal chance of equal satisfactions. Resources are, after all, not ends in themselves but means to achieve human purposes. Further, the fact that this equality of resources does not adjust for major differences in tastes and needs would appear to entail 'discrimination' against those with tastes or needs for goods which are scarce and in high demand (which is a matter of fortune) or which simply require more than average amounts of a given resource to satisfy. Which new oppressed minorities would emerge from this desert island fantasy it is hard to determine, but it is clear that there would be some such. The Dworkinian scheme could only take account of these inequalities if they are of such magnitude and likelihood that the average immigrant to a new social arrangement would think it wise to insure against them. Dworkin however admits that there will be systematic underinsurance in that it will not be rational to pay high enough premiums to ensure full compensation for misfortunes, particularly where misfortunes include the absence of advantages that, given better luck, persons might have had.

It is not intended to argue comprehensively in this section against Dworkinian equality, or to prove that rights cannot be powerful instruments for the protection of minority interests. In fact a constitutionally entrenched system of rights embodied in rules rendered specific in the course of a history of judicial decision-making and political debate may well serve as an important means of protecting minorities against unjust treatment at the hands of majorities. It is often of immense value when faced with a decision which favours most but not all of the members of a society to be able to point to considerations which veto that decision on grounds which cannot be overturned by utilitarian considerations alone. Rules which give entitlements that are inviolate against majority decisions both symbolise and protect the objective of justice for all.

What is in question, however, is whether, in the effort to formulate the content or scope of such rights, it is of much use to appeal to some preexisting 'moral' rights for guidance. Our discussion of Dworkin's account of justice confirms that, once we go beyond the identification of rights with rule-protected interests and move into the realm of general moral principle (and here I use the term 'principle' in its ordinary sense in which it implies vagueness as well as variable moral weight), we rapidly enter the arena of general moral and political argument in which the issues are to do with what rights we should have and what weight these rights should be given, rather than what 'trump' rights we, in some obscure sense, already have and can therefore call to our aid in a peremptory manner. The sort of basic or fundamental rights which Dworkin seeks to provide us with through the efforts of Hercules, the infinitely able and knowledgeable judge, or through the imaginative model of clamshell auctions and hypothetical insurance markets, cannot serve as the basis for an appeal to entitlements which preclude the necessity for further moral debate, as should be the case if we are dealing in rights as they feature in their characteristic contexts and distinctive uses.

What we have, instead, is a series of significant moral considerations which are on all fours with competing moral arguments based on such factors as merit, need or choice. In other words, at this level of justificatory argument, talk of rights has nothing distinctive to contribute beyond a sense that judicial procedure is an appropriate forum for the allocation of values. Indeed it may be dangerous terminology in that it leads people to expect that we may discover certain self-evident deontological truths to which we can give absolute practical priority. There may be serious epistemological and, in the end, moral objections to the pretensions set up by the proposition that there are fundamental moral rights which are there to be discovered once we have acquired the necessary insight or refined the most illuminating set of distinctions and techniques of legal and political argument. The history of the thesis that justice is a matter of treating persons in accordance with their rights is a warning that there are no short cuts to the determination of what is just. In the end Dworkinian rights leave us in a muddy pool of moral argument from which we are unlikely to be rescued on the chimerical life-raft of so-called moral rights, however fundamental and legally rooted they are alleged to be.

5 Justice as Contract: Rawls and Welfare

In many respects Rawls's major work, *A Theory of Justice* (1971), still sets the current agenda of issues to be discussed in any theory of justice and provides the terminology in which much policy debate proceeds. This is, in part, because he combines a sophisticated (contractarian) methodology with substantive views on what is just which are both appealing and coherent. It is important therefore that both the force and the limitations of Rawlsian contractarianism are appreciated and that careful consideration is given to the relationship between his method and the principles of justice which are said to flow from its application. As we will see it is possible to adopt Rawls's approach to the epistemology of justice without endorsing his views as to what is just, and vice versa. However, the impact of Rawls's theory depends largely on the combination of a promising method and attractive applications of that method.

In the 1970s Rawls, almost single-handed, restored the theory of social contract, which was at the time written off as incurably flawed, and at the same time helped to revive political philosophy from a period of decline and neglect. A social contract, as developed in the work of such giants in the history of political thought as Thomas Hobbes, John Locke and J.-J. Rousseau, is an agreement between potential citizens (or between such persons and a potential ruler or rulers) about the terms on which they are to enter into either social or political relationships (or both). Social contract theory posits a situation – called a 'state of nature' – in which persons who have no existing political (and perhaps social) rights or obligations reach (usually unanimous) agreement about the basis on which to establish a social and/or political system in which they do have recognised rights and obligations, including the obligations to conform to the agreement reached, respect the rights of other citizens and obey the appointed ruler(s). The social contract is used both to explain the general obligation of citizens to obey the law (and the possible limits of that obligation), and to provide a way of determining the proper content of the rights and obligations which bind members of a civil and political society. It serves, therefore, both to establish the grounds of social, political and legal obligation, and to justify a particular set of positive social and political norms.

The idea of a social contract came to the fore in political philosophy during the period when a non-theological moral foundation was being sought for the emerging modern state as an independent political entity. The state came to be seen as an omnicompetent institution within which the sovereign has the right to make binding laws in accordance with a constitutional structure that sets out the scope and content of the powers of the ruler and the duties and rights of the citizens. The social contract model took many different forms which varied in their descriptions of the state of nature, in their analyses of human nature and in the terms of the contract reached. In Hobbes's *Leviathan* (1651), the horrors of the state of nature and the egoistic rationality of Hobbesian man go with a contract between citizens that established almost unlimited allegiance to an almost unlimited sovereign power. The less serious drawbacks of the state of nature, together with a more balanced view of man as a creature with moral capacities, depicted in Locke's *Second Treatise of Government* (1690), produce a social contract between potential citizens that established governmental power as something which is entrusted to the sovereign who had to rule within the law of nature and maintain a degree of continuing consent from his subjects in order to retain his legitimacy. Rousseau's yet more attractive state of nature, outlined in *The Social Contract* (1762), in which uncivilised people enjoyed certain physical freedoms and securities, although little economic and moral development, leads to the affirmation of a democratic system in which each citizen would continue to bind himself by his own legislative enactments alone as a way of protecting his natural freedoms and enjoying the benefits of civilisation.

Clearly the notion of a social contract is a form into which many different political views can be fitted, but all these views involve some recognition of the significance of acquiring the consent of individuals to the norms which limit their presupposed initial freedoms. As such social contract models assume an individualistic view of society according to which persons are the sources of their own political rights and duties, and embody the liberal view that encroachment on the freedom of such individuals requires justification. In all its variations social contract theory encourages us to see actual political societies as a form of association whose object is to secure the interests of their members in a way which is consistent with the intrinsic equal autonomy of all.

Within this framework two rather distinct interpretations of the state of nature and social contract emerged early on in its development. In the first, considerable weight is placed on the historicity of the phenomenon, so that it is assumed that there were persons in a state of nature who did enter into actual agreements. This claim is clearly important if political obligation is said to derive directly from the social contract since only actual agreements are binding.

Developing awareness of the historical implausibility of the contract led to its modification, first into a view of what *might* have taken place (see Chapter 3 on conjectural history), and then into the idea that the actual agreements involved are being made all the time in that persons in actual political societies continuously make tacit or implicit agreements (for instance by not choosing to leave the polity), a modern variation of which is the idea that voting in an election is a tacit agreement to abide by the outcome of that election and adhere to the political system as a whole.

The second, more radical, approach is to abandon entirely the idea of a historical or actual contract and reinterpret the concept in hypothetical terms so that the contract becomes the agreement that persons of a certain sort in a certain type of situation *would* have reached. The rationale for this second, hypothetical, interpretation of the social contract is more epistemological than justificatory. Imagining and thinking through the implications of a hypothetical state of nature is a way of getting to know the content of the social and political rules and the system of government that ought to be created and sustained in the here and now. Those arrangements which would be agreed by free and equal individuals in a hypothetical state of nature are those which ought to be adopted as the basic norms of social life. Thus Locke, in a theory which mixes actual and hypothetical strands, appeals to 'reason' as well as to historical fact, to establish his conclusion that government is entrusted to certain designated persons to protect the individual's rights to life, liberty and property, an agreement which may be terminated if the people believe that this trust has been abused.

The intelligibility of this hypothetical approach to the social contract depends crucially on the characterisation of the imagined state of nature, including the qualities of the persons who participate in it. In the historical version of the contract these matters could be settled by considering what, given a certain view of human nature, life must have been like without the benefits of social and/ or political organisation and the reasons, such as the fear of death and the desire for economic security, which would motivate people to reach agreements on the basis of social order.

Hypothetical contractual theorists, on the other hand, do not speculate on what pre-social life must actually have been like, although they do tend to follow the same basic lines in that the imaginary contractors are described as free and equal, and are said to be living without the benefits of political arrangements, so that they are motivated to secure an agreement which is mutually beneficial. However, the characterisation of the state of nature changes, from the simple absence of social and political constraints on the one hand and the approximate physical and mental equality of persons on the other, into a more idealised and artificial model in which freedom is a matter of autonomy (uncoerced and informed choice) and equality has to do with equal capacity to bargain on the basis of equal procedural rights and equal claims on the outcome.

The effect of these developments is to render more plausible the claim that the outcome of such an agreement is just, since it seems intelligible and perhaps attractive to say that what persons who are free and equal in these ideal senses would agree to has a claim to be regarded as acceptable. Whereas the historical contract can be viewed as an agreement between desperate people with little bargaining power, in the hypothetical contract the situation in which the agreement is made can be made to appear much more fair. It is uncoerced and based on no unreasonable advantages of initial precedence. If the circumstances of agreement are fair it seems proper to regard the outcome as reasonable and the rules which would be agreed to as just.

Extending this line of thought it is also possible to base political obligation on such a hypothetical contract by adding the premise that citizens have an obligation to obey just laws. They may have made no actual promises, but they do receive the benefits of society and they have a natural obligation to support just laws. Since just laws are identified as those which would be agreed to in the ideal

hypothetical situation we can say that the hypothetical contract is
the basis for political obligation.

Since their inception there have been major doubts raised about
the social contract approaches. In some historical versions, at least,
the theory is self-contradictory. If, in the state of nature, people
have no rights or obligations, then any 'promise' made in the state
of nature cannot be binding, since there is no institution of promising in existence on which to found promissory obligations. In the
case of Hobbes, for instance, his empirical claims include the thesis
that, in the state of nature, men have no moral obligations while, in
his theory as a whole, he has to contend that men have a pre-
political obligation to keep their promises, otherwise there could
be no moral basis for our obligation to conform to the original
contract. How can a contract which is entered into in an amoral
context set up the moral presuppositions required to make that
contract itself binding?

If, in order to avoid this problem, like Locke, we attribute
preexisting rights and duties to denizens of the state of nature,
then the social contract becomes much less important and may
be bypassed altogether by founding political obligation directly on
these pre-social and pre-political 'natural rights'. According to
Locke we have natural rights to life, liberty and property, and we
institute government to protect these rights. While this may seem
logically more satisfactory, it has the disadvantage that the contract
cannot now be used to justify these basic rights which exist prior to
the contract and these must therefore be given a justificatory basis
elsewhere. Moreover the Lockean modifications may undermine the
basis for an agreement in the historical contract because of the
differing moral views of the contractors. In the historical contract
this reduces the prospects of agreement and in the hypothetical
contract it reduces the moral relevance of the contractual model,
since we will not be inclined to accept its outcome unless we share
the particular moral outlook of the contractors.

In both historical and hypothetical interpretations of the contract
theory there is an unresolved tension between fact and speculation
which until recently had been thought to be fatal to that theory. In
order for the choices to be made in the state of nature to be
predictable and relevant the state of nature must have major
similarities to our current social and political experience. Yet agreements made in such familiar circumstances do not sufficiently transcend the realities of current social and political life to provide any

sort of external justification or critique of our current norms and culture. If to counter this impoverished theory we devise a state of nature which is radically different from our familiar circumstances, then we have difficulty establishing what such strange people in such unusual circumstances would say or do, and the further difficulty of determining the relevance of such speculations about what they might or might not agree to for the determination of how we should make our own social and political arrangements. This is the argument which has been restated in current communitarian critiques of the contractarian tradition. Too much similarity to the present in this context inevitably renders the contract which is entered into morally suspect because it does not meet the conditions of free agreement and does not transcend our existing attitudes and beliefs. Too little similarity to our current condition renders the approach speculative and irrelevant. Actual societies are not fair and contracts in them reflect unequal power and wealth. Contract theorists are therefore in great difficulties when they seek to characterise a state of nature which has sufficient similarity to empirical reality for us to see its connection with our own nature and social experience, and yet is still a situation in which any agreement reached, whether actual or hypothetical, is fair, in that it is not the outcome of the sort of coercion, inequality or material ignorance which is commonplace in actual societies.

These are formidable difficulties which had long been considered to count decisively against the idea of a social contract in political theory. The choice between empirical accuracy and moral relevance seemed unavoidable. However the stakes involved are high and the advantages of a successful contract theory considerable. If it is possible to found social and political obligation in the idea of voluntary agreement, this not only gives strong support to the value of individual autonomy (and so of individual rights) but provides the best possible justification for having binding laws, namely that those bound have in some sense agreed to be bound by them, so that the obligations involved are self-imposed. Moreover, the idea of the social contract appears to offer the prospect of reconciling differing individual interests and values by a familiar device of compromise and discussion in which apparently incompatible objectives and incommensurable values can be brought under a single decision procedure. It is perhaps not so surprising therefore that the most striking contribution to the theory of justice in recent times has been a restatement of the hypothetical social contract as a counterposition to the utilitarianism which had for so long dominated political philosophy. Nor is it surprising that many of the criticisms which have been made of this neo-contractarianism echo the traditional attacks on the classical contract theories.

Justice as fairness

Justice as fairness is the theme elaborated by John Rawls in *A Theory of Justice* (1971) and developed in his subsequent writings. Rawls's model is based on the idea of the procedural fairness of an 'original position', which is his version of the hypothetical state of nature. This procedural fairness is based on the strategy of ensuring that all causes of bias and partiality are excluded from the original position, thus achieving an impartial and fair outcome. The fairness of the original position transfers to the principles of justice which would be agreed in the original position as applying to the basic institutions of actual societies. In other words, a fair bargaining is assumed to produce fair results. As far as the original position is concerned there is no antecedent standard by which to assess the results, as there would be in what he calls 'perfect procedural justice' where the idea is to have the most efficient procedure to get a result which is independently known to be correct. The acceptability of the result of the agreement reached in the original position depends solely on the acceptance of the procedure. Rawls calls this a matter of 'pure procedural justice' (1971, p.85).

Rawls insists on the procedural purity of the original position, not because he thinks that we cannot more directly assess the principles chosen in the original position, but because he wishes to present the contract as an independent justificatory source. Indeed the basic strategy of his method is to demonstrate that the principles adopted in the original position coincide with those which his readers would in any case accept once they had reflected systematically upon them. His hope is that 'the principles which would be chosen [in the original position] match our considered convictions of justice or extend them in an acceptable way' (1971, p.19). There are thus two sets of moral standards at work in Rawls's synthesis. One represents the limitations on argument we do in fact accept when we argue about justice. These are embodied in the description of the original position. The other represents our moral intuitions or judgements about what is just once these judgements have reached a condition which he calls 'reflective equilibrium'. It is only when – perhaps after further processes of compromise and adjustment – the two independent moral bases produce a common outcome that we have reason to think that we have the appropriate principles of justice.

The method of reflective equilibrium involves selecting our strongest and surest moral convictions as the provisional fixed points and then working backwards to the principles which would justify such intuitions. Thus we are certain that slavery is wrong and justify this conviction by reference, perhaps, to the idea of the fundamental equality of all persons. In this way we move towards the elaboration of a set of consistent principles which, together with knowledge of social circumstances, lead us to make the judgements we do for the reasons we make them. In pursuing reflective equilibrium we then seek to apply such principles to other everyday situations with respect to which our intuitions are more obscure and less certain and then determine whether the principles we have arrived at produce acceptable results in these more difficult cases, always being prepared to revise our original intuitions on the grounds that they may be 'distorted' or 'irregular'. And so, by a to-and-fro process of reflection in which judgements are developed and revised and principles tested and refined, we finish with an 'equilibrium' of consistent judgements and principles with which we can proceed to tackle more controversial moral issues. It is these 'considered convictions of justice' which coincide with the principles chosen in the original position that constitute the liberal ideal of justice.

The idea that in a hypothetical situation of equal liberty, rational and disinterested persons would choose the principles which accord with our sense of justice is said both to explain and to justify a particular conception of justice. The explanatory force comes from the demonstration that the principles of justice would be adopted by rational persons as the basis for social cooperation, it being assumed that there is some rationality in human affairs. The justificatory force comes from the coherence of considered moral judgements with the principles chosen in the original position.

The excitement initially generated by Rawls's theory arose from the fact that we appeared to be offered an epistemic or cognitive theory through which we could discover what is objectively just or justified. By imagining ourselves in the original position and working out what we would opt for by way of foundational rights and duties in society, and then checking these against our considered opinions, we could hope to come by reliable knowledge as to how a just society is constituted.

However, the rather loose and *ad hoc* way in which the original position is described is, as we shall see, a barrier to the acceptance of the authority of its outcomes. Moreover, the elaborate coherence theory of moral appropriateness developed by Rawls is vulnerable to the charge that the fundamental intuitions on which it appears to rest are not themselves reliable raw data on which to proceed. What, it might be asked, is the point of establishing a reflective equilibrium based on moral intuitions if we cannot show that these intuitions provide at least an approximate insight into moral truth? Such questions are particularly pressing if we have to take account of the variety of 'senses of justice' which have existed and do still exist and the difficulties which arise in trying to mould them into a consistent position.

Rawls's initial response to such questions is to limit the application of his theory to the sense of justice which is pervasive in modern liberal democratic societies. These are not specified, but he clearly has in mind principally the United States of America and other western democracies. Further 'justice as fairness' is restricted not only to a particular type of society, but, within that, it is confined to questions of justice in relation only to the basic institutions of society; in particular his concern is with the distribution of the benefits and burdens of social cooperation.

In his later writings (1980, p.518), Rawls is more explicit in his rejection of any deep philosophical underpinnings for his theory of justice. Not only does he reject the idea of rational intuitions as a justificatory test of universal moral truths, but he also abjures any search for epistemological or metaphysical bases for justice as fairness. Instead he argues for the autonomy of political philosophy as an activity aimed at furthering a consensus of fundamental political ideals in a particular polity as an essential prerequisite for the attainment of what he calls a 'well-ordered' society. His claim is that, despite the variations of political belief even within his own country, there is a degree of underlying agreement as to the terms of cooperation between citizens, and further there is a prospect of obtaining further consensus, a goal to which he hopes his own theory will contribute. The coherence of moral intuitions is not based on a philosophical ideal of moral truth but on this pragmatic political objective. His social contract approach is now no more than a method which facilitates a desirable consensus in one type of society. However, despite these disclaimers, Rawls's followers are often less restrained in their ambition for his method of political argument and take it to be a basis for more universal standards of justice.

Rawlsian justice

The essentials of Rawls's theory of justice lie in his account of the original position and the resulting principles of justice, including the now famous 'difference' principle.

In order to achieve fairness, persons in the original position must be free and equal. By 'free' Rawls means not only that the parties in the original position are uncoerced and not under any prior obligations or constraints but also that they are independent and autonomous sources of claims on the benefits of social cooperation. They are not limited by prior moral conceptions in the pursuit of their own interest. Rawls denies that the parties are egoists since they do not seek to harm anyone else, but says they are mutually disinterested in that they care only about their own welfare, taken in isolation. They have normal human desires although they feel no envy, and are not interested in benefiting or harming others for its own sake. In pursuit of their disinterested claims the parties are free to propose and argue for the principles of justice that they believe would be of greatest benefit to themselves and it is assumed that they, as rational persons, will agree only to the best bargain they can obtain in return for the benefits of social cooperation. People in the original position possess what Rawls calls 'rational autonomy', a property he equates with the notion of rationality found in Kant's hypothetical imperative or in neoclassical economics, in other words, the rationality of the intelligent and prudent person, the capacity to discover and follow the most effective means to a chosen end.

'Equality' in the original position applies first to equal freedom as defined above, including equality in procedural rights for the debate in the original position, and equality as equally important sources of valid claims on societal resources in relation to basic social institutions. All parties have 'equal worth', have the same characteristics and are situated equally in the original position. They are 'symmetrical with respect to one another' (1980, p.521).

The nature of this equality is not, however, completely abstract, for it is grounded in the equality of persons as moral agents, a notion to which Rawls traces the entire rationale of the contract model. He calls this method 'Kantian constructivism'. It is Kantian because it embodies the idea of persons as moral agents. This, for Rawls, means that each person has, first, a conception of the good (that is, a set of convictions about what personal goals are worth pursuing) and, second, a sense of justice (that is, a set of beliefs about the terms of fair social cooperation). It is also assumed that persons are capable of acting on a long-term basis in relation both to their conception of the good and to their sense of justice. The method is 'constructivist' because the content of the principles of justice is generated from the ideal of the moral person through the model of the original position. From the point of view of the original position this means that the constructing parties are equal in that they all have the minimum properties necessary to be moral persons and also that their claims are of equal force and validity despite the fact that, in the original position, they do not know what their moral values are or what their sense of justice will constrain them to do.

In order to ensure that this theoretical equality is given effect in the original position, Rawls introduces his novel conception of a 'veil of ignorance' which is designed to remove all possibility of unfairness in the decision to be made by rendering each of the parties entirely ignorant of any particular fact about themselves which might lead them, as rational choosers, to favour themselves at the expense of those with different qualities. They do not know their talents, or lack of them, their place in society, or even the type of society or the generation in which they will live. While they know that they have a conception of the good, they do not know its specific content, and cannot, therefore, slant the principles of justice to suit their particular goals, values or religious beliefs. Similarly they know other general facts about human nature and society, but not their own particular nature, their sex, their social class, their size or intelligence, or talents. In this way we 'nullify the effects of specific contingencies which put men at odds and tempt them to exploit social and natural circumstances to their own advantage' (1971, p.136).

Furthermore, the parties are, *ex hypothesi*, ignorant of the content of their sense of justice for even though this might not divide them in the same way as their knowledge of their own conception of their interests or their good, it is essential for the logical independence of the contract method that the motivation of the parties is the furtherance of their own interests, albeit they know that they are creatures who will have a sense of justice in actual society.

As important as the characterisation of the free and equal parties is the specification of what it is they are called upon to decide. Fundamentally their choice relates to the principles which will be used to construct the basic institutions of their society which will in turn determine the distribution of the benefits and burdens of social cooperation. They know, however, that in making this choice, they must have in mind life in a 'well-ordered' society. This involves a number of crucial features which relate to the type of social existence appropriate for morally autonomous agents with a sense of justice. The parties know that, in actual society, they will move beyond the rational autonomy of the original position to *full* autonomy, which is 'that of citizens in everyday life who think of themselves in a certain way and affirm and act from the first principles of justice that would be agreed to' (1980, p.521). The implications of this condition are considerable. It means that, in the society to which the principles of justice are to apply, there will be an effectively regulated public conception of justice, so that the rules will be known, accepted as 'reasonable', and largely followed. Further the members of society will have mutual regard for each other as free and equal moral persons and thus as independently legitimate sources of varying and developing demands on the common pool of resources and people whose cooperation can be expected only when arrangements are fair and 'reasonable', rather than merely instrumentally 'rational'.

Under the rubric of a public conception of justice Rawls takes in what he calls 'the formal constraints of the concept of right' which require that the rules of justice be general, universal, public and capable of ordering social claims with finality and comprehensiveness. In this way he brings in some of the basic idea of the rule of law as it relates to equal treatment and impartial adjudication. These formal constraints of right rule out 'first-person dictatorship' in which the will of one person is paramount and also ensure that there are no 'free-rider' arrangements whereby named individuals are granted special privileges. More specifically, since the principles of justice apply to the basic structure of society, the parties are to choose 'a public system of rules which defines offices and positions with their rights, duties and immunities and the like' (1971, p.55) in the main spheres of social life, rules whose proper administration is a matter of formal justice in that 'similar cases are treated similarly, the relevant similarities and differences being those identified by the existing norms' (1971, p.58).

All these factors are given to, rather than chosen by, the rational individuals who are parties to the social contract. The parties in the original position are taken to 'represent' the full autonomy of moral persons in a well-ordered society, but they are allowed only such knowledge as is necessary for them to choose the principles of justice. Knowledge that it will be a well-ordered society does not in itself enable them to determine a particular set of principles so they must proceed on non-individuated knowledge about the nature of man and the empirical realities of social life, including economic and sociological information, and the general conditions on which social cooperation is necessary and possible.

If all divisive information is removed from the parties it appears that there is then nothing for them to bargain about, for each individual will have the same set of considerations to take into account, the same motivation and the same ability to reason. It has therefore been argued that the Rawlsian contract needs only one party since equality entails identity of relevant features amongst the contracting parties. Nevertheless, Rawls assumes that there will be residual differences of opinion not related to arbitrary differences between the parties which will give rise to actual debate, although it is not clear to what these disagreements might amount. At any rate we are asked to accept that the contracting parties will know, or will be able to work out, that there are certain 'primary goods', that is, things which any person will require in order to pursue any conception of the good in a well-ordered society which respects the individual's moral powers to follow out in his life a conception of the good and an ideal of justice.

Primary goods, that is, the social background conditions and general all-purpose means normally necessary for developing and exercising the two moral powers and for effectively pursuing a conception of the good, include the basic liberties, such as freedom of thought and liberty of conscience, necessary for developing moral agency, freedom of movement and free choice of occupation, income and wealth, and 'the social bases of self-respect', by which he means the conditions necessary for individuals to maintain a feeling of their worth as moral agents. Primary goods are those things which are necessary for the pursuit, not of any human objective, but of any objective which is compatible with the exercise of moral agency.

Given that the parties in the original position have sufficient information and motivation to agree on what constitutes primary goods the question then arises as to how these goods are to be distributed. Here Rawls assumes that it will be rational for the contractors to proceed with caution. After all, they are dealing with the vital matters affecting the ground rules of their society. The contracting parties are unlikely, therefore, to take risks.

Rawls also assumes that they will not adopt a number of disparate principles but will seek an ordered set of guidelines which will give precedence to some considerations over others. In particular they will use the idea of 'lexical' ordering, according to which it is required that one consideration which is said to be lexically prior must be satisfied before going on to deploy the other considerations which may also be lexically ordered *vis-à-vis* each other.

The description of the original position is not, of course, based on any historical reality. Rather, it is intended to reflect the assumptions about fair procedure which are broadly accepted in the sort of society with which Rawls is familiar. Most of the characteristics of the original position are designed either to ensure impartiality or to exclude existing moral beliefs (which would render the method circular since these beliefs would be used to select the principles of justice). The object is to conjure up the principles of justice from a mix of self-interest and impartiality. If this can be done it removes moral issues from the realm of intangible metaphysics and makes moral debate a down-to-earth and manageable process. However, as we might anticipate from the earlier discussion of the contractual method, it may be difficult to know what rational egoists with extensive general knowledge but no particular information about themselves and their moral beliefs are likely to select as the basis for their future shared existence within the same political society.

Rawls conjectures that two principles will be agreed in the original position. The first is that 'each person is to have an equal right to the most extensive total system of equal basic liberties compatible with a similar system of liberty for all' (1971, p.250). This principle, he contends, is lexically prior, so that it must be met before we can turn to the second, which is that 'social and economic inequalities are to be arranged so that they are both (a) to the greatest benefit of the least advantaged and (b) attached to offices and positions open to all under conditions of fair equality of opportunity' (1971, p.83), with the proviso that (b), fair equality of opportunity, is lexically prior to (a), the 'difference' principle. In other words, once basic liberties have been maximised to the highest point compatible with their equal distribution, unequal distributions of other goods may be introduced if they have the effect of maximising the lot of the worst-off group (the 'maximin' strategy), provided that there is genuine equality of opportunity with respect to the inequalities licensed by the difference principle. In all these respects the 'right' is prior to the 'good' in that the requirements established by the two principles of justice take priority over the maximisation of any desired objective. Hence the contrast between the Rawlsian contractual approach and the moral theory of utilitarianism which gives exclusive priority to the maximisation of pleasure, or good things, and the minimisation of pain, or bad things.

The basic liberties which are to be equally distributed and given priority over all other considerations are in part those which are included in the set of primary goods already identified, particularly freedom of expression and liberty of conscience, but he extends basic liberty to cover those democratic rights which are necessary for the protection of other individual interests, and also to freedom of the person, the right to hold some private property and other liberties involved in the idea of the rule of law, such as freedom from arbitrary arrest. To some extent, therefore, both the content of the primary goods and their priority is predetermined by the choice presented in the original position. But beyond this there is a sense in which political liberties are seen as an indispensable safeguard against unacceptable treatment. Priority is given to these liberties because, it is alleged, no rational chooser would risk putting themselves in the position where their interests (which might turn out to be those of a small minority) are endangered by a non-democratic regime. It is only safe to put such liberties first. The rather controversial thesis that fundamental liberty should be sacrificed only for the sake of other fundamental liberties and never traded to any degree for greater economic prosperity is, however, not applied where these liberties cannot be secured, or where the economic development of the society is at some unspecified low level.

The second principle of justice takes in what Rawls terms 'efficiency', in that it proposes maximising other primary goods provided these are equally distributed and permits inequalities where these benefit the worst-off class of persons (the difference principle). The assumption is made that a measure of the self-centredness of the original choosers will carry over into actual society so that people will sometimes require incentives to make a contribution to socially productive enterprises. Hence inequalities will emerge as a result of the operation of incentives. Envy is ruled out as a reason for rejecting such inequalities, which explains the rather *ad hoc* way in which its influence is excluded from the original position. On the other hand, individuals who use their superior talents to gain higher benefits do not have any intrinsic right to these benefits arising from their personal merit, or, as in the case of Locke and Nozick, because they own their own bodies and hence may appropriate the product of their own labour.

It is the rational decision to avoid risk by the parties to the contract which leads them to choose this difference principle as grounds for limiting social and economic inequality. The parties to the contract are concerned to guard against the worst possible outcome for themselves as participants in actual societies and will not hazard their future security by adopting, for instance, the utilitarian principle of maximising the total quantity of such primary goods without reference to the way they are distributed. They do not know how likely it is that they may find themselves much worse off than under a maximin strategy and are unwilling to take the risk of coming out badly despite the fact that, on the basis of probability, they are likely to do better under a utilitarian arrangement. In these circumstances it is as well to insure against catastrophic bad luck.

Nor, as rational persons, will the parties permit inequalities in positions for which they might not be able to compete on equal terms. This requires not only equality of legal rights but also of the educational and material resources necessary for the development of the individual's inherited talent. This does not mean that positions will not be given to those best qualified – that is an acceptable requirement of efficiency – but it does mean that irrelevant factors related to family, wealth or education of the citizens will be inoperative as causes or grounds of the selection to office. If this is ensured then we will have 'fair equality of opportunity' and the second proviso of the second principle of justice is satisfied.

There are many ramifications in the working out of what Rawls calls his 'special conception of justice'. For instance, he outlines four stages in the emergence of an actual system of social institutions: in the first the two principles of justice are chosen, in the second there is a constitutional convention to set up a system of government, in the third ordinary laws are legislated and in the fourth these laws are applied by judges. During this process the veil of ignorance is progressively lifted somewhat so that at the second stage the constituent assembly knows the nature of the society in question, at the third stage the legislators know the basic economic facts about their society and at the fourth stage the veil of ignorance is totally removed so that for the first time citizens know their own circumstances and characteristics.

In order to place some limits on what can count as a person's good for the purposes of the theory, Rawls makes a number of empirical assumptions about human desires, needs and abilities, the most controversial of which is the 'Aristotelian principle' according to which, 'other things being equal, human beings enjoy the exercise of their realized capacities (their innate or trained abilities), and this enjoyment increases the more the capacity is realized, or the greater its complexity' (1971, p.426). This follows the precedent of John Stuart Mill's modification of classical utilitarianism to distinguish between the 'higher' pleasures of Socrates and the 'lower' pleasures of pigs (Mill, 1863).

However Rawls does not seek to justify in detail the way in which basic liberties and other primary goods are derived, nor does he say what sort of democratic constitution and specific legislation will be adopted. His aim is rather to set out a method for understanding the role of justice in society and to gain general acceptance for it as a method of political reflection in a liberal society.

The primary normative objective is to provide an alternative basis for social choice to the prevailing utilitarian outlook, which, he contends, does not take seriously enough the 'distinction between persons' (1971, p.185). By submerging the interests of the individual in the welfare of all, utilitarianism encourages the erroneous idea that society is akin to one individual who may rightly sacrifice some of his desires in order to further others. It is for this reason that he favours his own path to impartiality over the alternatives represented by the 'ideal observer' theory derived from Adam Smith, or the 'universalisability' theory derived from Kant, both of which, in his view, also tend to submerge the individual in society as a whole.

It is also in order to counter the attractions of utilitarianism that he insists on a closely integrated set of principles of social choice which determine priorities in cases of conflict. One attraction of utilitarianism over the pluralism of competing incommensurable moral outlooks has long been that it is able, in principle at least, to provide a solution to all distributive problems because of its unitary standard of rightness. Rawls believes that his own theory provides a viable alternative to utilitarianism in this respect as a social decision procedure, while providing a central place for fundamental rights and duties as a framework within which the individual pursuit of well-being can take place.

Problems for Rawls

Even if we are denied the prospect of using Rawls's method for the discovery of principles of justice which apply in all societies at all times, there is much that is attractive about a theory which promises to provide a means whereby citizens of liberal societies, with their emphasis on individual autonomy and commitment to toleration of individual and group differences, can reach working agreements as to the basic normative structure of society, an overlapping consensus which makes for more than a merely convenient temporary agreement. And it is hard to reject the view that there is some objectivity and universality in the method in so far as it incorporates and institutionalises the role of impartiality in moral debate and political decision-making. There is also much to be said in favour of reflective equilibrium as a method for refining and harmonising our moral beliefs, despite the lack of foundations to support the authority of moral intuitions.

The principal weakness of Rawls's approach is the uncertainty which surrounds the original position and its outcome. For instance, some of the most damaging criticisms of Rawls's theory are to the effect that persons in the original position would in fact adopt average utility as the rational choice in such conditions of uncertainty since this offers them the best chance of the best life. To many it seems desperately *ad hoc* for Rawls to rule this out by insisting on the unrealistic proviso that rational individuals would not be prepared to take the risks involved in such a strategy and do not know the probabilities involved. Yet, if he does not introduce these arbitrary provisos, there seems little to choose between contractarianism and direct appeal to the principle of universal beneficence as the basis for social choice.

Similarly it seems far from obvious that basic liberties must be given priority by purely self-regarding individuals with a sound knowledge of human nature, for actual people are prepared to forgo political rights for economic gains well beyond the point of economic subsistence. Rawls's carefully constructed method of settling these points of competing priorities is therefore always in

danger of lapsing into pluralism. Controversy has also attached to
the exclusive emphasis which the difference principle puts on the
situation of the worst-off group. Surely, it is argued, more weight
would attach, for instance, to those whose position is only marginally better than this one class of persons?

That these issues are hard to settle one way or the other is a
further problem for the hypothetical contract approach in that it
seems impossible to know what such unusual individuals in such
special circumstances would decide. The danger is that in attempt-
ing to use the model we will simply hold on to our own moral
assumptions about natural justice. Certainly it seems wildly optimistic to regard this process as a form of 'moral geometry' through
which we can discover 'the only choice consistent with the full
description of the original position' (1971, p.121).

More specifically, the degree of ignorance which is required to
ensure fairness takes away much of the information that is required
for rational choice-making, in that the individual's particular conceptions of the good can have considerable relevance to the basic
structure of society. For instance, it is evident that differing tasks
and differing ideals will make differing demands on economic
resources and political organisation. The pursuit of pleasure is in
general more expensive than the pursuit of learning and the interests
of the physical activist are less dependent on political structures
than those of the political enthusiast. The fact that knowledge of
different interests affects partiality does not mean that these factors
are inherently irrelevant to the choices proffered in the original
position. In particular the comparison of persons in terms of their
needs cannot be carried out on the basis of primary goods alone. As
we shall see this problem is especially acute if the 'least advantaged'
group is identified only in terms of the primary goods they possess.
The fairness of the contract appears to be promoted at the expense
of the realities of moral choice so that decisions of those behind the
veil of ignorance seem to lack relevance and content. Thus, while
Rawls struggles to distinguish those primary goods which we all
desire and do have knowledge of in the original position, from
particular conceptions of the good life which are to be left outside
the terms of the social contract, it is far from clear that the rational
contractor in the original position would not wish to take account
of his knowledge that, in the real world, people have strong moral
convictions that the 'secondary' goods of some ways of life are
morally superior to those of others. Hence his own rather arbitrary

introduction of the Aristotelian principle to ensure that there is an authorised preference for complex over simple pleasures.

A particular version of this line of criticism focuses on the extreme methodological individualism of Rawls's position, which, when combined with the highly abstract terms in which the individual in the original position is depicted, produces, if anything, a model for society which is lacking in the specific ties of culture and particularity which give our lives meaning and content at their core. No wonder that what emerges from the original position neglects the centrality of community, including obligations we have to members of our own groups, and the non-instrumental role of politics with respect to basic social and political institutions. Further, doubts can be raised about the usefulness of the very idea of an abstracted acontextualised individual without a particular set of social involvements and commitments being able to make choices which bear any meaningful relationship to real life, in which being a person means being someone whose existence is embodied in a particular culture and community. Even if we could know what choices a socially unsituated 'self' would make in an original position, would these choices produce a society in which concrete human beings would flourish? This is the gist of the communitarian critique of Rawls exhibited in the work of MacIntyre (1981) and Sandel (1982), to which I have referred in Chapter 2. For these theorists, the perplexity over what will emerge from an original position is simply a symptom of a defective method which ignores the 'embeddedness' of individual existence in particular cultures and groups, separated from which the individual lacks all sense of direction and values. This can be seen in the questions which are raised about Rawls's conviction that civil liberties are always the bedrock of any constitution, and more generally on his affirmation of the unvarying priority of justice over other, more sociable, values and his original confidence in the universal relevance of this theory to different cultures when in fact, as he has come to realise, it has strong ethnocentric and ideological affiliations.

Rawls's response to such difficulties is in part to reassert that he is not taking a morally neutral approach to the problem of distribution but is in fact seeking to explicate a particular moral point of view, namely that in which the autonomous moral agent is supremely valued. This is in fact his main justification for identifying and protecting basic liberties and insists on equality of opportunity. It is also the reason why he insists that in a well-ordered society there will be a public system of justice with general rules that allow individuals to cooperate on the basis of mutual respect. Again his Kantian starting-point is the fact that self-respect depends, not on wealth, but on the dignity of autonomous living and enables him to erect tolerance as a prime value protected by the veil of ignorance. It also enables him to accept so readily the empirically questionable Aristotelian principle.

Moreover, there is nothing in the theory that prevents individuals in the original position taking into account their general knowledge that, as real members of a society, they will wish to live in communities of a distinctive type and to be involved in shared enterprises with others which involve deep personal commitments.

While these responses may formally save Rawls's theory from being anti-communitarian in its values, they do undermine the methodology of the original position because getting the right result involves making changes to the original position with respect to the 'knowledge' attributed to the participants. Moreover, the values of fairness embodied in the original position and from which its description is derived can themselves be regarded as limited by the liberal assumption that everything in a society ought to be the outcome of a process of choice. In a communitarian world, free and informed consent may not be a touchstone of political legitimacy, but it is in a liberal society. Sandel, in particular, argues that the very question posed in the original position, which concerns how the benefits and burdens of social cooperation are to be distributed, predisposes the theory to an outcome which gives priority to individual autonomy and to the autonomy of a particular sort of individual, one whose self is identified entirely with a metaphysical core that stands outside the particular activities and relationships which constitute the actual life of actual individuals in actual societies (Sandel, 1982, p.17).

And so, either at the level of values, or at the level of methodology, it would appear that the Rawlsian theory of justice embodies contestable liberal assumptions which are presupposed by the theory and not proved or justified by it. We could as readily arrive at the same substantive result without all the paraphernalia of the original position.

Surprisingly, however, there is one element in the traditional liberal doctrines which Rawls does not endorse, and that is the significance of natural desert in the allocation of resources. Taking the view that the capacity to develop natural endowments is as much inherited as the natural endowments themselves, he takes all abilities as in principle part of a social pool of common assets on which no one has a prior claim. He argues that desert requires that there be a public set of rules laying down the rewards for certain performances which generate legitimate expectations, something which can come into existence only after society has been set up and after the principles of justice have been chosen. Thus, once the requirements of fair equality of opportunity have been satisfied, the inegalitarian outcomes of the chance distribution of natural resources remain unchecked by considerations of desert.

This is one way in which the logic of the original position does seem to have overborne our collective considered judgements in reflective equilibrium. Moral intuitions in themselves would surely have found some place for the idea that those who have earned our praise and thanks by socially beneficial and effortful activity would be allocated extra goods on that basis, and for that reason. Rawls might argue that this is never fair in the case of primary goods or in relation to the basic institutions of a society, but this is hardly beyond contention. Indeed, it is not clear why participants in the original position would not choose to incorporate an element of desert into their distributive criteria. It may be that they could have had, as part of their general knowledge, information to the effect that human beings do not have the sort of freedom of will on which Rawls's intellectual forebear, Kant, based his analysis of the moral nature of human beings. Similar points may be made about the other information that is or is not available to those in the original position, including the general 'facts' about human nature and economic systems on the basis of which the participants make up their minds.

The issue of desert is complicated by Rawls's initial analysis of justice which takes in any morally relevant consideration which bears on the distribution of the benefits and burdens of social cooperation. This means that the intuitions on which he bases his reflective equilibrium are not really connected with 'justice' as a specific type of distributive consideration but must include any rationale which is 'overriding' in this context, including the subsidi-ary parts of his complex lexical system of principles which promote efficiency. He does not therefore ask us to confine ourselves to things which are specifically identified by the language of justice and fairness, rendering it doubly difficult to specify the intuitional bases of our sense of justice. This is particularly evident when he

intrudes into justice the forward-looking criterion of the appropriate level of incentives to produce maximally efficient returns.

A particular example of this overly dogmatic concept of justice is
that it excludes the discourse of justice from an area of social life in
which it seems to play an important but subordinate role. Thus, it
has often been pointed out that Rawls is inconsistent in holding that
justice concerns all the basic institutions of society but in practice
excludes it from so-called 'private' spheres, such as the family (see,
for instance, Kearns, 1983).

Rawls rightly notes that in the family, mutual affection and
solidarity often make considerations of justice seem out of place.
Identification of the least well-off person and applying the idea of
equal opportunity to father, mother or child seem inappropriate.
Such considerations, which fit neatly with his assumptions and
principles, lead him to systematically ignore the unjustified inequalities of power, opportunities and resources which characterise
family relationships in most societies. Making, as he does, 'heads
of families' the representative participants in the original position
may simplify the model, but it seems designed to avoid the issue of
domestic justice. Maybe this difficulty could be rectified by including all women and men in the original position, although this opens
up yet another contentious issue concerning the possible distinctive
differences between male and female modes of thought which may
persist even behind the veil of ignorance as a barrier towards reaching a working agreement on such matters as justice in the family and
selection of primary goods (Okin, 1987, pp.65–72).

When considering these problems for Rawls's theory, it must be
noted that he has adapted and developed his theory, partly in the
light of such criticisms, over a number of years. When, in the essays
drawn together in *Political Liberalism* (1993), Rawls emphasises
that his theory is 'political not metaphysical', he means that it is
designed to assist the growth of consensus in a liberal society, such
as the USA, and not to establish any profound truths about the
nature of human beings or an objectively correct ideal of justice
which transcends cultural boundaries. Pluralism, in the sense of a
flowering of radically different but equally valid ways of life,
requires a state which provides a framework of individual rights
that are neutral with respect to different lifestyles. His theory is
directed, he now says, to facilitating the identification of those
aspects of these different cultures which overlap to any extent that
enables a core of right to be fixed as a basis for a diversity of good

and desirable ways of life. Political liberalism does no more than try to 'answer the question: how is it possible that there could be a stable and just society whose free and equal citizens are deeply divided by conflicting and even incompatible religious, philosophical and moral doctrines?' (Rawls, 1993, p.133). The 'overlapping consensus' required for such stability and justice has to be, he argues, much more than a compromise of conflicting interests, a mere *modus vivendi*. It must be a firm moral commitment to the mandatory system of justice that protects everyone's right to pursue their own good and values and is given overriding priority over this diversity. This political consensus rules out only such doctrinally-based lifestyles that are not 'rational', in that they cannot gain the respect of those who disagree with them, but is otherwise not only sceptically tolerant but actually supportive of the diversity of rational world-views.

These developments are helpful clarification of 'justice as fairness', and they do insulate Rawls from criticism relating to his alleged universalism and the apparent arbitrariness or cultural parochialism of some of his premises. However, it remains something of an article of faith that none of those matters which are judged to be overriding and hence legitimately part of the coercive framework of a liberal society are matters on which there are irreconcilable or incommensurable doctrinal or philosophical differences about acceptable ways of life. In particular, the defence of Rawls's theory, even within a liberal society, must involve ultimately unargued rejection of those communitarian claims that prioritise those forms of society which provide individuals with a firm community framework in which to live out a less than fully autonomous existence.

Justice and welfare

Justice has inescapable and firm ties to the treatment accorded to those who fare worst in whatever social arrangements exist in a society. Not only is 'social' justice closely associated with the relief of poverty and the care of the less fortunate members of society, but justice in general is inextricably linked to the idea of the interests of the oppressed, the weak and the exploited. Any theory of justice must, therefore, have regard to its implications for the most needy persons within a community. This does not mean that 'need' as such must be the prime criterion within an acceptable conception of justice, but no approach which does not address itself adequately to the problem of what constitutes 'fair' treatment of the most deprived citizens can be seriously considered as an acceptable normative theory of justice. It is a point in favour of Rawls's principles that this is recognised.

The connection between justice and welfare is obscured by the use of the term 'welfare' in welfare economics to cover the satisfaction of any human preferences which can feature in economic choices, so that the maximising of welfare is adopted as the modern equivalent to the maximisation of utility. Interpreted in this way a concern for welfare may be regarded as distinct from justice in so far as the former is a matter of aggregation and the latter a matter – at least primarily – of distribution. In contrast, the relevant connection may be between justice and welfare in the sense of the satisfaction of the basic needs of those who are unable to provide adequately for themselves, an objective which is often given priority over the demands of others upon the same scarce resources. This relates welfare, in the sense in which it is tied in with justice, to some conception of fundamental human needs.

The basic need analysis of welfare is, however, as it stands, rather restrictive if we are seeking to take in the characteristic activities of the 'welfare state' whose operations cover more than helping those who cannot provide the essentials of material living for themselves. The welfare state extends to the provision of general health and educational services for everyone, including those who would be able to see to these matters for themselves and their family, if they had to do so. The crucial features of the welfare state are that its services promote the well-being of citizens and are provided more or less free of charge through a system of insurance or taxation rather than a payment for services received at the point of delivery. Normally the fiscal arrangements for such services are such that the poorest persons in society do not in fact pay for what they receive, in that insurance is paid by those in employment or, more substantially, through a system of progressive taxation. Services are then provided on the basis of need rather than ability to pay, hence the affinity between caring for the poor and the welfare state. The conceptual boundaries here are fuzzy in that there is no clear distinction between giving direct material aid to those in need and providing an environment in which those previously unable to care for themselves have the effective opportunity to do

so, but the general drift of welfarism is clear enough – it is directed
to the satisfaction of fundamental needs and thus has to do particularly with those in greatest need, although this may be within a
system of universal benefits funded via the fiscal mechanisms of the
state.

It is interesting to see how competing theories of justice deal with
making provision for basic needs. Merit-based theories can either
justify the relief of poverty on the grounds that gross suffering is in
general undeserved and therefore unjust and requiring remedy, or
else they may classify poverty relief as a matter of beneficence or
prudence rather than justice, a strategy which need not carry the
implication that it is not a proper activity for states. Need-based
theories have no immediate difficulty in accommodating welfarism
but require, along with other theories, to identify what counts as a
fundamental need, and to assess the relative fairness of the mechanisms they propose to use for the promotion of need-satisfaction.
Rights-based theories, which characteristically interpret rights in
terms of respect for individual choices, have more difficulty in
determining what should be done about persons who fare badly
under such a choice-based system, either through making bad
choices, or through not having the wherewithal to make effective
choices in relation to their own well-being, perhaps through lack of
capacity, ability or wisdom. The first move of rights theorists is
often to equate welfarism with providing individuals with the
opportunities to develop and deploy their abilities as rational or
moral agents, but this leaves untouched the problem of those who
are unsuccessful in making use of these opportunities, to say nothing of the wider problem of the possible injustice of the unequal
outcome of even a strongly interventionist form of 'fair' equality of
opportunity, which must still depend in part on morally contingent
matters such as inherited natural endowments and favourable
family circumstances.

One of the attractions of Rawls's theory is that it appears to
marry the entitlements of human choice with a lively concern for
the less fortunate members of society. Once the equalities of basic
liberty and fair opportunity are taken care of as inviolable rights,
the difference principle sees to it that such inequalities as emerge are
only permitted in so far as they benefit the least advantaged in
society. This seems not only strongly egalitarian in its tendencies,
but tailor-made to a system which gives the sort of priority to the
well-being of the poor which is to be looked for in a conception of

justice. The worst-off group in society not only enjoy the self-respect
which comes from the possession of full and equal political rights
and the material assistance which is necessary for them to develop
their abilities to the same level as those of similar ability and
motivation, but the whole subsequent economic system appears to
be directed to ensuring that they are not excluded from its benefits
of increased wealth which comes from social cooperation. No
inequalities are allowed which do not improve their position. This
in itself is interesting in the light of feminist criticisms of liberal
justice as excluding caring and loving, whereas for Rawls justice is
allied with fraternity and 'the sense of justice is continuous with love
for mankind' (Rawls, 1971, p.434).

Deeper investigation of Rawls's difference principle and related
features of his theory which bear on the lot of the worst-off segment
of society does not entirely bear out these expectations. This is
hardly surprising in view of the recurrent problems which arise in
bringing together in one system the prime-value freedom of choice
and the virtues of fair contracts on the one hand and effective
commitment to the provision of welfare on the basis of need on
the other. Not only does it turn out that Rawls's scheme permits far
greater economic inequalities than might be imagined, but it also
becomes clear that the difference principle is not directed primarily
at those most characteristically identified by the concept of fundamental need. Consequently it becomes difficult to see how the
Rawlsian approach can adequately operationalise the provision of
welfare at an acceptable level to essentially needy groups.

One of the features of the original position which is taken to be
'realistic' in that it is also a feature of actual societies – at least
modern democratic ones – is that a free-market economy is efficient
as a means for coordinating the efforts of economic agents, who are
assumed to be basically self-interested. People are taken to require
incentives to work and to develop their socially useful talents. Rawls
holds that there is no effective way of ascribing relative values to
resources except by recourse to the laws of supply and demand as
the crucial determinants of who gets what in an economically efficient system. However he contends that 'there is no essential tie
between the use of free markets and private ownership of the
instruments of production" (1971, p.271) and takes up a neutral
position between private and public ownership of the means of
production and exchange, simply assuming that both property systems are compatible with a market economy.

From Rawls's point of view the economic efficiency of the free market is a fortunate empirical fact since the liberties which are essential to the operation of a free market – including the absence of slavery and the right to a measure of private property – also feature amongst his list of basic liberties. However, beyond the requirements of efficiency and basic liberty, there is an independent insistence that the competition be 'fair'. This is spelt out in his full conception of equality of opportunity which requires large transfers of resources to ensure that all those with similar abilities and motivations have similar educational opportunities, not just formally, but in effect, through the provision of adequate facilities and material support. This is extended to cover equal economic rights in a free market which is then seen as a case of 'pure procedural justice'. If markets are reasonably competitive and open then the fairness of the competition transfers to the fairness of an outcome which is not independently known to be just.

Despite the happy coincidence of economic efficiency and pure procedural justice, which gives Rawls's economic theory the flavour of Adam Smith's 'invisible hand', Rawls does not believe, any more than Smith, that the fair competition of the open market can be sustained without proper governmental background institutions. Accepting that there is a tendency for wealth and power to accumulate, thus distorting competition and undermining equality of opportunity, he requires the state to police economic activities to prevent monopolies and trade restrictions, which threaten both efficiency and fairness. He goes further than Smith, however, not only in the substance of his ideal of fair equality of opportunity, but also in his use of the difference principle to justify taxing the better-off members of society to provide a 'social minimum' of resources for the least well-off group through what he calls the 'transfer' branch of government. In Smith's system of natural liberty this tendency to more equal distribution happens naturally through the expenditure of the wealthy, and not artificially as a result of state-organised redistribution of resources.

Before looking into the significance of the difference principle in this context we must note that, once all these corrective actions and background fairnesses have been taken into account, it is still the case that some will use their talents better than others and that some have more talents than others, so that, given freedom of contract and freedom of choice in employment, significant inequalities are bound to emerge if different employments are rewarded differently as, *ex hypothesi,* they must be in an incentive system. However 'fair' the starting-point, therefore, inequalities will rapidly emerge and accumulate, for the individual is free to spend their income to pursue further wealth and opportunity. The general idea that differences in natural and developed abilities should lead to differences in income is not of major concern to Rawls. He does not hold that individuals have an antecedent natural right to use their capacities as they think fit to gain whatever they may, as Nozick contends, but he does not regard it as problematic that natural differences lead to material inequalities, given a free-market incentive system. If differential rewards need to be offered to increase the general wealth of a society, then those who, in a 'fair' competition, are chosen to fill such offices and positions on the basis of ability, 'deserve' or are entitled to these higher rewards. Anything less would be an infringement of legitimate expectations and a denial of basic freedoms of choice.

The question then arises whether the difference principle turns this apparent meritocracy into something more like a welfare system. The argument that it does so is to the effect that the inequalities in question all have to be justified by their beneficial effects on the worst-off group. However, while it might appear that this will produce a roughly egalitarian society, there is in reality no reason to think that it will do so. Self-interested individuals will be able to benefit from the possession of scarce skills, differentials which bring small increases in resources to the worst off may bring much larger benefits to other groups, and in general the outcome of the difference principle is compatible with very significant inequalities. Moreover, any tendency it has to equality is contingent on particular circumstances, in the same way as the alleged egalitarian outcomes of the principle of utility depend on the empirical variables which affect supply and demand. It is possible, therefore, that in a Rawlsian society the worst-off group may be very badly off indeed both in absolute and relative terms.

Anxieties of this sort are heightened by investigation of the membership of the worst-off group in society. It might be thought that this will include those unable to work through sickness, mental or physical incapacity, or lack of opportunity; but this is apparently not so. In the first place, such persons are in general not represented in the original position, where the parties are confined to those with the capacity to take part in society and who must, therefore, have the minimum requirements of moral agency: that is, they must, *inter alia,* have the capacity to have, and effectively pursue, a conception of their own good. This makes no allowance for the special needs of those without these capacities. Moreover, within the class of moral persons, the worst-off group are identified in relation to their possession of primary goods, particularly economic and material resources, and not according to their available satisfactions which are, of course, affected by their state of health and other sources of suffering and felt misery, and do not depend simply on the resources available to them irrespective of their physical and mental condition. Further, it turns out that Rawls, in thinking about this group, identifies them with the group which is in employment, but is paid least, rather than with those who are in what might be considered a worse position of being unable to work. The 'social minimum' is 'wages plus transfers' (1971, p.277).

It is not clear how basic to Rawls's theory is this characterisation of the least favoured group. He gets to this position initially through considering normal social and economic life, putting to one side the problem of those who do not come up to participant level in a society of free and equal moral agents: 'everyone is capable of honouring the principles of justice and of being full participants in social cooperation throughout their lives' (1980, p.545). However, this assumption may be considered to be a relatively superficial part of the model. Certainly the problem of the unemployed appears to be mitigated by the fact that the principle of fair equality of opportunity requires that governments ensure that there is a choice of suitable employments available, but this is a highly problematic practical suggestion in a free-market economy which cannot simply create jobs to provide employment without distorting the market and, if the problem is a large one, creating massive 'distortions' in the economic system, thus reducing the wealth available to help the worst-off group. Further, in an incentive system, jobs that are created to provide employment in this way must presumably be paid less than the lowest-paid socially useful job, which may be very low indeed. And, of course, this solution, even if practicable and possible in a free-market system, does nothing for those unable to work, whose special needs may be much greater than can be met by the resources of the least favoured class.

Another tactic for reducing Rawlsian embarrassment on this point is to take the temporary conditions of childhood, unemployment, transient illness and old age into the normal life-cycle of the worker and see benefits in relation to such needy categories of person as part of the total rewards of employment. This would not, however, deal with those whose course-of-life needs of this sort are exceptional due to the abnormality of their health or accidental misfortunes. Also, such arrangements would not be confined to the worst-off group so that we are not here dealing with an application of the difference principle.

Moreover, to take special needs such as those of the seriously ill into consideration would be to make a major change in Rawls's assumptions. Clearly, even an equal share of resources will be insufficient to redress such imbalance of satisfactions and medical care in itself will not greatly alter the situation. Does this mean that the difference principle would involve putting more and more resources towards marginal improvements in the lot of persons with such a low quality of life? Society would then become one large hospital or welfare institution, to which end all social co-operation would be ultimately geared.

The reason why Rawls does not take this to be the result of his difference principle may be that he does not take persons disadvantaged in these ways to be 'normal' members of society, in that his model is designed to deal with the distribution of the benefits of social cooperation to which all members contribute. He sees society as an organisation for mutual benefit in which everyone participates to some degree and from which all should benefit, hence the justice of viewing natural abilities as a form of collective asset whose fruits can legitimately be used to improve the lot of the least well-off set of contributors.

To allow non-contributors to be represented in the original position would be to remove the basis for a bargained agreement, but to exclude them seems inhuman, especially as Rawls is prepared to allow representatives of future generations a say in the contracted outcome, in so far as the parties to the contract do not know in which generations they will be born. We seem, therefore, to have a clash between the logic of the original position and the sentiments of justice which the outcome of the social contract is said to match.

In the end Rawls's system, using as its basis the original position, comes down in favour of choice and opportunity for those with the ability to grasp it, rather than of a sort of full-blooded commitment to satisfaction of needs which is bound to undermine a free-market system but nevertheless seems to be an element in our sense of justice. This is evident, for instance, in his identification of self-respect with equal political rights rather than equality of economic resources, and his consequent readiness to accept a degree of economic inequality which marginally increases the lot of the least advantaged group of employed persons. This accords with the priority of liberty, political and economic, but it may do less than justice to those who are really worst off in the community of free and equal moral persons. It seems then that, in the event, there is an unresolved tension between the libertarian ethos of the original position and the reflective equilibrium of our considered moral judgements which incorporate treatment in accordance with basic need.

It is another question again, however, if distributions which are based solely on need are, in any case, a matter of justice, rather than humanity or benevolence. Rawls's broad definition of justice as having to do with 'the way in which the major social institutions distribute fundamental rights and duties and determine the division of advantage from social cooperation' (1971, p.7), and his emphasis on the overriding force of justice, do not enable him to exclude the provision of basic welfare from the sphere of justice without undermining its social and political priority. If we broaden the scope of justice to make it a relevant factor in all those situations which we routinely assess in the terminology of justice and if we drop the insistence that justice must always take priority over all other considerations, then we might clarify the issues of social choice by contrasting the claims of need with those of justice. Rawls's rejection of desert as an element within justice debars him from making the alleviation of undeserved need a matter of justice, thus closing off another way of bringing at least some categories of need within the scope of justice in distribution. Finally, his individualistic model of a liberal society makes it difficult for him to base fundamental welfare duties on the community ties and relationships which communitarians see as lacking in his vision of justice.

6 Justice as Efficiency: Posner and Criminal Justice

Although it is common to draw a sharp distinction between justice and utility, utilitarians themselves vigorously dispute the validity of this antithesis, and claim that utilitarianism can account for the significance of justice as a subordinate ethical and political standard whose importance can be explained by the ultimate ethical principle that the right act is that which maximises overall utility. In contrast, non-utilitarians often ascribe to justice those moral judgements which are routinely used to curb the application of utilitarian reasoning, while some go so far as to define 'justice' as a distributive ideal which totally excludes the aggregative goal of bringing about the greatest quantity of good (see p.17).

Inevitably, therefore, utilitarians are on the defensive when articulating and defending their conception of justice and they usually feel impelled to demonstrate that adherence to utilitarianism does not radically conflict with common-sense notions of what is just. Often, in the process, they reinterpret classical utilitarianism so as to accommodate the demands of justice. Indeed, one contemporary theorist of justice, Richard Posner, whose work is very much in the utilitarian tradition, presents his theory almost entirely by way of contrasts with his interpretation of utilitarianism. Later in this chapter I shall consider Posner's 'economics of justice' and its applications to criminal justice. But first, by way of introduction, the main elements of the justice versus utility debate are reviewed.

Justice and utility

Utilitarianism – in some shape or form – has been, for over a century, a working hypothesis for most western economists and constitutes a fair reflection of the concentration on economic growth as the central policy goal in modern politics. Present-day utilitarianism is, perhaps, best exemplified by 'welfare economics' which adopts as the basic economic norm the maximisation of human utility or 'welfare', an approach which has also been applied to democratic theory and, more recently, to the common law.

The central tenets of utilitarianism constitute a powerful combination of empirical and normative dogmas, expounded first by the nineteenth-century Philosophical Radicals, particularly Jeremy Bentham and – in a less orthodox vein – John Stuart Mill. The Philosophical Radicals held the apparently contradictory theses that (1) as a matter of fact, all persons seek to maximise their own pleasures and minimise their own pains (sometimes called 'psychological egoism'), and (2) as a matter of value, the morally right act is that which maximises the pleasures and minimises the pains of *all* those affected by it (which I will call 'ethical utilitarianism'). With these premises, the classical utilitarians embark on a detailed critique of social arrangements which do not maximise utility, and produce a multiplicity of specific proposals detailing ways in which the self-centredness of the individual could be harnessed to generate happiness for all. What, for Adam Smith, had been a wonder of divine design whereby the individual's pursuit of his own economic benefit, in the context of free-market competition, results in the 'wealth of nations', becomes, for Bentham and his followers, a mechanism to be developed and improved in all spheres of social life by the scientific methods of human social engineers. Thus Bentham proposes to reform the criminal law by having effective sanctions to deter harmful conduct and supports the extension of the democratic franchise to provide similar market-type controls over the behaviour of politicians who promote the general happiness only in order to be reelected. Smith's 'natural' harmony of interests is thereby transformed into an artificial harmony whereby the manipulation of incentives produces 'the greatest happiness of the greatest number', a slogan which is taken to mean the largest possible quantity of pleasure over pain in a community where every member's pleasure and pains are given equal weight in the calculus of social happiness.

Given that this historical association of psychological egoism and ethical consequentialism – which became the dominant orthodoxy of late nineteenth-and early twentieth-century capitalism – still features in many public policy debates, it is difficult to treat the twin pillars of classical utilitarianism separately, particularly as the psychological doctrine is frequently deployed to demonstrate how ethical utilitarianism may be used to support ordinary standards of justice. This is done by showing the need for rules which allocate benefit and burdens as inducements for self-interested individuals to act as the general happiness requires. Indeed, although utilitarianism is usually considered to be an essentially ethical doctrine, many theorists are counted as utilitarians more because of their adherence to the postulate that people are rational maximisers of their own happiness (or interests) than on account of any unshakeable commitment to the normative consequentialist thesis that general utility-maximising is the sole ethical and political value. However, the two elements of the classical theory are, in principle, separable and both have been developed in different ways from the various forms of modern utilitarianism.

In modern economics, the psychological doctrine concerning the self-interestedness of human motivation has been transformed, for theoretical purposes, into a working hypothesis to the effect that, in order to predict the outcome of economics and social arrangements, it should be assumed that people act rationally, in that they consistently choose those options which bring most benefit to them as individuals, the associated assumption being that economic agents base their choices on relatively constant preferences or desires. The theoretical standing of this hypothesis depends on the extent to which it can be used to generate verifiable predictions concerning the social effects of economic or legal change. Its effectiveness as a postulate does not, therefore, depend directly on the extent to which it applies in fact to the reasoning processes of particular individuals. Thus the idea of maximising behaviour has been described as 'a useful fiction for analysing the behaviour of groups' (Burrows and Veljanovski, 1981, p.3), although it is clearly intended by most of its proponents to be a realistic, if selective, fiction, which adequately encapsulates the dominant tendency in human behaviour.

For Bentham, utility-maximising means choosing pleasant and avoiding painful sensations – pleasure and pain being the two 'masters' of human conduct – but the implausibility of this view in relation to many forms of behaviour led to the substitution of 'want-satisfaction' as the measure of utility, a more open-ended variant of psychological egoism which enables the maximising assumption to achieve the status of a truism at the price of excessive vagueness. To render this interpretation of utility operational the test of want-satisfaction is taken to be the preferences of individuals as expressed in the choices they actually make. This turns the max-imising hypothesis into the tautological truth that people choose what they choose, since the satisfactions which are said to determine choices are evidenced only by the choices which are made.

In economics this vacuity is remedied by concentrating on strictly economic preferences that involve the effort to gain com-mand over scarce resources by increasing purchasing capacity, and hence gaining control over goods and services which rational max-imisers hope to obtain through their choices. Since, by extension, anything may be given a 'price' according to what individuals are prepared to pay for it in an open market, all want-satisfactions can in principle be given a monetary value by the application of such ideas as 'opportunity costs', whereby the value that a person places on an apparently non-monetary activity may be equated with the amount of money they could have earned in that time (this repres-enting the 'opportunity cost' of their indulging in the activity in question). In this way we pass from happiness to want-satisfaction, and thence to monetary wealth, as the value which individuals or aggregates are said to pursue. In the case of wealth, however, it is not always clear whether – unconvincingly – wealth is taken to be the ultimate objective or – more plausibly – wealth is assumed to be a measure of the enjoyment value of the resultant experiences, the capacity to achieve felt want-satisfaction, or some such further objective for which wealth is merely the instrumental or proximate goal.

The normative principle of ethical utilitarianism has undergone similar modifications in the face of comparable difficulties. Thus the empirical problems of measuring pleasures and pains or other psy-chological states, such as feelings of satisfaction, has prompted the abandonment of happiness-maximising as the all-inclusive ethical value, in favour of some form of preference utilitarianism according to which utility-maximising is giving people what they want or choose rather than what will actually enable them to increase their pleasures or enjoyments. Again there is often an ambiguity here about whether realising preferences is a means of increasing happi-ness or obtaining felt satisfaction, or is itself the valued objective. In the latter case what may be called preference utilitarianism approx-imates to its standard rival – the ethics of autonomy – in that it treats the exercise of the capacity for choice rather than happiness or satisfaction as the ultimate moral value.

Preference utilitarianism, as an ethical doctrine, looks almost as circular as its behavioural counterpart since, if moral principles are intended to guide choices, it appears to suggest that we ought to choose that which we do in fact choose, in which case it cannot offer guidance about how we ought to exercise our capacity for choice beyond requiring us to be consistent in our preference orderings. However, as we have seen, the ethical dimension of the maximising principle relates not to individual choices directly, but to social choices – that is, to choices which affect the welfare of many or all members of a social group. Ethical utilitarianism, abridged in terms of preferences, is the principle that the right act is the one which gives as many people as possible what they choose. In economic matters this becomes equated with maximally increasing purchasing power and, again, by extension, promoting those non-monetary preferences for which people would pay most.

The preference version of ethical utilitarianism has the advantage of helping to circumvent one of the major difficulties of the classical theory, namely, how to make interpersonal comparisons of utility, particularly when utility is equated with such subjective factors as pleasure or pain. Despite Bentham's valiant efforts to provide a 'felicific calculus' for the aggregation of the hedonic experiences of a community by measuring such factors as the intensity, duration and pleasurable or painful nature of their sensations, it has always seemed impossible to ascertain the truth of claims such as that one person's pleasure is four or five times as great as that of another, or that one person's intense but brief pleasure can be counterbalanced by another person's weaker but longer-lasting pain.

Preference utilitarianism avoids interpersonal comparisons of this sort by attending to the choices that individuals make rather than the pleasures and pains they experience. The principle of utility can then be met by giving everyone what they say they want. However, since this can rarely if ever be achieved, particularly when social choices about institutional arrangements are under consideration, in practice it is necessary to resort to a democratic interpretation of preference utilitarianism by making social and political choices in accordance with the wishes of the majority, despite the fact that this may have the disadvantage of effectively excluding the interests of minorities. The move to democratic utilitarianism can be resisted if utility-maximising is given a more restricted democratic interpretation by requiring unanimity in the making of social choices.

This approach is exemplified by the use of the idea of 'Pareto optimality', according to which one situation is superior to another if at least one person is better off (or prefers that situation) and all other persons are equally well off (or think that the situations are equally acceptable). The Pareto optimal situation is that which it is impossible to change in a way which improves the lot or meets the wishes of at least one person without at the same time conflicting with the welfare or wishes of other people who are affected by the change. This uncontroversial concept is not only of very limited application in practice but has the disadvantage of giving to every member of a community a veto over any proposed changes, thus giving unjustified weight to the status quo and in effect making an infinite number of different social situations Pareto optimal, since there will always be those who stand to lose by alterations in existing arrangements.

An apparently more classically utilitarian variant of Pareto optimality is the Kaldor–Hicks principle according to which one social situation is to be preferred to another if the gains to some members of the community would be sufficient to compensate those who are the potential losers in the change from one to the other. The changes so justified do not depend on obtaining agreement of all those involved or actually paying the compensation to those who stand to lose from them, so that, while the Kaldor–Hicks approach has the flavour of a happiness-maximising principle, it removes the element of consent involved in the Pareto principle, which potential losers could use to block proposed changes. One problem with the Kaldor–Hicks principle is that, when we seek to establish appropriate levels of compensation, it takes us back into the problem area of interpersonal comparisons, for the measurement of gains and losses involves comparing the satisfactions of the different persons involved.

The empirical realism conferred on the normative principle of utility by the Pareto optimal formula has to be offset against its diminished political applicability. Nearly all political choices benefit some at the expense of others. Of more direct bearing on the topic of this book is the objection that Pareto optimality rules out criticism of existing social arrangements as unjust, at least as long as they are more beneficial to at least one person than the suggested alternatives. The Kaldor–Hicks formula has more political uses and in its talk of compensation seems to be moving in the direction of justice, despite the fact that the compensation is notional rather than actual. But this too assumes that justice must take a status quo as a reference point for determining compensation. These normative limitations of tests of general social welfare illustrate one of the most serious criticisms of utilitarianism in general, namely its failure to take seriously the distribution of the valuable goods it seeks to maximise. This criticism can be made most forcibly from a meritorian standpoint, according to which it is essential to justice that benefits and burdens are allocated on the basis of the praiseworthy and blameworthy conduct or character of those affected by the distribution, but similar criticisms are put forward by everyone who considers some degree of egalitarianism to be an essential ingredient of justice.

An initial utilitarian response to such charges is to reiterate the Benthamite dictum that, in the calculus of pleasures and pains, 'each counts for one and no more than one'. However, this form of equality means only that no one's pleasure and pain are to be excluded from the calculus, or given less weight than a similar pleasure or pain experienced by any other person. While this requirement is entirely consistent with utilitarianism, and does rule out certain decision procedures on grounds which have at least a semblance of justice, it is still compatible with the many gross inequalities which are routinely denounced as unjust. It permits the 'victimisation' of minorities whose sufferings can be outweighed by the increased pleasures these sufferings bring to others (perhaps in the form of slave labour), and lacks the ability to make relevant moral discrimination between different types of enjoyable and painful activity.

Utilitarians have a number of further arguments with which they hope to accommodate their theory to common sense notions of justice:

1.   Drawing on the concept of diminishing marginal utility, according to which the enjoyment to be derived from a given quantity of any commodity diminishes as the individual obtains more of it (so that the wealthy person derives less pleasure from receiving an additional sum of money than the same sum of money brings to a poor person), it is to be argued that an approximately equal distribution of money or other desired commodity will maximise the sum total of happiness in a society. To this extent utilitarianism has distributive implications which may be described as 'egalitarian', since it tends to produce an outcome of approximate equality of holdings.

2. According to ethical utilitarianism, an act is right if it maximises the happiness of all those affected by it and wrong in so far as it causes suffering to others; this means that the best utilitarian social arrangements will reward those who act altruistically and punish or burden those who cause suffering to others. It is not, therefore, the case that utilitarianism is indifferent to the moral quality of the behaviour of individuals for, through a system of incentives and penalties, those who act rightly will tend to be allocated a greater share of society's resources than those who act wrongly. This may not mean rewarding moral goodness, if this is seen as doing good for its own sake, but it does give credit for socially beneficial behaviour, thus avoiding the charge of moral insensitivity.

3. The distinctive importance placed on justice as a political value is compatible with utilitarianism because the happiness of human beings is particularly vulnerable to certain types of injury or harm, so that utility is maximised by prohibiting actions which tend to inflict such serious damage. These prohibitions may be regarded as the particular sphere of justice which has to do with the prevention of the major forms of human suffering in contradistinction to the wider utilitarian objective of encouraging the performance of socially beneficial actions. In a variant of utilitarianism – called 'negative' utilitarianism – it is held that pains or pleasures are not commensurate in that a pleasure cannot outweigh a pain and, in addition, the relief of suffering is said to take moral precedence over the increase of pleasure. This position is associated with the thesis that law should be concerned solely with the prohibition of pain-causing behaviour, leaving the pursuit of happiness to the private sphere.

4. Finally, stressing again the function of justice as a political ideal rather than an ethic for private life, the utilitarian, drawing on the premise of psychological egoism, can demonstrate that a society organised on utilitarian lines will be a society of rules and therefore of formal justice. Not only will social decisions be taken according to certain generalisations about the normal consequences of types of behaviour, but these types of behaviour will be encouraged or discouraged by the enactment of rules laying down appropriate sanctions (both negative and positive). While these rules, or laws, will be evaluated on utilitarian grounds, so that the net sum of harms prevented and

pleasures elicited will maximally exceed the totality of pains inflicted by the imposition of negative sanctions (such as punishments or taxes), individual actions will be judged in accordance with the rules and not by a direct appeal to utility. This 'rule-utilitarian' approach is to be distinguished from the classical 'act-utilitarian' theory, according to which it is the individual act, rather than the rule, which is assessed by the utilitarian standard. Under rule-utilitarianism, it is argued, individuals will be treated with the formal equality required by ordinary standards of justice and the problem of victimisation will thus be reduced, if not eliminated. In this way the rule-utilitarian thesis explains why justice is essentially a matter of social organisation rather than personal morality.

In combination, these points constitute a formidable defence of utilitarian justice, but each is open to objection. One general difficulty is that most of them appear unfortunately *ad hoc,* in that they rely on contingent facts, rather than moral principle, to produce acceptable results. Thus, if diminishing marginal utility does not hold in a particular context, can its standard egalitarian consequences be ignored? Or, if punishments do not deter certain types of harmful behaviour, does this mean that they should not be penalised? If disobeying a generally useful rule increases happiness can it not be ignored in that instance? Even when utilitarianism does get the morally right answer, it does not appear to do so for the right reasons.

It is also doubtful whether the combination of arguments (2) and (3) above really meets the full charge of moral inadequacy. Critics are concerned not simply with the fear that the unmerited sufferings of some will be inflicted or permitted just because they maximise overall utility. They also have the feeling that some pleasures, such as those of the sadist or the racist, ought not to be counted at all in the calculus of social values, because they have, if anything, negative moral quality. In a milder version of the same point it is argued, along the lines of Rawls's Aristotelian principle (see p.111) that some types of pleasure are inherently superior to others in a way that does not relate to their felt intensity.

The admission that it may be necessary to pick and choose amongst pleasures and pains undermines hedonistic utilitarianism, according to which these are the only values of consequence, and thereby takes away one of the main advantages of utilitarianism, namely its unitary measure of value. However, there are various types of 'ideal' utilitarianism according to which the rightness and wrongness of acts (or rules) depends on a number of different types of valued consequences. These versions of utilitarianism, which can accommodate the significance of beauty and truth as well as pleasure and pain, are, in general, morally more acceptable, although they do not directly confront the distributional issues characteristically posed by justice.

Rule-utilitarianism does appear to meet some of the distributional objections to making utility the sole measure of political rightness but, if taken strictly, it appears to be a radical departure from classical utilitarianism. The genuine utilitarian surely cannot be committed to following a rule even when this does not – and sometimes this must surely be the case – maximise utility? Moreover, not only is rule-utilitarianism a departure from the classical purity of the theory, it does not in practice avoid all forms of victimisation, some of which are group rather than individual victimisations, and may therefore be perfectly compatible with rule-based institutions, such as slavery or other routinised forms of discrimination.

For reasons such as these, the consideration of utilitarianism tends to generate a search for a more stable basis for the minimal equalities and particular protections against victimisation which are felt to be prerequisites of any tolerably just society. Typical in this context is John Rawls's critique of utilitarianism's failure to take seriously the distinction between persons and his attempt, through the idea of the social contract, to provide a basis for rights which limits but does not eliminate the application of utilitarian considerations. However, if absolute rights – whether or not they are based on contract or mere moral conviction – are deployed in this way, it is open to the utilitarian to counter with the charge that these rights tend to place unjustifiable restraints on the pursuit of the general welfare and in practice serve in large part to protect the interests of a privileged minority over against the prospective advantages of the majority. Rawls's defence of the priority of liberty and, more evidently, Nozick's stand on the unlimited transactional rights of the property-owning individual can be taken by the tough-minded utilitarian as exemplifying the moral inadequacies of non-utilitarian theories of justice.

More generally, the utilitarian can cast doubt on the common assumption that justice is always an overriding moral consideration and adopt the view that the rights protected by utilitarian rules are indeed quite properly no more than positive rights which may be overridden, when appropriate, by wider considerations of utility. This hard-line utilitarian approach may involve overturning some accepted ideas about what is just and requires us to revise our views on the significance of justice within the overall moral framework, but utilitarianism has traditionally been a reforming and radical philosophy and it may be that, in the last resort, the utilitarians' best line of defence is the characteristically iconoclastic one of attacking the questionable outcomes of non-utilitarian principles. A contemporary example of such tough-mindedness is the work of Richard Posner, to whose economic theory of justice I now turn.

Posner's 'economics' of justice

The title of Posner's book *The Economics of Justice* (1981) suggests that his concern with justice is principally to do with the cost-effectiveness of the administration of law. This is certainly one of his interests, but it is a theme which is more central to his later work, *The Federal Courts, Crisis and Reform* (1985), in which he deals with the case-load crisis facing the federal judiciary in the United States of America. *The Economics of Justice,* on the other hand, focuses more on presenting an economic conception of justice which equates justice with economic efficiency, particularly within the sphere of common law. While this book by no means sets out a systematic and rigorous defence of the idea that justice comes down to the benefits of wealth maximisation, it is noteworthy as a rare attempt to argue for a modern utilitarian analysis of justice (although it must be stressed that Posner himself sharply distinguishes his theory from Benthamite utilitarianism). Since Posner is a leading advocate of what is called the 'economic analysis of law' (EAL), his account of justice provides us with important insights into the contemporary implications of a type of theory which has close associations with the normative economics of free-market economists such as Milton Friedman. Posner's achievement has been to apply the type of individualistic economic theory to the substance of common law doctrines in areas such as negligence, contract and criminal law.

In terms of general ideological standpoint, Posner's theory of justice closely resembles that of Nozick, for both offer vigorous defences of capitalist libertarianism, giving general endorsement to private ownership of productive resources and free exchange of goods untramelled by government interference. However, while Nozick's position is based on the assumption of socially preexisting rights to life, liberty, the product of one's labour and the outcome of voluntary agreements, Posner adopts a typically utilitarian scepticism regarding moral rights and argues instead, on basically consequentialist grounds, for positive rights which, in the event, turn out to be extensionally identical to Nozick's fundamental moral rights. This is in line with his general thesis that social and political arrangements are subject to the test of 'wealth maximisation' – the essential tenet of EAL, which seeks to articulate an economic perspective on law that will help us both to understand and assess legal process in the light of economic 'efficiency'. Like most overarching theoretical approaches EAL is partly descriptive in that it claims that, at least in common law, decisions, whether intentionally or otherwise, are determined by considerations of economic efficiency and partly normative, in that laws are criticised if they are not consistent with the basic economic logic of the law.

Posner's version of EAL is well set out in a series of essays contained in *Economic Analysis of Law* (1977), where he defines 'efficiency' as 'exploiting economic resources in such a way that human satisfaction as measured by aggregate willingness to pay for goods and services is maximized' (p.4) or, alternatively, 'the aggregate satisfaction of those preferences...that are backed up by money' (p.61). An efficient society is one in which goods are in the hands of those who are able and willing to pay the highest price for them, since these are the persons who value them most highly. In other words, in the traditional language of utilitarianism, 'utility' is increased through voluntary exchanges in which one person purchases something from another. Those exchanges would not happen unless the purchasers valued the objects concerned more highly than the sellers, so that such exchanges, by placing goods in the hands of those willing to pay most for them, maximise overall social wealth.

Generalising from this assumption, maximising utility (or wealth) is achieved in the main through the operations of a free market in which participants are allowed to produce what they wish and offer their products in the market-place for potential consumers to purchase according to their wishes, means and the other available alternatives. This form of preference satisfaction uses the rational maximising assumption of classical utilitarianism that is part of the standard utilitarian defence of the capitalist system of private production of goods for exchange in a free market: self-interested producers will compete to provide the goods and services demanded by self-interested consumers at the lowest feasible prices, thus unintentionally contributing maximally to the overall wealth of the economic community. Given a reasonable number of non-impoverished consumers, a pool of potential producers ready to enter into competition, and inexpensive ways of entering into bargains on the basis of adequate information (that is, low 'transaction costs'), the economic system will gravitate to a specific form of Pareto optimality in which neither producers nor consumers can improve their wealth in one respect without reducing it more in another.

EAL is an extension of this economic mode of analysis to law, which is interpreted as a way of regulating, in the interests of overall social utility, the behaviour of wealth-maximisers through a system of rules and sanctions administered by lawyers and judges who are themselves motivated by the same considerations as the agents whose interactions are regulated by law. Citizens break the law if the economic benefits to themselves outweigh the advantage of law-abidingness and litigate their disputes if the likelihood of equivalent economic benefits is greater than the likelihood of equivalent economic burdens. Further, judges determine the cases that come before them in the most economically efficient way, attaching the strongest sanctions to the most economically destructive behaviour, allocating rights to those litigants who would be prepared to pay most for them in a free market, and determining liability and damages so as to ensure that resources are in the hands of those most able to capitalise on them.

The law of tort, for instance, concerns itself with the efficient distribution of the costs of accidents in terms of the losses caused by accidents, the costs involved in guarding against them and the processes for allocating these costs, the general principle being that liability for accidents should rest on the party who could have avoided or minimised the risk of such accidents at the lowest cost to himself so that, according to Judge Learned Hand's now famous judgment in *US* v. *Carroll Towing* (1947), negligence is a failure to take care when the cost of care is less than the probability of the accident, multiplied by the loss if the accident occurs. The application of this principle gives an incentive to reduce accidents, and hence the resultant losses, to those who can do this with least impact on the community's total wealth. Similarly, efficiency is best served by having a system of property giving individuals exclusive use of 'possessions' which can be alienated only by voluntary transfer, so that rights in property will be acquired by those able to make the most productive use of them.

Posner holds back from the contention that judges always decide cases on such overtly economic grounds. Nor does he believe that all citizens routinely alter their behaviour as the result of conscious economic calculations. But he does maintain that the economic model is theoretically sound in that, in general, it enables accurate predictions to be made about the common law legal process.

It should be noted that EAL, as it is presented by Posner and others, is restricted in scope, in that its descriptive application is primarily to judge-made common law, although there is a suggestion that the common law is ethically superior to the legislative decisions of political authorities which tend to depart from efficiency norms. It is also important to realise that 'wealth maximisation' is a specific form of economic analysis which goes far beyond the more limited assumptions of simple Pareto optimality and presents a standard for choosing between various possible Pareto optimal situations. A society bent on placing all goods and services in the hands of those able and willing to pay for them is 'efficient' in a highly specific way which has no claim to be *the* economic standard of efficiency and is, in general, more resonant of the pretensions of classical utilitarianism than the more cautious normative claims of modern welfare economics.

The practical implications of EAL might appear to be that legal process be replaced by purely economic transactions, at least in civil as opposed to criminal matters, leaving courts to do no more than enforce bargains which are concluded in the market-place. For instance, those who are liable to suffer from accidents will agree to pay those who are able to be the cheapest accident 'cost-avoiders' to take the necessary precautions, and the law will then enforce such agreements. This, however, ignores the crucial place of transaction costs in actual markets. It may be prohibitively expensive for individuals acting alone or in concert to gain the information and make the agreements necessary to achieve economic efficiency. In such situations, therefore, law has the more positive role of helping to reduce the market inefficiencies which result from high transaction costs. The contention is that the courts do, or should, allocate rights to those who would pay most for them if there were a relevant free market with no transaction costs.

Similarly, other problems arise in real markets because of 'externalities', that is, the uncompensated losses which fall on third parties as a result of such factors as pollution, environmental damage or accidents which do not feature in the 'cost' of the activities as paid by the voluntary participants. The function of law is to mitigate these market 'failures' also:

> 'Not that judges can or do duplicate the results of competitive markets, but that within the limits set by the costs of administering the legal system...common law adjudication brings the economic system closer to the results that would be produced by effective competition – a free market operating without significant externality, monopoly or information problems.' (Ibid., p.6)

Posner's thesis about the function of the common law is derived from the work of R. H. Coase who, in an influential article ('The Problem of Social Cost', 1960, p.1), argues that in situations where there are assumed to be low transaction costs the actual allocation of legal rights is immaterial with respect to the efficient outcome since the party who values a right more highly will always purchase that right, or its benefits, from the party to whom it is allocated by the courts. One way or another, therefore, the right in such hypothetical circumstances will end up in the hands of the party willing to pay most for it, which is the wealth-maximising solution to economic conflict between litigants. In the real world of high transaction costs the law best promotes efficiency by adopting the solution which *would* have emerged in a costless free market.

Posner's thesis, then, is that 'the common law method is to allocate responsibilities between people engaged in interacting activities in such a way as to maximize the joint value, or what amounts to the same thing, minimize the joint cost of the activities' (Posner, 1977, p.178). Furthermore he contends that, in so doing, the common law is 'just', a surprising conclusion in view of the fact that the maximisation of wealth, as he defines it, gives weight to preferences of individuals in proportion to their capacity to pay for what they want, which appears to be an embodiment of the sort of stark economic inequalities which are routinely denounced as unjust.

In the first part of *The Economics of Justice* which deals with 'Justice as Efficiency', Posner defends this equation of justice with wealth maximisation by pointing to its alleged advantages as an ethical theory over classical utilitarianism. He argues for the view that 'the criterion for judging whether acts or institutions are just or good is whether they maximize the wealth of society' (1981, p.115) by seeking to demonstrate that it is a satisfying blend of Benthamite utilitarianism and Kantian autonomy.

The defects of Benthamite 'happiness' utilitarianism are said to be, first, the indefiniteness or 'sponginess of the utility principle as a guide to policy' (1981, p.42) due to the absence of an empirical method of identifying, measuring and comparing happinesses (see 1981, p.54) and, second, the notorious 'moral monstrousness' of utilitarianism with respect 'both (a) to its inability to make distinctions amongst types of pleasure and (b) its readiness to sacrifice the innocent individual on the altar of social need' (1981, p.57).

The problem of indefiniteness is overcome by substituting wealth for happiness since wealth, it is argued, can be objectively measured by market mechanisms: utility thus becomes 'the sum of all goods and services in society weighted by their values', which is 'based on what people are willing to pay for something rather than on the happiness they would derive from having it' (1981, p.60).

Whatever advantages wealth maximisation may have in terms of precision, at least where actual markets exist, it has no evident intrinsic moral relevance. The value of wealth would appear to depend entirely on its contribution to other goals, such as the utilitarian satisfactions from which it is designed to extricate us. In fact Posner allows that this is indeed its moral grounding, for 'Value and happiness are of course related: a person would not buy something unless having it would give him more happiness, in the broad utilitarian sense, than the alternative goods and services (including leisure) that he must give up to have it' (1981, pp.60 ff.), but he goes on to argue for the difference between wealth and happiness as a criterion of justice by saying that the measure of wealth does not generate satisfactions for *all* since it excludes, for instance, the preferences of the destitute. While he is on relatively strong ground in arguing that there are limits to the moral force of happiness-maximising, he gives no good reason for the particular limitations imposed by wealth maximisation, as there is no clear reason why an increase in wealth, as he defines it, has any moral significance in itself. Indeed, the fact that wealth as a measure of justice gives systematic preference to the producers over consumers and to the wealthy over the needy, is directly counter to the use of the language of justice to denounce unjustified inequalities of wealth.

As Posner's defence of justice as efficiency develops it becomes clear that, in the end, he does not found it on efficiency as the ultimate moral standard but regards it as merely the subordinate instrument whose significance depends wholly on the further values served by efficiency. This is only to be expected, given that efficiency is an instrumental term which always invites the question: efficient for what purpose? Any answer to this question in terms of wealth creation, if this is interpreted in monetary terms, simply raises the same question about the purposes for which money may be used. It is part of Posner's utilitarian flavour that he brings us back to the value of wealth for satisfying human desires and eschews any moral evaluation of these desires. However, he also justifies wealth-maximising as a way of increasing liberty, for in the wealth-creating markets he describes individuals are free and able to make choices according to their own preferences and personal desires. Echoing Nozick, his claim is that the maximisation of wealth also involves 'greater respect for individual choice than in utilitarianism' (1981, p.66), a claim he bolsters by arguing that participants give implied consent to the outcome of all market transactions, provided these are not the result of fraud or duress (see 1981, p.94).

Posner's commitment to freedom of choice is not, however, open-ended, for he equates it with the protection of those freedoms which are a necessary part of a free-market private property system. In other words, overriding importance is given only to the positive rights which are intrinsic to capitalism. It is only because these rights are not vulnerable to 'the appeal to general utility' that he is able to claim that wealth maximisation provides more adequate protection for individual rights than does utilitarianism, a theory which, in his view, justifies constant infringements of personal liberty. It turns out that wealth maximisation limits as well as protects liberty, for it requires that effective restrictions be placed on some activities, such as the formation of monopolies, which restrict the creation of wealth.

We are, therefore, left with the ambiguous position that wealth maximisation is an intermediate objective ultimately justified by its effectiveness in increasing happiness and liberty and yet also serving as a limiting consideration which enables us to discount certain forms of happiness and favour some liberties over others.

In *The Economics of Justice,* Posner retains the utilitarian's willingness to subordinate rights to utility by allowing that, where transaction costs are high, certain matters cannot be left to voluntary agreements for 'rights are not transcendental or ends in themselves' (1981, p.71). Logically this vulnerability to the claims of utility must apply to the most basic rights of all, including the right to sell one's labour, but Posner argues that, because transaction costs are high, 'the wealth-maximizing principle requires the initial vesting of rights in those who are likely to value them most, so as to minimize transaction costs' (ibid.). In this way he can ascribe to everyone the basic rights of liberty and freedom of contract, although he cannot maintain that these rights are in principle absolute.

As many critics have pointed out, this represents a rather unstable basis for the defence of rights, for it might turn out, for instance, that slavery in some form or other is in some circumstances the most efficient wealth-creating system. Moreover, as with all such *ad hoc* utilitarian justifications of rights, this approach seems to reach the right answer for the wrong reasons, in that our objections to slavery are based on considerations other than its disutility. Few would agree with Posner that apartheid is wrong simply because it is 'unlikely that ostracism, expulsion, or segregation of a productive group would actually increase a society's wealth' (1981, p.85). Nor might we feel that the utility monster has been slain if the sadist's pleasure is admitted into the system provided that he pays for his pleasures even though, as Posner points out, the high cost of indulging his tastes will place some limits on his activities. Similarly, while it is welcome that the satisfaction of envious desires is given no moral weight, it is a disappointment that the reason given for this gesture to ordinary moral sentiments is that envy is felt primarily by those without market power, whose desires are therefore irrelevant to efficiency.

The strategy of Posner's defence of justice as efficiency is the familiar utilitarian combination of showing, on the one hand, that wealth maximisation is a satisfactory rationale for standard moral views about such matters as honesty, truth-telling and promise-keeping – the 'conventional pieties' (1981, p.67), which are vindicated by the fact that they are vital for a flourishing commercial system (see 1981, p.84) – and, on the other hand, in effect modifying the purities of crude utilitarianism by introducing counterbalancing considerations to formulate a more 'enlightened utilitarianism'

(1981, p.107). Posner leaves obscure what happens when the pronouncements of enlightened utilitarianisms conflict with ordinary moral intuitions. It is also unclear how we are to establish the correct balance between utilitarian and non-utilitarian elements which Posner is happy to interpolate into his system. The attractiveness of Posner's thesis, at this point, is that it does offer us what is in effect a device for determining that balance, and hence avoids intolerable vagueness, but in the end he gives us no good reason to suppose that wealth-maximising is a reliable guide to the correct mix of utility, liberty, merit and equality which he seeks to uphold. Moreover the actual and possible consequences of the application of the wealth-maximising test are often morally unpersuasive, and are so in a way which runs counter to precisely those moral considerations which are specifically the domain of justice.

Thus, with apparently breathtaking callousness, Posner allows that in the case of a feeble-minded person and others whose 'net social product is negative' there is 'no right to the means of support even though there was nothing blameworthy in his inability to support himself. This result grates on modern susceptibilities, yet I see no escape from it that is consistent with any of the major ethical systems' (1981, p.76). This means that the interests of those who cannot support themselves are on a par with the interest of animals if these are thought to have significance only in so far as they are valued as producers. The reverse side of this particular implication is that he is able to draw on quasi-meritorian considerations by pointing out that, although wealth maximisation has nothing to say on the initial distribution of wealth, his system does see to the reward of talent and skill. However this nod in the direction of desert is not developed, perhaps because of the serious limitations which any extensive cognisance of desert would impose on permissible inequalities of wealth and the fact that he would have to define desert in terms of wealth productivity, thereby introducing further circularity into the theory.

Conceptually, a difficulty with Posner's account of justice is that it makes no effort to distinguish between justice and other political ideals, a weakness which can be traced in part to his acceptance of the Rawlsian catch-all definition of justice as encompassing whatever relates to the assessment of the basic structure of a society. Morally, the shortcomings of 'justice as efficiency' is its inability to provide anything more than contingent justifications for any idea of real equality of satisfactions. Even the classical utilitarian principle that each is to count for one and no more than one is swept aside by the fact that suffering, unless accompanied by the capacity to pay, is irrelevant to economic 'justice'. The appeal to the satisfaction and liberty-promoting tendencies of wealth maximisation might have more force if it were tied to something like Ackerman's notion of an initial situation of adult resource equality or Dworkin's idea of equality of resources, but Posner is not prepared to countenance the degree of redistribution that such principles would require.

Posner's own proposal – that resources be distributed where they are most productive of wealth – is methodologically as well as morally flawed. Wealth is a matter of the individual's ability to pay and cannot, therefore, without circularity, be used as the standard for determining the proper distribution of wealth. Because the distribution of wealth determines whose preferences are to be used to measure a society's wealth, Posner can, at most, proffer a theory of corrective justice. Given that the existing distribution of resources affects which laws are economically efficient, Posner is not able to provide the clear and objective test for evaluating law reforms which is promised as one of the improvements on the alleged 'sponginess' of the principle of utility. Moreover, as we shall see when considering the application of EAL to criminal behaviour, these theoretical difficulties are compounded when non-economic activities are taken into account. The general thesis that people are wealth-maximisers lacks substance when persons who choose to put such factors as leisure or status above an increase in their wealth are then said to be 'purchasing' them by forgoing actual wealth-producing activities, rather than admitting that they are acting for non-economic reasons. In non-economic areas EAL analysis makes the 'economic' analysis of human behaviour a vacuous and unverifiable hypothesis compatible with any consistent pattern of actual choices.

Posner has, in recent years, acknowledged the strength of the methodological and moral criticism of his approach (see Posner, 1990, chapter 12; and Posner, 1995, Introduction). He now accepts that EAL explains only a part of social behaviour and is only a default rule or presumption. He also accepts that there are strong moral intuitions which count against some of his conclusions, such as those about slavery and the importance of luck. Nevertheless he still utilises the methods of EAL himself and others, often less sensitive than he to its limitations, continue to follow his lead.

Posner now recommends a more pragmatic approach based on the general economic success of societies which operate on the wealth maximisation principle.

The economic analysis of criminal law

Although EAL has made its most striking contributions to legal theory through its application to the civil law of negligence and contract, Posner follows in the tradition of Bentham in deploying it in relation to criminal law for which he regards it as particularly well-suited. The Benthamite approach is to define crime in terms of acts which cause sufficient harm or suffering to others to justify the enactment of rules backed by sanctions which prohibit such behaviour. The efficacy of such rules depends on the assumption that the potential criminal will refrain from socially harmful activities which would benefit him or her if there is a sufficiently high risk of their incurring an unacceptably high level of pain, by way of the infliction of an official sanction, were they to be caught and convicted. In other words citizens are regarded as rational and prudent maximisers who will be deterred from 'criminal' activities if the 'price' is too high. Criminal legislation is justified if the end result is a maximal positive balance of pain prevented by the deterrence or prevention of harmful acts over the pain inflicted by way of punishment, together with the costs of administering the criminal justice system, including its penal institutions.

Bentham himself has wider consequential considerations in mind than simply deterrence since, believing as he did in the malleability of human nature and the efficacy of a rigorous system of negative and positive sanctions, he believed that a properly organised and designed prison could reform the criminal, deter potential criminals and even pay for itself.

Posner follows the Benthamite mode of analysis, but with more emphasis on costs than on suffering and a greater attention to the financial efficiency of the criminal process. For Posner 'a "crime" is simply an act that subjects the perpetrator to a distinctive form of punishment that is meted out in a distinctive kind of proceeding' (1979, p.163), and 'the purpose of the criminal law is to increase the costs of unlawful conduct where conventional damage remedies are insufficient' (p.164). He is careful to include in these costs not only the expected punishment but also the price of the equipment required to perpetrate a crime and the opportunity costs of the criminal's time. Similarly the benefits to the criminal include not only any material gains resulting from successful crime but also the 'intangible satisfactions' of non-pecuniary crime, such as rape. Consequently crime levels can be varied by altering levels of unemployment, which affects the opportunity costs of crime, as well as by varying the severity of penalties and the incidence of detection.

It is, however, on punishment that Posner concentrates his analysis. His model for 'optimal criminal sanctions' is worked out in the first place in monetary terms with the example of theft. Taking the 'expected punishment cost' to be a combination of 'the probability that the punishment will be imposed and the cost to the criminal if it is imposed', and assuming that the offender is 'risk-neutral', he argues that the expected punishment cost should be 'at least equal to the damage to the victim of the criminal act' (p.169). If the benefit to the criminal was higher than the social cost of the crime then its perpetration would be a contribution to welfare and therefore presumably justified. In fact he is prepared to concede that on occasions theft is indeed value-maximising, as when a hungry person steals food from an unoccupied cabin in the woods. This follows from his general assumption that social welfare is increased when resources are in the hands of those willing to spend available cash to buy them, which means that he has to allow that theft may be a justifiable activity when transaction costs are so high that they make the transfer of goods impracticable.

Such cases must be regarded as exceptional in a system whose wealth-creating power depends on flourishing voluntary transactions in conditions of low transaction costs, and it is this fact that makes theft a crime, for it undermines the normal incentives of the market system. With this in mind, punishment is inflicted to encourage the potential thief to enter rather than bypass the market. To do this we must set the expected punishment cost higher than the social cost of the object. In this case, assuming that the thief knows they will be caught and punished, purchasing an object will always be more rational than stealing it. Adding the costs of administering coercive sanctions to the social costs of the violation gives the appropriate level of fine, at least for those situations where it is thought desirable to encourage market transactions. In the extraordinary cases in which theft is 'justified' because of inordinate transaction costs, the criminal law may not deter but it may still exact the full cost of the thief using the legal system as a surrogate for the market.

The level of fine will of course have to increase as the probability of detection and enforcement decreases, although it is not clear why this should apply in the same way to 'justified' theft – which it is presumably not desirable to deter – as well as to genuinely harmful cases of theft. However, Posner often seems more concerned with recovering the costs of the administration of justice than with the calculation of efficient levels of deterrence, two aims that are clearly not always compatible.

Given the poverty of the average criminal, the obvious inadequacy of fines for recouping the costs of the criminal justice system is countered by the argument that imprisonment is an alternative way of imposing economic costs on violators. 'Imprisonment imposes pecuniary costs on the violator by reducing his income during the period of confinement and, in many cases, by reducing his earning capacity after release as well (the "criminal record" effect). It also imposes non-pecuniary benefits as well' (Posner, 1979, p.167). However, imprisonment is costly and these costs are not offset by any benefits which accrue to victims. Moreover imprisonment decreases the opportunity costs of future crime, for ex-prisoners are usually unable to find work because of their criminal record. Imprisonment can, therefore, hardly be efficient unless it acts as an effective sanction.

Posner does no more than sketch the tortuous calculations required to reckon the social cost of acts which are thereby defined as criminal as weighed against the social costs of effective enforcement of the criminal law. Nor does he make it clear how this method can be applied to non-pecuniary crimes like assault and homicide. He is clearly in difficulties when he moves from crimes and penalties to which measurable financial costs can be ascribed. As soon as it comes to questions about what value to place on a human life, or what a term of imprisonment 'costs' an unemployed man in terms of shame and suffering, or the degree of 'satisfaction' gained by those who perpetrate crimes of sexual passion, then the economic model of crime becomes nebulous and speculative. It can even be extended to include the 'satisfaction' felt by the vengeful citizen who likes to see offenders punished even if this does not reduce crime.

There is undoubtedly something of importance in calculating the cost of genuinely economic crimes such as theft, fraud and the destruction of property and weighing these against the cost of the administration of a criminal justice system which is aimed at reducing these offences, but the attempt to incorporate into this scheme the web of complex social judgements that go into the criminalisation of non-pecuniary offences and the determination of appropriate penalties even for pecuniary crimes is not successful at the level of sociological analysis and, in general, blurs the distinction between punishment and taxation.

The economic analysis of criminal law opens up the whole debate about the purpose and function of the criminal law and in particular the dispute between consequentialist theories of punishment (whether deterrent, preventative or remedial) and those which incorporate an element of retributive reasoning according to which punishment, whatever its consequences, is an appropriate response to harmful and wicked conduct. The strength of consequentialist theories is that they seem to justify existing practices without drawing on the morally questionable idea that the infliction of pain on an offender is a good thing in itself, but their weakness is that they license acts and institutions which are even less acceptable than pure retributivism. Whether it be the Benthamite objective of minimising the pains resulting from harmful and therefore criminal acts, or the Posnerian goal of minimising the wealth-reducing effects of 'crime', the efficient way of going about this – assuming the rational maximising hypothesis of human behaviour – must involve the unfairness of imposing penalties out of all proportion to the wickedness of those criminals who get caught, the possible victimisation of innocent persons in order to obtain strong deterrent effects and the discriminatory injustice of varying penalties according to such morally irrelevant factors as the possibility of deterrence and the cost of criminal law administration, thereby perpetrating systematic inequities between equally 'guilty' groups of people.

Posner attempts to deal with a number of such difficulties. Noting the apparent unfairness of imprisoning those who are unable to pay fines, which will in practice discriminate against the poor, he suggests that the 'rate of exchange' should be varied according to the wealth of the offender. If this means that a wealthy person has to pay a larger fine to equate with the same period in prison than a poor man, this solution could be more efficient as well as fairer than flat-rate fines for specific offences, but Posner's requirement that the social cost of crimes be recouped means that the actual result would be quite different. The fines for rich and poor would have to be the same, with the variable rate of exchange affecting only the lengths of the equivalent prison sentences for rich and poor, for the poor will pay less than the rich to avoid imprisonment. And so, whichever way the trade-off between liberty and ability to pay is taken, it illustrates the inegalitarian implications of the economic analysis of law that the liberty of the poor man is of less value than that of the rich.

Even less attractive is Posner's response to the objection that low detection rates require high penalties, thereby imposing heavy sanctions on those few who are caught while the vast majority escape altogether. This he compares to a lottery which is fair as long as the *ex ante* costs and benefits are equal, whatever the eventual outcome. If all have an equal chance of getting caught, high deterrent penalties are said to be fair. One does not have to be a retributivist to be disturbed by the analogy between criminal law and a lottery.

The problem of keeping penalties proportional to the seriousness of the offence, especially where there are maximum penalties, is simply noted as 'another factor to be considered' (1979, p.170). Scarcely more consideration is given to the absence of an efficiency rationale for harsh treatment of persistent offenders or the punishment of attempted crimes.

The familiar problems to which utilitarian theories of punishment give rise have been dealt with much more extensively and sensitively by others, but Posner's relatively simplistic wealth-maximising version of the Benthamite method is a useful exemplar of the practical effects of translating questions of justice into arguments about efficiency. Even when it can be demonstrated that the efficiency approach to criminal law would not be quite so inegalitarian and morally offensive in its disregard for the moral merits of those caught up in its operations, it systematically fails to capture the real reasons why it is unacceptable, for instance, to punish the insane or incarcerate the morally and legally innocent. The sphere of the criminal law is thus peculiarly suited to bringing out the moral indecency of EAL, thus drawing attention to the need for a conception of justice that will hold in check the dominance of purely economic modes of thought.

7 Justice as Desert: Sadurski and Remuneration

In historical terms the idea that justice is a matter of people getting what they deserve is perhaps the most common and tenacious conception of justice. Indeed the internal connection between justice and desert used to be standardly cited as part of the very concept of justice itself. In recent times, however, desert has had to take its place as, at best, only one amongst many competing criteria of justice and sometimes it is excluded altogether from the list of relevant justicising considerations.

For many, desert carries the flavour of a past age characterised by overindividualised forms of social relationships, dominated by a combination of moral book-keeping and the glorification of unfettered competition. For others, the idea of desert is associated with discredited 'intuitionist' accounts of ethics according to which we are alleged to have direct knowledge of self-evident moral 'truths', such as the unqualified duty to tell the truth or to execute murderers. Further, the belief in desert – the very idea that anybody ultimately deserves anything – seems to run counter to the common contemporary assumption that individual behaviour is, in the end, almost entirely the outcome of heredity and environment, with little if any significance being attributable to people's autonomous choices. The 'free will' assumptions behind traditional ideas of desert are certainly hard to fit into a scientific and determinist world-view according to which human decisions are simply one part of a continuous causal chain. For all these reasons, it is tempting, therefore, to regard desert-based theories of justice as no more than historical curiosities.

Nevertheless the conviction that people should be treated in accordance with their deserts is not readily abandoned in practice and remains as an unstated assumption in many theories which purport to exclude it. Presuppositions about desert lie at the root of many of the central moral 'fixed points', to which appeal is made to determine whether situations are to be called 'fair' or 'just', and it is the strength of our instinctive feeling about the evil of inflicting unmerited suffering that lies at the core of our doubts about the reduction of justice to utility. Moreover any argument which brings in the intrinsic importance of rewarding people according to their labours has strong meritorian overtones.

It is unsurprising, therefore, that, given the acknowledged moral limitations of utilitarianism, there has recently been a return to the idea that desert is a central feature of justice, a return which is fostered by a growing recognition of the substantive emptiness of theories based on nothing more than the concepts of equality or impartiality and the perceived need to provide an underpinning for fundamental rights, particularly in the sphere of criminal law. While desert may never be reestablished as the sole relevant moral criterion for the distribution of benefits and burdens in society, the contention that desert is the most distinctive criterion of justice remains a powerful one, particularly if justice itself is seen to be only one of many types of moral factors which bear on issues of social, political and economic equality.

It is not difficult to document historically an authoritative line of desert theorists from Adam Smith and Immanuel Kant to John Stuart Mill and Henry Sidgwick, but, although there has been a general resurgence of retributivism in the philosophy of punishment, there is perhaps no one recent theorist who is well-known for championing a desert-based theory of justice in general. Despite many careful analyses of the nature of desert we do not have a recognised contemporary exemplar of a desert-based theory of justice, although one philosopher has recently claimed that 'everyone agrees that justice, almost by definition, is giving people what they deserve' (Sterba, 1986, p.1). However, an impressive work by Wojciech Sadurski – a Polish–Australian philosopher now living in Italy – develops a largely desert-based analysis of justice which covers both legal and social justice. Sadurski's 'equilibrium' theory makes desert central to the idea of a hypothetical balance of benefits and burdens which justice in all its forms seeks to establish. While his is not a pure desert theory, Sadurski makes important moves towards rendering the idea of desert intelligible and realisable, thus overcoming two of the major drawbacks of traditional meritorian theories of justice. His important book, *Giving Desert its Due: Social Justice and Legal Theory,* serves as the reference point for the issues raised in this chapter.

The attractions of desert

The basic contention of what I call the meritorian theory of justice is that justice requires us to treat people as responsible for their actions and therefore to praise or blame, reward or punish them, in accordance with their conduct and character in so far as these are the outcome of their own efforts and choices. Thus if someone chooses to perform socially useful actions, particularly if these involve the expenditure of time, effort or personal resources, then they are deserving of praise and/or reward. If a person chooses or is willing to perform socially harmful actions, particularly if they produce benefits for that person, then they are deserving of blame and/or deprivation of benefits, or punishment. Meritorian theorists hold that a society is just when the distribution of benefits and burdens is in accordance with the distribution of good (that is, 'positive') and ill (that is, 'negative') desert. Just actions are those which seek to maintain, achieve or restore this proportionality, particularly through the administration of appropriate rewards, punishments and compensations. Justice requires that, other things being equal, people ought to get (or be given) what they deserve.

The term 'desert' can be used very widely to cover, for instance, the use of the term in the evaluation of such things as works of art when they are said to be 'deservedly' famous, or in the opinion that smoking 'deserves' its reputation as being dangerous to health. In the analysis of justice, however, 'desert' is normally taken to mean moral desert in two senses of 'moral'. Thus the meritorian conception of desert is of a 'moral' concept, first because its preferred idea of desert is contrasted with conventional or institutional 'desert', which is acquired merely by satisfying established requirements. In contrast, the meritorian's moral desert is 'natural' or 'raw' in that it does not presuppose preexisting social norms or distributional rules. We may say – perhaps metaphorically – that a person 'deserves' a scholarship solely because they have met the criteria set for the award, whether or not this reflects their choices and efforts, but conventional or institutional 'desert' of this sort is more a matter of entitlement than desert. Certainly it is not the sort of desert with which the meritorian is principally concerned. In contrast to mere entitlement, moral, natural or raw desert features as a reason for establishing such conventional rules so as to ensure that scholarships and other benefits are distributed in accordance with what is antecedently thought of as deserving.

'Desert' may also be taken to be 'moral' in a second sense of that term in which it is now contrasted with 'natural' when this is equated with what happens 'naturally', that is, without human choice or intervention. Desert is then analytically tied to the notion of making choices and acting knowingly or intentionally, in contrast to 'natural' events which happen according to the normal processes of cause and effect. Thus responsibility, in the sense of accountability and liability to praise, blame, reward and punishment, is said to be attributable solely to agents, that is, to persons who can intentionally alter the course of 'natural' events through their own deliberate actions and according to their own purposes. Only the actions of such moral agents are said to be deserving or undeserving in the meritorian sense.

Sadurski's account of desert is moral in both these senses. Having distinguished desert from entitlement, he goes on to argue that the idea of desert is used 'to screen out all those features that are "unearned", that are beyond human control, that are dictated by dumb luck, and for which the person cannot claim any credit'. On this score, when considering desert in relationship to justice, 'what counts is conscientious effort which has socially beneficial effects' (Sadurski, 1985, p.116). For reasons which will become apparent when we consider his theory in more detail, Sadurski stresses that it is the effort to bring about socially beneficial consequences, rather than those consequences themselves, that is relevant to desert, a point which fits in with the idea that desert excludes 'dumb luck', since people cannot always be held responsible for the actual results of their conduct, which is often not completely in their control.

Sadurski points out that desert, so conceived, is (1) 'person-oriented', in that it is always attributed to persons on account of their conduct, (2) 'value-laden', in that it involves an assessment of this conduct as good or bad, and (3) 'past-oriented' in that 'when talking about desert, we are evaluating certain actions which have already happened' (1985, p.118).

Many meritorian theorists would incorporate in their analysis of desert the requirement that desert has necessarily to do either with moral goodness or badness, or at most with some other morally praiseworthy or blameworthy motives. Sadurski, however, while accepting that desert covers only *intentionally* effortful activity directed towards socially valuable ends, emphasises that his 'theory of desert is not concerned with the "moral worth" of an individual, but with his socially valuable effort' (1985, p.222). This means that desert takes in effortful behaviour which happens to benefit society even though that is not its motivation. We shall see that this broad conception of the concept of desert makes it easier for him to encompass all of justice within the ambit of desert, but it does tend to undermine the link between desert and morality, which looks beyond intentionality to motivation.

A further question relating to the analysis of 'moral' desert is whether or not it should incorporate the evaluation of prudential behaviour, that is, the rationality of a person's actions in relation to their own interests and welfare. The failure of persons to take obvious precautions to protect their interests, when it is well within their knowledge and capacities so to do, is not immoral but it is imprudent, and yet we often say that such people deserve the ill consequences of their foolish conduct as well as the good consequences brought about by their own efforts. Meritorian theory can readily assimilate this use of the language of desert, since it accords with the common view that it is not unjust that people are left to enjoy the benefits of their prudence and suffer the burdens imposed by their own imprudence. On the other hand some meritorians regard this as an unacceptable dilution of the moral force of desert-based theories. Since Sadurski constantly stresses the importance of the social benefits of deserving behaviour, he would presumably exclude purely prudential conduct from the ambit of desert.

The most distinctive aspect of Sadurski's analysis of desert is his contention that desert, at least in so far as it relates to justice, always involves conduct which is in some way burdensome. Hence his emphasis on the effort involved in deserving conduct. He also counts as burdensome anything which incorporates an element of 'sacrifice, work, risk, responsibility, inconvenience and so forth' (1985, p.116). This, as we shall see, has advantages for his general theory, but it rather ignores the fact that we morally praise, and consider deserving of reward, conduct which is in no obvious sense effortful or burdensome as long as it exhibits morally admirable characteristics such as unselfishness or sensibility. The kind person who sends flowers to a sick friend or the rich person who employs a member of a socially deprived group is deserving of thanks and perhaps reward, even though their actions cause them literally 'no bother'.

Following some linguistic usages, Sadurski also restricts the concept of desert to behaviour which is 'deserving' in the sense that it manifests good rather than ill desert. When he comes to discuss the punishment of crime, for instance, he distinguishes this from rewarding desert, and so seems to deny the meritorian nature of his theory of punishment. However it is clear that no sharp conceptual distinction is intended here, since he views the function of punishment as balancing 'undeserved benefits', and presents himself as a retributivist in the theory of punishment and thus as someone who believes that 'criminal guilt is the sole reason for punishment' (1985, p.223), going on to analyse criminal guilt in moral rather than purely legal terms. His thesis is, in fact, that socially useful conduct which is burdensome to the agent deserves reward, while socially harmful conduct which is beneficial to the agent deserves punishment. This is evidently a desert-based analysis of criminal law.

Whatever refinements we introduce into the analysis of desert, the idea that society should be organised so as to bring it about that valued and disvalued things like pleasure and pain, psychological satisfaction or material resources, are distributed in accordance with desert has many practical and theoretical difficulties which are discussed in the next section. It does, however, also have powerful justificatory and explanatory features.

In the first place, the idea of due deserts has the advantage of explaining the centrality of human agency in the idea of justice, and hence the close association of justice with such notions as respect for persons, autonomy, self-determination and human dignity. Justice is important in human society not simply because we care about who gets what, but also because we wish to be treated as human beings whose actions and choices are to be taken seriously and given respect. As Sadurski remarks, 'principles of justice are of fundamental, although not of absolute, moral importance. This importance stems from the links between the principle of desert and respect for persons' (1985, p.251).

It may be this insight that provides the essence of the common belief that there is a sense in which human beings are equal, which is at the same time a basis for treating them differently. The fundamental equality involved here can be based on the idea that all persons are the source of choices which have equal worth, in that they should receive equal respect as the initiators of choices. This means that a concern for justice involves a commitment to the idea that people choosing for themselves is something worthwhile in itself and therefore to be valued and fostered for its own sake. Moreover, to accord proper respect to agents, it is not sufficient simply to foster their agency, although, other things being equal, that is what is required. Respect for agents also involves evaluating the choices and actions to which the exercise of agency capacities gives rise. This means responding to persons in terms of the quality of their action choices and intended conduct. Respect for the equal worth of each individual is thus felicitously combined with attention to their unequal worthiness.

Also, meritorian theorists have no difficulty in accounting for the backward-looking nature of justice, in contrast with the forward-looking focus of utilitarian theorising, for, as Sadurski points out (1985, pp.118ff.), desert is essentially a matter of evaluating past choices and conduct. In this respect meritorian justice is not, in Nozick's terminology, a pure patterned theory in which holdings are matched to present properties of individuals. Desert, like justice, has an essential 'historical' reference in that it is logically tied to past events and individual responsibility for them.

Viewing justice in terms of desert also enables us to explain the dual aspect of justice as involving both the maintenance of a pattern of distribution and the process of rectifying 'injustices'. All claims that situations are unjust imply that there is a baseline or presupposed balanced situation against which the background of judgements of injustice are made. They also imply that corrective action is in order. Desert fulfils this dual role, not by proposing a baseline of strict identity of situation, but by erecting an ideal of proportionality of desert, positive and negative, to experiences, good and bad, with the implication that, other things being equal, differential treatments should be instituted to achieve and restore that proportionality. In Sadurski's words: 'whenever an ideal, hypothetical balance of social benefits and burdens is upset, social justice calls for restoring it' (1985, p.101).

Justice as desert can also account for the fact that, while not all actions which upset the baseline balance are unjust (the evil of torture, for instance, is not usually regarded as wrong because it is 'unjust'), nevertheless it is a matter of justice that the perpetrators of such acts be punished and the victims compensated by the offender.

This is explained by the fact that intentionally harmful acts are wrong and hence merit punishment and the associated idea that the perpetrators of unjustified wrongdoings ought to compensate their innocent victims. The idea of rectificatory justice, both punitive and compensatory, covers such individual treatments and balances. However justice is more than taking account of the negative desert of wrongful actions. Justice takes in the pursuit of the general objective of matching benefits and burdens to appropriate degrees of positive and negative desert, even when no one can be identified as responsible for existing imbalances. Justice may require the compensation of undeserved suffering brought about through natural causes as well as recompense for suffering deliberately and unjustifiably inflicted by others. Indeed, it is this 'intuition' about the appropriateness of compensation from which Sadurski extrapolates to formulate his entire theory of justice.

The defence of the thesis that justice is essentially a matter of desert requires us to give an account of how other suggested criteria, such as need or choice, can be so readily, if erroneously, taken to be the bases for conceptions of justice. Sadurski does this by demonstrating first that, in general, where such criteria have to do with justice they are crucially related to desert and, second, that where those criteria are not related to desert they are not criteria of justice.

Thus utility, which, it is universally agreed, may often properly be allowed to affect the distribution of benefits and burdens, is excluded from justice when it is not the product of intentional and effortful contribution to the social welfare. Sadurski could take the same line with need and argue that 'need is a criterion of justice only where it happens to be associated in some way with our ideas of merit and demerit' (Campbell, 1974, p.14). Distribution in accordance with need could then be regarded as a matter of humanity rather than justice, unless it is related to desert in some significant manner. Interestingly, Sadurski takes a different view and argues that the satisfaction of basic needs (Sadurski 1985, p.159) – defined as those needs which 'may be said to constitute obviously and inherently a burden such that their satisfaction is a necessary condition of a person being able to fulfil his or her other needs and desires' – is unconnected with desert but nevertheless is an essential ingredient of the hypothetical balance of benefits and burdens on which all judgements of justice depend.

A purer form of meritorian theory distinguishes between the satisfaction of basic needs *per se* and the significance of taking account of those undeserved needs which contribute to making individuals worse off than they deserve to be. That we have good, perhaps overriding, moral reason to relieve need, particularly in its acute forms, is not in doubt. What may be doubted is whether this is a requirement of justice. The relief of basic need may be a matter of justice where the need is undeserved, in that it is not the result of the foolish or immoral choices of the persons in need. That is, a person's needs may be a measure of the extent to which they fall below that level of benefits which is appropriate to their degree of merit. The relief of need is also a matter of justice when the need is the result of the blameworthy actions of other persons, in which cases there is an initial supposition that those responsible for the need should see that it is met. This applies also where persons are in need because of the benefits they have bestowed on others who, in justice, ought to repay them. It can also be argued that the satisfaction of basic need is a prerequisite of acting autonomously, and thus of being a person who can rightly be praised or blamed for their behaviour. But where need is not connected in some way with the deserts of those involved, while its relief may be a matter of humanity or benevolence, it may be confusing to say that satisfying even basic needs is a matter of justice. Sadurski is unhappy with this thesis because it seems to downgrade the priority of basic needs, but this does not follow unless it is assumed that justice is always the overriding social value. Further, throughout his book he brings in reference to undeserved burdens as a justicising factor, a rubric into which he could readily fit sufferings and incapacities derived from the frustrations of basic need. It might, therefore, require a relatively minor shift of emphasis to render his theory more purely meritorian.

Justice as desert can also account for the important but limited role of choice in the determination of what is just. For instance, Nozick argues that people own their own body and natural abilities and are therefore entitled to do what they like with the fruits of their labours, quite irrespective of whether or not they may be said to 'deserve' them. However, as Sadurski points out (Sadurski, 1985, pp.135f.), while there is a natural sense in which people's bodies and skills belong to them in that they are their own rather than anyone else's, this is not itself a matter of right, but of natural fact. It is a separate question whether or not the product of 'my' capacities is 'owned' in a way which gives rise to property rights, since it is not itself a matter of logic that the product of 'my' capacities is 'mine'. This inference can be supported if we presuppose a principle of liberty which requires non-interference in the use of our bodies and the right to enter freely into agreements of others, but there is no reason to suppose that such principles are absolute and unlimited in their scope, or that they are to be equated with justice. Indeed it would seem to be a characteristic problem of social organisation that such liberties may conflict with justice.

Desert theory can explain this situation by pointing out that while people, through the exercise of wise choice and effort, may often deserve the fruits of their labours, these fruits may greatly exceed the degree of their merit. In such cases we may wish to leave them in possession of their surplus gains on the basis, for instance, that liberty is a significant independent value, but it is also open to us to override considerations of liberty in favour of other objectives, including the redistribution of wealth on the basis of desert, for some choices can produce for the individual benefits far beyond that which is proportional to the effort or wisdom involved. In other words meritorian theorists can explain why free choice is often relevant to justice and yet justice may often be more important than liberty.

Meritorian theory also explains the ambivalent place of promise-keeping in relation to the concept of justice. For some people, to break a promise is considered to be unjust. To others promise-keeping seems to be a completely different form of wrong-doing. The desert theorist can accommodate aspects of both these views. He can agree that, at one level, promise-keeping is simply one of the many moral duties whose violation can result in ill-desert and is therefore justly blamed, adding that, when it results in actual harm to some other person, either in disappointed expectations or losses incurred through reliance on that promise, justice may require the payment of compensation, or even punishment, as a matter of rectificatory justice. This does not make promise-breaking in itself unjust. Indeed, as Sadurski argues, 'to say that a person is entitled to some contractual benefits is not the same thing as to say that he deserves them' (1985, p.120), and 'the duty to fulfil promises is not really a matter of justice because promises themselves (or rather, the structure of distribution produced by their fulfilment) may be assessed by standards of justice' (1985, p.28).

On the other hand, at a deeper level of analysis, since the idea of keeping one's word is so closely associated with responsible moral agency and entitlement to respect as an autonomous person, it is natural to look on promise-keeping as the mark of a just person in the sense of a person who invites us to treat them in accordance with justice, that is, to hold them accountable for their actions. It is even possible to argue that breaking a promise is an undeserved injury to the promisee. Nevertheless, the reason that it seems odd to regard promise-breaking as such as a form of injustice is that the promisee is not normally thought of as 'deserving' what they have been promised.

Finally, it is an advantage of meritorian theory that it enables us to make sense of the ambivalent relationships between the formalities of rule application and the concept of justice. It might be thought that the connection between desert and formal justice is best explicated by making treatment in accordance with existing rules a matter of desert. But we have seen that this involves a conflation of desert and entitlement, which weakens the moral force of the theory. In the light of the moral thinness of pure formal 'justice', Sadurski wisely does not seek to incorporate formal justice under the rubric of desert by using the truncated conception of institutional desert. This is in line with the general meritorian view that justice arises only where the substantive rules have some relationship to the natural or moral deserts of those to whom they apply.

However, we have already seen, in Chapter 1, that if we adopt a broader and more substantial ideal of the rule of law, the governance of rules does relate to desert, and so to justice, in that much of its content has to do with treating persons as responsible agents, answerable for their actions, who ought to be given fair warning of possible penalties (and indeed of possible rewards) so that they can adapt their behaviour accordingly. Hence the requirements of technical 'natural justice' or 'due process' and the more general insistence on public and prospective legislation. These ideals are rooted in the same set of ideas as treatment in accordance with desert, namely that people are to be treated as responsible beings. Hence the close connection between the sphere of justice and developed ideas of the rule of law and the connections, also emphasised by Sadurski, between justice and respect for persons.

Problems of desert

As is to be expected with such a basic notion, desert gives rise to many problems, some of which are frequently considered fatal to its proper use in the political arena. Most often the idea of desert, perhaps because of its close connections with personal morality, seems to many people to belong to that aspect of human conduct which is least amenable to political administration. Meritorian justice, if there is such a thing, is said to be a matter for the judgement and execution of God, not man.

For instance, it is argued that there are insuperable theoretical and practical difficulties in measuring desert. Not only are there conflicting beliefs about what sort of conduct is deserving, but all these beliefs seem to require that we have considerable knowledge of the inner workings of the minds and emotions of the persons involved. This is particularly so if we take a narrow motivational view of desert which incorporates the morality of the motives of conduct, but it is pertinent also to the evaluations required by Sadurski's analysis, which are dependent on knowledge of intentions.

As an argument against the possibility of attaining complete meritorian justice this seems invincible. However there is nothing in the concept of justice itself which entails that its fullest realisation is practicable in human society. On the contrary there seems good reason to hold that human justice will always be somewhat controversial in theory and radically imperfect in implementation. The criticism is serious only if it can demonstrate that we cannot even approximate either to a consensus as to what actions are deserving or to reliable knowledge of the nature of individual actions. Yet there is no doubt that in many of the affairs of everyday life we work with a fair measure of normative consensus and rely on rebuttable presumptions that we have a rough idea of what persons intend to do and even why they perform certain acts. In any case, the problem is certainly diminished if we follow Sadurski and base desert on the intentions rather than on the motives of acts.

Critics of desert-based theories of justice also contend, however, that they encourage unwarranted coercive intervention in the lives of citizens, thus eroding the important boundary between morality and law. However, there is no analytic connection between justice and justifiable enforcement, or between substantive justice and law. Justice need not be taken as either a necessary or a sufficient condition for creating mandatory requirements or making coercive interventions in the lives of citizens. No doubt it is an acceptable legislative philosophy that extensive and manifest injustices be corrected by the process of legislation and that where state action is legitimated on other grounds it should be as far as possible in accordance with substantive justice and the rule of law. But the automatic and insistent enforcement of justice in all aspects and in all spheres is an unattractive and dangerous ideal if only because of the necessarily varied views which coexist in modern society regarding what counts as meritorious behaviour and the consequent imposition of distributive rules on unwilling subjects. On the other hand, it is correct to say that meritorian justice is logically related to a belief in the appropriateness of gratitude and reward for positive desert, and of condemnation and punishment for negative desert, so that raising considerations of justice necessarily brings up questions about how we are to respond to the behaviour of others in these respects. This response need not, however, involve the mandatory application of distributive rules and, in the light of the difficulties involved in determining desert, there are good reasons for caution in moving from praise and blame to reward and punishment.

There is, however, no way of avoiding the political necessity of dealing with the choices which have to be made about the permitted system of economic allocation, educational opportunity and various forms of advantage-taking. Ideas of desert have relevance in all these areas and societies have to do the best they can to devise means of gathering information about the merits of their members and evolving a consensus as to the value judgements involved. Institutionally this requires reliance on the assumption that certain external behaviours are standard manifestations of characteristic intentions and motives and that contribution is a sound, if defeasible, measure of effort. That this will lead to mistakes is inevitable and of major relevance to enforcement, but that the attainment of meritorian justice is utterly impractical and therefore morally unenforceable is unproven. Indeed it is clear that actual societies do operate to some extent on a consensus as to what sorts of actions are meritorious and that it is often possible to be reasonably accurate in identifying the motivation of the actions of others.

The difficulties involved in assessing the merits of persons are compounded by the fact that every agent works within the framework of their inherited potentials and the limitations of their social environment so that it is not possible to make an accurate estimate of the extent to which a person can take genuine credit for any of their actions. Given the pervasive influences and effects of environment and heredity it is by no means clear that any aspect of human conduct is unaffected by factors which are beyond the control of the individual.

Carried to its logical extreme such an approach amounts to the espousal of determinism in that it implies that every action is the necessary product of the previous state of the universe, or some part of it. In other words, there is no such thing as 'free' or 'contra-causal' action. An all-pervasive scheme of cause and effect seems to negate the idea of moral responsibility and leave no more foothold for speaking of the desert of a person than of the deserts of a hurricane or a frog.

Sadurski accepts this implication of determinism but offers the pragmatic argument that, if determinism is true, we have no real choice as to whether or not we seek to treat people in accordance with their deserts, so that there is no point in worrying about the issue. While this is hardly an entirely intellectually satisfying way of sidestepping the problems which determinism sets up for the desert theorist, there is no agreement amongst philosophers of action that determinism is true or even that a distinctive sense of agent respons-ibility and determinism are mutually exclusive postulates. Certainly most of those who adhere to determinism still retain working con-ceptions of what distinguishes actions from movements and what sort of phenomena can sensibly be praised or blamed. As long as some notion of self-determination can be retained in practical situa-tions, such as, for instance, when we are seeking to influence the conduct of others by praising or blaming them, then there is no clear impropriety in speaking of desert in a determinist world, although, in the view of many philosophers, the metaphysical significance of the concept may be unacceptably diminished if determinism is in fact true.

Even so, we are left with the difficult practical problem of unscrambling the different contributions of heredity, society and the individual, something which must be done if we are to make sense of the idea of individual merit as having to do with that which is in the agents' control and so can be credited to them. We have to be able to separate out the non-creditable from the creditable in the behaviour of persons if we are to determine deserts. By and large this can only be done by seeking to measure the impact of the various 'external' factors and then discounting their influence, leaving the individual's personal contribution as a residual cat-egory consisting of what remains after these deductions have been made.

In some instances the non-creditables that we are concerned with are the necessary prerequisites of action, such as the possession of a body, sound mental capacities and the absence of external obstacles to movement. These are relatively straightforward in contrast to the more complex matter of the extent in which more specific factors, like temperament or family background, make the performance of certain activities easier or more difficult for the individuals concerned. The nature of the development of human personality is such that it is often not possible to identify features of adult behaviour which are clearly creditable since all action is enmeshed in a continuing 'use' of inherited and environmental non-creditables.

Desert theory is also plagued by incommensurables. It is hard, some say impossible, to make the necessary interpersonal comparisons, not only of the relative deserts of individuals, but also of what would count as an equal reward or punishment, since individual preferences and tastes affect the way in which different treatments are actually experienced by different people. Moreover, even if it is possible to establish a scale of merit and a scale of punishments and rewards, there is no single way in which the degree of negative or positive desert can be matched to an obviously appropriate level of blame or praise, and reward or punishment. It seems arbitrary, for instance, to think of zero merit (neither negative nor positive desert) equating with zero allocation. A more realistic possibility might be to equate average merit with average benefits and average burdens, the baseline being that which would result from an equal division of the benefit and burdens or, in other words, a quantity equal to the average distribution. Even if this is possible, awkward choices have to be made about the degree of negative and positive desert which matches the various levels of reward and punishment. Thus if 'effort' is what counts, and can be measured in an objective manner, we still have to decide the extent to which differences in effort are to be reflected in differential rewards.

Sadurski's main contribution to desert theory is to propose a scheme which avoids these baseline difficulties by incorporating all justice-relevant considerations in the general idea of a balance of benefits and burdens. His contention is that 'whenever an ideal, hypothetical balance of benefits and burdens is upset, social justice calls for restoring it' (1985, p.107). Generalising Feinberg's idea of 'compensatory benefits' (Feinberg, 1970a, p.59), according to which many onerous jobs 'deserve' economic rewards so as to bring those who perform them back to a position of equality of burdens with those who do not have such strenuous occupations, Sadurski takes as his moral fixed point the intuition that certain burdens 'deserve' compensation to the point where a presupposed equilibrium of benefits and burdens is attained. This is then applied to all types of justice. The thesis is not simply that justice is about the distribution of benefits and burdens, but rather that it is always about striving for a balance of the burdens borne by each person and the benefits enjoyed by that same person, so that the benefits and burdens are 'equal' or 'equivalent'.

Sadurski accepts that talk of 'bringing someone back to a position of equality' is metaphorical in that the idea of balancing benefits and burdens cannot be taken literally since no actual scales are available to 'weigh' and therefore equalise the two elements. 'Burdens' – another metaphorical term – carries an image of weight not shared by the concept of a benefit, unless burdens are regarded as the absence of benefits, which is a rather artificial way to look at such benefits as social status or job satisfaction. The plausibility of Sadurski's theory depends, therefore, on giving a convincing cash value to the language of weights and balances.

The idea is not, I think, that one individual's burdens should always exactly match that same person's rewards, although there is an idea of the proper proportionality of burdens and rewards, as of benefits and punishments. Rather it is that the balance of benefits and burdens in each person's life should be equivalent to the balance in the lives of other members of the same society. Thus the person born with gross handicaps must be compensated with benefits which make their position as equivalent as possible to the balance of benefits and burdens in the lives of the non-handicapped. This has a similar form to the idea that the efforts of the socially useful worker be rewarded to bring them back to the position they had occupied before they performed the work, which is assumed to be the measure of equivalence which puts them in the same (no doubt hypothetical) position as everyone else. Similarly the criminal who steals something reaps the benefit of breaking the law and is punished to the extent that this benefit is taken away and they are restored to the same position as the non-criminal. In each case some type of compensation is at work. Because of this equivalence of form these are all different aspects of justice, hence the idea of 'justice as equilibrium' (Sadurski, 1985, p.3).

Sadurski does not attempt to develop an idea of an all-encompassing balance of benefits and burdens of all types in all spheres of life. Instead he concentrates on only three characteristics of the particular balance of benefits and burdens which he incorporates into his analysis of justice. The first is 'a social condition character-ized by a state of mutual abstention from harm, that is to say, by a mutual respect for liberties. It is an equilibrium, in the sense that, in the situation of full respect for each person's sphere of autonomy, all enjoy equally the benefits of autonomy and the burdens of self-restraint' (1985, p.104). This equilibrium presupposes rules which lay down what constitutes harm to others and hence an area of individual negative rights to be left alone. If this balance is upset by illegitimate intrusions into the sphere of autonomy of another per-son, then the balance may be restored by punishing the offender, and perhaps by compensating the victim. This gives substance to the idea of retribution in punishment and explains the renewed signific-ance attributed to compensating victims through criminal as well as civil law.

'Secondly, equilibrium is characterized by equal satisfaction for all persons of basic material conditions of a meaningful life: no-one suffers burdens which make his subsistence, or participation in community life, impossible' (1985, p.105). This is the area of basic human needs, the 'means of meaningful life', or 'the conditions of self-realization', whose satisfaction Sadurski considers an element of social justice. These burdens, but not burdens in general, call for compensation.

'Thirdly, social equilibrium means that everyone's work, effort, action and sacrifice, yield a benefit equivalent to the contribution; in other words, that a person's "outcomes" are equal to his "inputs"' (1985, p.105). Thus persons who do more for others than they take from them should be compensated by the amount of this imbalance. Extra benefits restore the equilibrium which has been upset by socially beneficial effort.

Clearly this scheme has the advantage of limiting the range of benefits and burdens which are of relevance to justice and aids comparability by distinguishing between three distinct spheres of justice, each with its own equivalent balances. On the other hand, from the theoretical point of view, it has the appearance of arbit-rariness in what it excludes and includes. This is particularly so with the inclusion of only basic needs as requiring compensation rather than a more egalitarian position which takes as relevant all needs which affect a person's quality of life. In fact it would appear that, in this sphere, Sadurski is concerned to include only basic needs because these are the needs which he believes ought to be met by government action. It is, perhaps, for this reason also that he includes the compensation of basic needs in his account of justice at all, instead of bringing need into the sphere of justice only where it is related in some way to desert.

In general the assessment of Sadurski's innovative equilibrium theory requires detailed investigation of the sense which he can give to the ideas of benefits and burdens in each sphere, and the meaningfulness of the notions that these can be balanced and that these balances can be seen to be equivalent to each other. Thus, in the criminal sphere, he is less than convincing in categorising all crime as a form of illicit benefit-taking which can be measured and then balanced by appropriate punishment. Since not all crimes benefit the criminal, the 'benefits' which criminal acts confer have to be conceptualised in terms of avoiding the burdens of self-restraint imposed by the criminal law when it establishes that persons have rights to life, liberty, security and property. All these rights confer benefits, but the enjoyment of rights depends on the exercise of restraint by others. 'This self-restraint which is a precondition for the effective enforcement of rights, can be perceived as a burden. Indeed it is a limitation on the freedom to do as one wishes. If such freedom is a benefit, its limitation is obviously a burden' (1985, p.226). In some such way, Sadurski has to maintain that conformity to the criminal law is always a burden, even if it is not felt to be so.

Despite these qualms about the general applicability of the idea of balancing benefits and burdens to all situations which are judged in terms of justice, the idea of 'justice as equilibrium' does help to give content to the often persuasive but too often obscure idea that there is a profound moral connection between moral deserts and just distribution.

Just remuneration

An important criticism of the analysis of justice as desert is that it is incoherent in practice because institutionalising the requital of desert undermines the basis on which desert is acquired. This argument assumes that, if a reward is offered for a naturally good form of behaviour, then this behaviour will thereafter be done in order to gain the reward, thus negating the putative moral deserts of its performers, whose motives are now purely self-interested. Similarly a person who refrains from naturally criminal acts because of the threat of sanctions is not said to be deserving in the same way as a spontaneously good person.

This critique is at its strongest where positive desert is taken to be moral desert in the narrow sense in which this involves either moral goodness (duty for duty's sake) or the desire to perform the action in question for the reasons that make it a good action, rather than for some ulterior self-interested motive (spontaneous goodness). On this moral interpretation of desert, it is a powerful critique of any organised system of rewards and punishments that it tends to undermine the scope for those forms of moral desert which are maximised by permitting the widest scope for alternative possibilities of action so as to bring out the best and the worst in people. Distribution by moral desert is best served by the minimisation of externally imposed rewards and punishments which muddy moral choices and mask moral goodness. On the other hand, since the whole point of a theory of justice is to provide a basis for justifying differential benefits and burdens, it seems incoherent to use the theory to argue against carrying out such distributions in a systematic and predictable manner.

The problem is reduced if we take in prudential conduct as a type of desert base, since the avoidance of sanctions and the pursuit of proffered rewards may be regarded as standard examples of prudential behaviour. These manifestations of prudence, however, are parasitic upon the prior existence of a system of rewards and deprivations and give no guidance as to the nature of the system that ought to be established. As far as natural or 'raw' desert goes, we have to consider what constitutes admirable prudence prior to the artificially contrived prizes and punishments. This can take in, however, the endorsement of such distributions as arise from the self-interested actions of individuals as they seek to fulfil their own desires, as long as these distributions are the outcome of their own efforts and skill. The pursuit of justice on this basis would require, in addition to the general legitimation of prudential behaviour, that individuals be not permitted to harm each other in the course of their self-interested activities. In other words, prudential deserts may be diminished or outweighed by moral demerits.

This approach takes us somewhere near the classical liberal scheme of free competition within a framework of restraints on

harming others, as exemplified, for instance, by Nozick's entitlement theory of justice. In contrast to Nozick's relative free-for-all
society, a more scrupulous but still basically prudential meritorian
theory will require that the resultant differential benefits and burdens are indeed related to different prudential achievements rather
than to other circumstances, such as luck, or the altruistic actions of
others. Where rewards outstrip prudential merits, or deprivations
are in excess of prudential demerits, reallocation is called for. On
this basis, a scheme of rewards can be seen as an effort to adjust the
consequences of self-interested behaviour in such a way as to
approximate to a distribution which matches the levels of prudential
desert. Thus gross incomes, which emerge from the self-interested
rational conduct of individuals, may be subject to taxation in such a
way that the net result is one in which people are rewarded according to the achievements for which they can take the credit.

Liberal philosophies standardly attach some, albeit variable,
weight to self-directed individual achievement of this sort, at least
in relation to the distribution of material benefits. The prudential
frame of reference is not so evident, however, with respect to the
systems of punishment, where demerit is more a matter of the harm
caused to others than people's failure to look after their own interests. Moreover, even in the spheres of benefit distribution, most
liberals extend their concept of desert to include rewards for conduct which benefits others. This approval of limited benevolence is
sometimes masked by the assumption that, in order to encourage
individuals to benefit others, it is nominally necessary to offer them
inducements, and hence to reward socially valuable work for utilitarian rather than meritorian reasons. It can be argued, however,
that a system of just – as opposed to merely efficient – rewards
requires that these inducements should not be higher than a level
which would match the deserts of those involved if they had been
acting without regard to such inducements. A hypothetical desert
scheme, which makes inducements and penalties equivalent to those
which are appropriate for useful behaviour when it is undertaken
for morally, as opposed to prudentially, good reasons, offers a
possible way round the paradox that rewarding virtue undermines
virtue. At least it does not penalise the naturally benevolent whose
actions are not affected by inducements. It is a scheme which gains
further point to the extent that it is believed that individuals are not
purely self-interested in their conduct and often do undertake
socially valuable work for partially altruistic reasons.

Sadurski's analysis sidesteps some of these problems by excluding the significance of motives and requiring only that deserving behaviour be intentional. He does not overtly apply his concept of desert directly to prudential behaviour, for he limits justice-relevant desert to intentional conduct which is socially useful. He is, however, able to take into account behaviour which is socially useful but is undertaken for prudential motives. Indeed, according to his scheme, which excludes motivation, this type of conduct must be viewed as just as deserving as altruistic conduct. Indeed it turns out that he does take into consideration effortful conduct which benefits the agent for, in measuring appropriate rewards, he proposes taking account of all productive labour:

> 'Social equilibrium means that everyone's work, effort, action and sacrifice yields a benefit equivalent to the contribution: in other words, that a person's "outcomes" are equal to his "inputs". A paradigm example of this aspect of equilibrium is that of a peasant who actually consumes the entirety of what he produces. At the initial, hypothetical stage of social equilibrium there is no exchange and no exploitation: everyone does everything for himself.' (1985, p.105)

Without going into whether or not there are any limits to the quantity of holdings that a person can accumulate by their own efforts, Sadurski points out that in normal economic systems people do make a contribution to the well-being of others. In general, Sadurski's model is similar to Rawls's in that he views modem society as a cooperative enterprise which produces an aggregate of benefits which fall to be distributed according to principles of justice. He differs from Rawls in holding that, in any situation where the individual's contribution is such that he or she creates a surplus beyond their own appropriations, then justice calls for compensatory rewards. More specifically, in the terms of his theory of equilibrium, one aspect, at least, of justice 'is achieved when the overall level is equal for all people, that is, when the ratio of one person's outcomes to inputs is equal to other persons' outcome/input ratio' (1985, p.106).

It is a further feature of Sadurski's account of just remuneration that the measurement of input is in terms of effort rather than results. It is required that such effort does produce socially beneficial results but the relevant measure of input is not the quantity of the benefit but the extent of the burden undertaken in producing the benefit. Sadurski takes this position 'mainly because "contribution" or "success" reflect, among other things, factors which are beyond our control and thus for which we cannot claim any credit' (1985, p.134). He does not specify exhaustively which features of a job performance are relevant inputs, but he mentions, as examples, the expenditure of energy, both physical and intellectual, and the degree of unpleasantness involved, whether this is due to physical conditions or mental stress. He is also prepared to take note of risks and opportunity costs in the form of sacrifices incurred in order to undertake a task and the general inconvenience of making the contribution in question. In principle, however, almost anything can be regarded as a burden and therefore as part of the creditable input in any particular task. All that the theory requires is a reasonable degree of consensus as to what is burdensome and what is not. Here Sadurski has an interesting discussion of how to take into account the fact that some tasks have their own intrinsic rewards. Most people enjoy a degree of responsibility, or the opportunity to perform a useful task, so that not all aspects of employment are burdensome. The attractive features of work have to be set against the unattractive ones in order to establish those aspects of a job that require compensatory rewards.

Sadurski can deal with the problems which emerge in relation to individual differences of taste, which mean that the same task is more burdensome for one person than for another, by pointing out that any system of remuneration has to operate in a rough-and-ready way on the basis of average tastes and typical situations. A more intractable difficulty for his theory is that effort itself is not always a burden, but may be welcomed and enjoyed. Since it is effort that is the principal link between his idea of justice and the notion of what is in the control of the individual, and therefore deserving of reward, the prospect of effort being a benefit rather than a burden undermines his model of due deserts as a proper balance of benefits and burdens. In the end, when arguing for the practicability of his conception of desert in relation to just rewards, his appeal is to the choices which the average person would make when presented with a range of employment, each with its own bundle of attractive and unattractive features. The evidence is, he claims, that roughly the same choices would be made by the vast majority of individuals in the same society. It is assumed that, for the majority, effort is, on balance, a burden.

A similar approach is appropriate to the determination of what is to count as remuneration, a concept which must take in not only the level of wages and salaries and associated material benefits, but also any pleasant features which particular employments may have. The appeal to a consensus of public values may also be required if we are to measure what is to count as socially beneficial effort. Sadurski is unwilling to leave this matter to the choice of the market, if only because it is not possible to put market values on all socially valuable work. Moreover, as we have seen in the discussion of Posner in Chapter 6, even in relation to consumer goods, it can be argued that the market gives disproportionate weight to the preferences of the already wealthy and is thus an inefficient measure of actual social value.

An important implication of justice as desert in relation to remuneration is that it encourages lower extrinsic rewards for intrinsically less burdensome jobs, thus running counter to the tendency for desirable high status jobs also to be the better remunerated ones. Noting the sociological prevalence of 'status consistency', that is, the tendency of high prestige to go with high income, he accepts that his theory may be out of line with contemporary moral views but nevertheless takes the line, reminiscent of Walzer's notion of undominated inequality, that material rewards need not be highly correlated with the distribution of other desired benefits, such as prestige and education.

These are important issues with which any theory of just remuneration must deal. It is to the credit of meritorian theory that it both reflects the complexity of the choices that have to be made and locates them in the need to reach agreed value judgements as to what is burdensome and beneficial, both in the performance and in the products of different employments. In this respect desert theory outstrips its more simplistic rivals in its grasp of the nature of the questions to be asked in relation to just remuneration. On the other hand, the problem of establishing proper meritorian rewards for labour is even greater than is allowed for by Sadurski's division of justice into three relatively independent aspects, for, if we take taxation systems into account as part of what is involved in the determination of net rewards, there seems no reason not to use this aspect in respect to the merits and demerits of individuals outside their employment and so seek an overall balance of benefits and burdens in all aspects of distribution. Meritorian theories lack other than purely pragmatic grounds for not taking all desert-relevant factors into one comprehensive assessment of the individuals' merits, whether these relate to economic, criminal or social circumstances.

Another major and distinctive problem for a meritorian theory of remunerative justice is in the determination of what it is that individuals can claim credit for. The particular difficulty with which Sadurski deals in some detail is that individuals cannot take credit for their natural endowments, or for their developed potential in so far as this is due to the environment and support provided by others. Natural ability is no more deserved than are wealthy parents or good schoolteachers, and yet such things are central determinants of what it is that individuals are able to contribute to society.

Sadurski, and other meritorians, must at this point fall back on seeking to isolate those ingredients of an individual's conduct that are the outcome of his own choices and efforts and see that these, rather than raw natural abilities, are rewarded. This is to reject Nozick's position that individuals own their capacities and are entitled to all the fruits of their use. Sadurski goes along with Rawls's idea of natural talents as common assets as 'there is nothing incompatible with the autonomy of individuals in the idea that the fruits of people's natural talents should be shared by all, since those natural talents are not deserved in any way' (1985, p.127), but does not accept that what individuals make of these natural talents should be submerged in the same 'common pool'. The problem is that not only may these ingredients turn out to be relatively minor but, as Rawls argues, they themselves may be the outcome of a combination of heredity and environment not chosen or worked for by the individual. Even if we reject the total determinism of all aspects of human conduct, it seems clear that, once natural talents are discounted, the capacity to make an effortful contribution to the common good is not dependent solely on the exercise of the individual's will, in isolation from the social environment which nurtures it.

There are meritorian answers to these problems, some of which are answers which are exceedingly radical in their implications. We can, for instance, propose that the social arrangements for education and upbringing be such as to provide an equal chance for all individuals to exhibit the choices and efforts which are considered meritorious in a society. This entails not simply providing the same provisions for all children but in arranging superior circumstances and education for the less gifted children. Sadurski is willing to contemplate such a sweeping system of equal opportunity, particularly through the preferential treatment of disadvantaged groups in order to equalise their chances of meeting the criteria of desert applied in their society: 'it is not correct to classify as "equality of opportunity" a situation in which some people are excluded from obtaining a certain good on "appropriate" grounds when the possibilities of satisfying them were clearly unequal' (1985, p.201). This requires, for instance, massive compensation for those born with such handicaps that they are deficient in basic need, but it presumably has similar, if lesser, implications for less severe incapacities which do not feature as fundamental deficiencies but nevertheless affect the individual's chances of obtaining higher rewards.

Even when this is achieved, however, natural differences will still come through and the inequitable results of employment in adult life have to be countered with other remedies, such as a tax system which disfavours individuals in proportion to their higher inherited capacities for choice and effort. Sadurski gives sympathetic consideration to the notion of a 'capability tax' which is 'based on the innate capabilities of individuals rather than their incomes, so that we do not tax the marginal efforts of persons' (1985, p.128). This device has the effect of pressuring people to enter employments which maximise their incomes, but Sadurski takes this to be in line with other standard uses of taxation systems and believes that it is in itself an intrinsically fair distributional mechanism.

When contemplating these radical implications of justice as desert, it is important to remind ourselves that the meritorian theory of justice does not commit us to the view that justice is the sole or even the most important objective of political organisation and legal intervention. Just as the principal object of criminal law may be to reduce harmful actions rather than mete out justice for its own sake, so in the allocation of many jobs, competence and promise may be more important than justice with its past-oriented response to praiseworthy efforts. Indeed the more pervasive ground for state action is the general welfare of citizens. Most rewards and punishments, and most strategies for the allocations of benefits and burdens, have been initiated with general utility rather than individual justice in mind.

The insistence that, for instance, whatever compulsory measures are introduced should be compatible with justice in general often serves the function of placing limits on the way in which the general good may be sought, rather than featuring as an overall justificatory reason for the measure in question. The distinct and sometimes competing values of the general welfare and the liberty and privacy of the individual may override the significance of due deserts in many circumstances. In relation to the justice of remunerating in proportion to past efforts Sadurski need not be committed to giving this dimension overriding force, certainly in the allocation of jobs. Further, in this context his commitment to the central role of desert within justice is weakest, for, as he notes, 'it often happens that distributive criteria other than desert (such as formal entitlements or basic human needs) override those of desert' (ibid., p.156).

When all this has been taken into account, however, it seems less than satisfactory to say that justice is a factor of major significance in relation to the level of remuneration, but of scarcely any importance in job allocation. Sadurski argues that, in most cases, we rightly follow utilitarian consideration in making appointments according to capacity and potential contribution: 'no reasonable person could claim that in a well-ordered society the allocation of jobs and positions should be based on compensatory criteria and that, for instance, the least able people should be hired for the most responsible jobs in order to have a general balance of benefits and burdens restored' (1985, p.153). This fails to take sufficient account of the fact that, without a job, the individual has no chance to make the effortful contribution which merits reward. Equality of opportunity in the preparation for a job is inadequate if there are no tasks available through which individuals can manifest the socially beneficial conduct that they are able and willing to undertake.

There is, in fact, no reason why a meritorian theory cannot use its major premise – namely that people are to be treated in accordance with their deserts – to argue that employment opportunities must be provided which enable individuals to display as well as develop their potential deserts. If, as has been argued, the moral basis of a meritorian theory is that it is right to treat people as responsible agents who are accountable for their behaviour, then it must be right so to arrange society that what happens to individuals depends on how they conduct themselves in conditions where they have a chance to demonstrate their responsibility. This must mean that all have a real chance to meet the preferred criteria of desert, which must include the availability of work appropriate to the individual's talents. This is a matter beyond the equal opportunity to compete for work. It is equality of opportunity to manifest desert in work. In other words, the 'equal worth' premise of meritorian theory requires that everyone have the same opportunity to exhibit their unequal worthiness.

While this is a perfectly coherent position for the meritorian to adopt, and may indeed be a model for a just employment system, it does bring justice into such practical conflict with economic realities that it may have the effect of displacing the pursuit of justice into radically utopian circumstances. Moreover it could be argued that rewarding in accordance with desert is not such an important moral goal that it justifies the reorganising of social and economic life in such a wholesale manner. On the other hand, if justice is only allowed to make a marginal difference to the level of remuneration and has little or no impact on employment distribution, then it becomes impossible to contend that existing social systems begin to approximate to what is just, a conclusion that most meritorian theorists have sought to avoid.

In the end Sadurski is left with an uneasy compromise whereby the lot of those unsuccessful in the employment stakes is taken care of by the aspect of justice which deals with the satisfaction of basic needs. Although the blamelessly unemployed may not have the opportunity to earn through contributing to the social good, their undeserved needs will be met in so far as these qualify as 'basic'. Interestingly such basic needs, while including that which is necessary for the individual to participate in society, do not appear to include the need to participate in the economic system as a worker. This possibility, however, constitutes another avenue through which we might arrive at a moral basis for full employment policies. Whether the provision of appropriate employment as a basic need would be regarded as a matter of humanity or justice will depend on the theory of justice deployed. For Sadurski, employment needs, if there be such, would be part of justice because of their status as basic needs rather than because of their connection with desert. An alternative view is that employment needs are grounds for claims of justice because their fulfilment is a necessary condition for the display of desert and thus a prerequisite for being treated with the respect due to a responsible being.

8 Justice as Critique: Marx and Exploitation

The fact that the bulk of innovative analytical philosophising about justice in recent years has originated in the United States of America explains, but may not excuse, the imbalance of attention given in this book to 'liberal' over 'socialist' theorists. While Rawls considers his contract theory to be compatible with both free-market and centralised economic systems, and at least some of the implications of Dworkin's rights approach are sufficiently egalitarian to count as radical liberal – in contrast to the rampant libertarianism of Nozick – to have only one chapter devoted to explicitly socialist theories of justice appears politically unbalanced, even after the demise of the Soviet Union.

This imbalance is in line with global hegemony concerning the merits of liberal democracy and general insensitivity to the problems of poverty within wealthy states and the gross poverty of most states in comparison to the affluence of an economically and ideologically powerful minority. The preponderance of liberal capitalist ideas within current theories of justice is in line with Marx's contention that rights and justice are essentially bourgeois ideas which impress the ideology of capitalist economic organisation. If justice is indeed an intrinsically capitalist concept, then it is predictable that those who propound a normative theory of justice will express the values of bourgeois individualism. If, as is stated in the *Manifesto of the Communist Party* (1872), 'communism abolishes eternal truths, it abolishes all religion, and all morality, instead of constituting them on a new basis' (Marx and Engels, 1958, vol.1, p.52), then it is mistaken to look for a communist ethic or to expect a normative theory of socialist justice. Within the Marxian tradition, the whole mode of theorising typified by traditional political philosophy is politically and intellectually suspect.

On this view, socialist theorising about justice is a matter of developing critiques of the idea that justice represents a trans-historical ideal applicable to all types of economic system, the assumption being that talk of 'eternal justice', like the rhetoric of natural and human rights, is essentially an ideological device for presenting bourgeois interests under the guise of allegedly universal values. The battle cries of Liberty, Justice and Equality are seen as ideological concepts which express and further the position of the dominant economic class within capitalism, 'justice' itself being no more than 'the ideologised, glorified expression of the existing economic relationships' (Marx and Engels, 1958, vol.2, p.128).

There is a good deal of textual evidence for Marx's theoretical amoralism and his anti-justice and anti-rights stances. Certainly Marx did not think that juridical concepts like justice have any significant role to play in the explanation of social structure and social change. However recent debate on Marx and justice takes up the question of whether there might be, at a deeper level of analysis, distinctively socialist normative conceptions of rights and justice which embody some of the values which can be realised only in a socialist society. This approach draws on Marx's clear abhorrence of the miseries engendered by capitalism and his allegations that capitalism, as a form of theft perpetrated against the workers, fails to match up to even its own moral ideals, a theme taken up later in this chapter.

More particularly, it is argued that socialist societies will at least approximate to, if not directly aim at, the genuinely socialist principle of distribution 'from each according to their ability, to each according to their needs', a maxim which Marx himself endorses in *The Gotha Programme* (Marx and Engels, 1958, vol.3). The communal egalitarianism implied by such a principle could be said to embody an aspect of socialism's moral superiority over other forms of political philosophy which is particularly relevant to justice. In brief, the socialist conception of justice can be regarded as distribution according to need of resources willingly created by others. The fact that there will be no scarcity of resources in an actual communist society may render justice less significant than it is in other societies, but this does not mean that socialist societies are not, in their own distinctive sense, just. Nor does it negate the claim that socialist justice is – in its proper historical context – to be preferred to other conceptions of justice or without relevance today. Echoes of this can be heard in A. K. Sen's analysis of real equality of opportunity based on the functioning of human capacities (Sen, 1992).

Marx's strictures on justice and his failure to denounce capitalism as 'unjust' can be interpreted as no more than a manifestation of his criticism of 'utopian' socialists, whose primary failure was to assume that historical progress could be brought about by drawing up imaginary blueprints of an ideal form of society and then exhorting people to set about transforming actual societies into the preferred utopia. The Utopians were alleged to have ignored the fundamental historical realities which make it impossible to realise a socialist society until the existing or emerging material conditions are appropriate to it. Imaginative thinking, moral insight and appeals to people's better natures are powerless before the underlying determinants of historical development.

It is possible to share Marx's sense of history and acknowledge the futility of ahistorical moralising, while seeking to specify the values which are relevant to the assessment of the moral superiority of one form of society over another. Doubtless this was not Marx's prime concern, but there is sufficient indication of the values which are presupposed in his critique of capitalism and in his clear preference for the fulfilments and freedoms of socialist societies over against the barbarities and degradations of capitalism to make it reasonable to develop a socialist set of values which include a conception of justice both for the critique of capitalism and for the description of communist society.

Formal justice and the critique of rights

Opinions vary as to the extent of Marx's rejection of morality and moralising. On a strict interpretation of the doctrine of historical materialism, all ideas, including moral ideas, are part of the 'superstructure', the effects rather than the causes of social phenomena, and hence utterly dependent on the material basis of the forces of production which are constituted by what a society produces and the manner of its production and distribution. It follows that moralising is not only futile but also baseless since there would seem to be no way of deciding that one moral opinion is better or worse than any other, all ethical systems being equally the products of non-rational economic forces. This reductionist assumption seems to undermine the purely evaluative as well as the prescriptive or exhortatory function of moral language and therefore renders nugatory the strongly normative aspects of the theories of justice which we have been considering. On such a strict interpretation of Marxian orthodoxy there is no way of demonstrating the moral superiority of the Rawlsian maximin principle over the wealth-maximising ideal of Posner or the Dworkinian conception of treatment as equals. Neither utilitarian calculation, nor contractarian imagination, can serve as anything more than the vehicle for pre-existing political prejudice.

On a looser interpretation of historical materialism, in which the superstructure of ideas may be allowed some causal efficacy, at least on the pace of historical development, there may be a place for timely moral persuasion, and there is also the possibility that an element of rational judgement may enter into the formation of political opinion, particularly as the necessities of capitalist society give way to the emerging freedoms of socialism. It is unlikely, however, that there can be any Marxian indulgence for the pretensions of those theories of justice which present themselves as the embodiment of universal truths which have application to any and every stage of historical development. Particularly vulnerable to the Marxian historical sensitivity are theories, like Nozick's, which are founded on unchallengeable natural rights and presuppose a form of individualism that ignores the interdependent and socially variable nature of man. Less vulnerable are the more modest objectives of later Rawlsian reflective equilibrium which seeks only to express and render consistent the political outlook of a particular historical form of social organisation.

A characteristic socialist critique of all liberal theories of justice is that they oversell themselves in so far as they purport to provide an impartial analysis which is neutral as between the interested groups which coexist even within a particular society. In our consideration of, for instance, Dworkin's practical applications of the idea that we should treat people as equals, we have noted that they cannot provide sufficient reasons for the conclusions they reach, in that the same principles can generate widely different practical recommendations for essentially similar circumstances. The same is true of all theories which posit the emergence of a rational consensus as to what is just, once partiality has been excluded by one device or another. The hidden selectivity involved in all potentially universalistic theories results in systematic bias in favour of certain social groups in a way which Marx predicts will occur with all aspiring consensual political theories.

The most evident example of this covert (or, in this case, not so covert) ideological slant must be the wealth-maximising model of Posner, which can readily be seen as a rationalisation of capitalist accumulation, but similar critiques can be mounted of Rawls's lexical priority of liberty and his apparent neglect of the unemployable. Similarly Sadurski's tendency to conclude that desert converges on socially valuable contribution is readily presented as a modern variant of the recurrent liberal thesis that those who come out on top in an equal opportunity competitive society somehow 'deserve' to do so. In general, however they are deployed, impartiality and neutrality have an uncanny knack of coming up with ideals which do not pose any real threat to the established economic inequalities of the liberal societies from which they routinely emerge.

Faced with such swingeing critiques of liberal theories of justice, socialists may think it wise to develop other terminology to express their counter values, but, given the rhetorical force of the language of justice and its constant reemergence as the expression of specific types of social criticism, it is hardly surprising that efforts are made to establish the credentials of a socialist conception of justice through which to communicate at least part of the vision of the socialist ideal.

The differing analyses of the Marxian concept of justice which have been put forward can usefully be approached in terms of the contrast between formal and material justice, the justice of adherence to rules as distinct from the justice of the rules themselves. Marx himself often appears to move between the idea of justice as conformity to the established practices of a social institution and the more substantial idea of justice as it applies to the assessment of these practices. It is clear that some of his observations on justice are directed at the idea of formal justice while others have more to do with material justice.

Thus it is when Marx is thinking of formal justice that he treats justice as a juridical concept which has to do with conformity to established rules and hence the administration of law or 'justice' within a particular system. From this point of view justice is always 'internal' to a particular form of social organisation, since it refers to no more than the efficient implementation of the norms of the system in question. This means that the language of justice cannot be used as the basis for an external critique of the organisation as a whole or to condemn its constituent rules. Societies can be unjust in so far as they fail to apply their own rules consistently, but the rules themselves are never properly described as just or unjust. For instance, the capitalist judge who applies the property laws of capitalist society is acting justly, as the feudal courts are just when they uphold the different rights and duties which constitute feudal ownership. Justice is therefore relative to, and can be no higher than, the existing system of economic relationships.

According to this interpretation of Marx, it follows that societies are unjust only in so far as they do not consistently enforce their societal norms and laws. Marx does not appear to attach any moral significance to such inconsistencies, except perhaps to note as one of the contradictions of capitalism that its laws are often selectively enforced to the benefit of the bourgeois class. It might appear, therefore, that justice, for Marx, is a morally neutral and entirely relative concept, equally at home in all societies and in principle applicable to socialist societies in relation to the consistent application of socialist rules and standards.

However this conclusion misses Marx's contention that law is an intrinsically capitalist phenomenon, and one which will play no significant part within a truly socialist or communist society. Law, along with the state, will wither away with the demise of class differences and economic exploitation, to be replaced by a spontaneous order of mutual cooperation untrammelled by the coercive apparatus of law and the restrictions of rigid social norms. In a society in which men are genuinely free to make their own relationships within uncoerced social groupings there will be no role for law and hence no place for justice.

There is no avoiding this conclusion if a strict juridical interpretation of justice is combined with a classical positivistic analysis of law which makes law, by definition, a coercive apparatus of the state. No Marxist could accept that a truly socialist society would have coercive laws backed by state sanctions. And yet, if justice is taken to include the quasi-juridical form of conformity to the non-legal rules or mandatory societal norms which lack the backing of formal sanctions, socialist communities would require a conception of justice to cover adherence to their non-coercive societal rules. Alternatively, by revising the crude sanctions version of positivism to allow for the possibility of there being laws which, while mandatory within a given territory, require no sanctions to attract adequate conformity, justice can be freed from its necessary connection with force and formal justice given an acceptable role in socialist society. Either way, there is no difficulty in making conceptual room for the idea of socialist formal justice, or socialist legality. As long as there are socially recognised rules which are authoritative within a territory and which are applied by specialist bodies with responsibility for their interpretation and adjudication in relation to particular cases, then there is law in a sense which is sufficient for the language of formal justice to gain a foothold.

Similar considerations pertain in relation to rights. If, following the discussion in Chapter 3, we bypass the idea of moral rights, and define rights in terms of the existing normative entitlements to which appeal may be made to protect the interests of the individual, all that is required for there to be rights is for there to be a set of needs-based binding rules according to which individuals regulate their interactions. In a socialist society the binding force of the rules rests on willing acceptance rather than the threat of sanctions or the inducements of reward, but there is no contradiction in the notions of continuing consent to obligations and free acquiescence in a body of shared rules. If part of formal justice involves treating individuals according to their rights, then we can have a working tie-up between quasi-juridical conceptions of rights and justice which have potential application to socialist societies.

It is true that some forms of Marxian anarchism have no place for rules of any sort and envisage all social cooperation as being purely spontaneous and transient, thus requiring no basis in expectations arising from an authoritative set of rights and duties. However this model lacks plausibility in a society involving modern production methods and large-scale social organisation. Moreover, what little Marx himself has to say on the nature of the ultimate form of communist society is compatible with the continued existence of non-coercive and, in this sense, largely 'administrative' rules, and hence with the idea of formal justice.

Difficulties over the assumed coerciveness of law are not the only ones, however, which prompt Marxist suspicions of formal justice, particularly when it is assumed that formal justice involves treating individuals in accordance with their positive rights. There are a number of other question marks which hang over the compatibility of rights and socialism. Some of these concern the alleged universality and overriding inalienability of rights as expressed in connection with conceptions of natural or human rights. Not only did

Marx castigate bourgeois moralists for presenting their class interests as universal interests, his sense of history led him also to reject
the idea that there could be any paramount rights applicable to all
persons in all ages.

I have already noted, in Chapter 4, that it is not necessary to
invoke the concept of human rights to explicate the thesis that
justice involves treating people in accordance with their rights, but
other socialist objections to rights apply equally to rights in general,
rather than to human rights specifically. For instance, it is argued
that rights are essentially individualistic in that they are the 'property' of individuals and have the function of protecting the interests
of their possessors against the perhaps otherwise justified claims of
other individuals and groups. The idea is that rights are devices for
legitimising possibly anti-social and certainly self-interested behaviour and hence get in the way of the organisation of a polity for the
welfare of the society as a whole. This is given backing by the
common jurisprudential analysis of positive rights in terms of the
legal power to control the behaviour of others in specified ways, a
power whose use is left to the discretion of the right-holder to use as
he or she thinks fit. This device is alleged to be a reflection of the
idea that a society is a collection of independent individuals whose
interests are protected through the institution of rights which
enables them to pursue their 'legitimate' self-interest.

The Marxian critique of rights in general can point to the increasing significance of rights in the legal systems of capitalist countries
and the affinity between the idea of rights and the belief that
obligations normally arise from the agreement of autonomous individuals in commercial-like transactions. The standard model is
economic man acting in accordance with his own judgements as to
his economic interests, a hypothesis which is given varying degrees
of endorsement by all the theories of justice which we have considered. Clearly a large-scale commercial society requires laws which are
framed in terms of rights and these rights dominantly assume a
context in which individuals are acting in accordance with their
own conception of their interests. Further, there is in historical
terms a powerful correlation between rights and the exercise of
individual autonomy in a manner which avoids the need to justify
itself in community terms. This is most evident in the work of
libertarians, such as Nozick and Posner, although, as we have
seen, the latter does, at least in principle, subordinate individual
rights to the social goal of wealth maximisation.

This historical picture does not in itself demonstrate that other forms of society would not require and endorse a system of rights which serves other purposes. There is nothing in the concept of a right which requires that it go along with the assumption that obligations, and hence their correlative rights, be primarily the outcome of voluntary agreement, let alone that this agreement is always made by essentially self-interested individuals. Nor is it necessary to analyse rights, as liberal theorists so often do, in terms of discretionary powers of right-holders, whereby they may call on others to fulfil their obligations or may waive the obligations in question. We also speak of rights where there exist obligations to further the interests of another, as in the case of children's rights, whether or not the right-holder is required to initiate any claims and even where the right-holder is not able to waive the obligations which correlate with rights, as with the right of an unconscious person to medical treatment. It is not even necessary to assume that a system of rights requires that violations of rights be dealt with only on the complaint and initiative of the right-holder, although this may normally be an efficient way to organise the protection of interests.

It is possible, therefore, that socialist doubt about a legal system involving rights is a result of the failure to realise that not only the content of rights but their *modus operandi* and justificatory rationales can be quite different from that which typically pertains in capitalist societies. Even within the assumption that rights are often discretionary powers wielded by individuals, it is unproblematic to envisage a function for such rights in societies in which individuals are not selfish and whose self-interest is not rigidly separated from the interests of others. As long as individuals have desires (however altruistic) on which they wish to act and as long as such actions are facilitated in a socially beneficial way by allowing the individual a range of legal powers with which to pursue their interests, then there is reason to have a rights-based system of rules. It is only the assumption that individuals are inherently and irredeemably self-interested that renders the idea of rights anti-socialist. And so, while the significance of formal justice does not, of course, depend solely on the rules of the system being construed in terms of rights, establishing the coherence of the idea of socialist rights does clear the way for an open-minded assessment of formal justice within socialist theory.

Much discussion of this issue has had to do with how far, if at all, the rule of law can mitigate the evils of pre-socialist government by injecting an element of impartiality into the exercise of political power in non-socialist systems. There has been little direct discussion of the significance of formal justice once socialism has become a reality. Of course, if there is reason to have rules within socialism then there must be reason to have these rules effectively, and that must mean by and large accurately, administered. The issues which then arise concern the reasons that there might be for curtailing the discretion of officials to vary retrospectively the application of rules where this seems to them to be for the public interest. This question is addressed indirectly in the debate about the alleged utilitarianism of socialism and the tendency of socialists who, in their concern for the happiness of the mass of the people, adopt an act-utilitarian rather than a rule-utilitarian approach. Act-utilitarianism makes the commitment to government according to law provisional in that the system is open to the principle that the general interest can routinely be used to justify interventions in the normal processes of formal justice where this is clearly beneficial in utilitarian terms.

It is, however, by no means clear that Marx himself is a straight-forward utilitarian either in his ultimate political values or in his attitude to rules. For instance, Marx is clearly committed to the importance of freedom within a communist society which requires that individuals and groups are able to pursue creative projects in cooperation with their fellows. His communitarian conception of the full development of a socialised human nature, which is manifested in the ideal of satisfying work in the service of genuine needs, leaves room for respecting the sort of individual and group autonomy that is furthered by giving the individuals and groups fixed sets of rules in the context of which they can plan and take responsibility for the outcome of their actions. Those aspects of the socialist ideal which stress the importance of creative endeavour, in addition to the simple pursuit of happiness, provide some basis for the view of man which relates respect for the individual to strict adherence to the rules which affect his or her welfare. Fixed rules provide a context within which socialists as much as capitalists can act responsibly in the light of the stability which such a system provides. Altruists, as much as egotists, are rule-dependent for the success of their projects.

There is nothing in Marx to suggest that he would give any weight to the value of the bare idea of treating like cases alike within a public set of rules, for this represents the sort of rule fetishism which places abstract rationality above human interests and frequently acts as an excuse for the perpetration of material injustice. However, since, as we have noted in Chapter 2, the independent value of formal justice is questionable, socialists need not be faulted for dispensing with it. Further, much of Marx's critique of justice can be seen as directed to the unimportance of formal justice in situations where the substantive rules are exploitative. This does not rule out the possible instrumental significance of formal justice in situations where the rules are materially acceptable.

Material justice, exploitation and desert

Exploring ways in which socialism might incorporate a conception of material justice requires us to have a reasonably clear idea what an actualised socialist society would be like. From Marx we can glean many negative descriptions of socialist or 'communist' society: there will be no classes, no exploitation, no conflict and no coercion. All this is due to the abolition of the private ownership of the means of production, in relation to which class membership is defined, through which exploitation occurs and because of which social conflict and coercion arise. The more positive aspects of socialist society are less clearly defined. The communal ownership of the means of production is said to achieve plenty, not in any crude materialistic sense, but in relation to the genuine needs of men and women in a society in which their social and creative natures can be expressed and fulfilled and true freedom experienced in the context of community life. This implies that there will be far less division of labour, and such as there is will be freely chosen. It also involves the end of market transactions as the prime determinant of production and distribution. It is also assumed that, once the various transitional stages have been gone through, there will be genuinely consensual democracy, so that all share in the direction of social organisation towards the satisfaction of needs and the expression of a freedom which involves the absence of practical as well as legal barriers to attaining the goals of human endeavours.

Interestingly this brief sketch of the telos of social evolution draws on the language of freedom and fulfilment and could readily have been couched in terms of equality, but the language of justice does not spring to mind as central or even essential to the exposition of the communist ideal, although there seems to be no awkwardness in asserting that a socialist society will not be unjust. The most straightforward explanation for the marginality of justice in social-ist terminology is that, in communist society, the so-called 'condi-tions' of justice do not obtain: there is no scarcity of goods to be distributed, no conflict to be resolved, no systems of punishments and incentives to be administered. It can therefore be argued that there is no scope for the ideas of justice and injustice within com-munism because society has passed beyond the stage at which these ideas have anything on which to bite. Thus, while it may be correct to say that communist society is not unjust, this has to be taken as a not very appropriate description rather than an evaluation (see Wood, 1983 pp.163–91).

If, however, we take up the broader analysis of justice according to which it has to do with rightness in distribution, it is clear that abundance and harmony do not in themselves dispense with the role of justice. In situations of harmony and plenty distributive issues still require to be dealt with, if only to ensure that the needs and welfare of all members of a society receive attention. Abundance of goods does not necessarily entail their proper distribution and it seems likely that proper distribution even of what is plentiful is a condition of the continuing absence of conflict. Indeed there is no suggestion that in a communist society abundance and harmony are achieved without conscious effort and good organisation which involve decisions about production and distribution being made in relation to the chosen objectives of that society. This would enable us to bring in the principle of distribution according to need and contribution according to capacity as a positive description of communist society, although not as an ideal to be striven for, although the capacity requirement can be taken as representing a pre-communist stage before fully spontaneous labour has been achieved (Elster, 1985).

Because of the doubts about the relevance of prescriptive cri-tiques based on justice with respect to a fully formed communist society, it is common to fall back on a socialist theory of justice which emphasises the injustice of non-communist systems, espe-cially capitalism, often utilising the idea of exploitation to identify the evil or unfairness of the capitalist system. In technical terms, exploitation is irretrievably tied to a narrow interpretation of the labour theory of value according to which labour is the sole source of wealth, so that, if those who are employed as wage-labourers in an industrial system do not receive compensation equivalent to the total value of what is produced, there is a dissonance or unfairness in the distribution of wealth. The intellectual basis of this position, according to which value is rooted in labour, is very similar to Nozick's thesis about self-ownership as the ground of the right to property rights over acquisitions and transfers. Indeed the common source for Marx and Nozick here is clearly Locke (see G. Cohen, 1995).

More generally, exploitation can be seen as a social situation where one group is in a position to take advantage of other groups in a way which is unfair. Thus, under capitalism, even if we reject the labour theory of value, it can be argued that owners of capital take a disproportionate share of the wealth created by socially organised labour. This can be given more objective formulations in terms of workers not receiving the full amount of the marginal increase in production which their labour makes possible. Another influential analysis is provided by John Roemer who traces the phenomenon of exploitation to the unequal distribution of productive resources, thus reducing the Marxian terminology to a more generalised critique of underlying economic inequality, albeit an inequality of economic power rather than consumer goods (Roemer, 1989).

Allen Buchanan (1979) retains something of the Marxian flavour in viewing exploitation in relation to the feelings of alienation, which feature centrally in the early work of Marx, that arise in the process of capitalist labour, something which cannot be taken away by higher wages alone but relate to the inequality and indignity of relationships in the workplace. In general, however, the language of exploitation features largely as a synonym for feelings of anger at excessive inequality of wealth and resources, which give rise to talk of robbery, theft and greed. In the end such discourse is rooted more directly in the conviction that the wealthy do not deserve to be so much better rewarded than the mass of working people. Thus the Marxian economic terminology of exploitation becomes reabsorbed in moral beliefs which relate reward to effort and contribution.

It may well be, however, that the reluctance of Marxian theorists to articulate the distributive principles of communist society in the language of justice is rooted in their awareness of the conceptual tie-up between justice and desert and their instinctive hostility to the notion of desert and its alleged moral significance within capitalism. Bourgeois ideology attempts to justify the inequalities of capitalist society by appeals to the notion of the value of the contribution made by those involved in production and its financing, and behind this there are the assertions that those who succeed in a free-enterprise private ownership system 'deserve' to do so through their wise choices, hard work, acquired skills and honest dealings. To Marxists this meritorian ideology is, of course, complete humbug, hence their scorn for appeals to justice in the context of capitalism. But the basis for their rejection of capitalist pretensions to justice vary and do not always carry the implication that the underlying ideas of meritorian justice are always without foundation.

Sometimes the denial of meritorian justice is based on the determinism of historical materialism according to which all human actions are the products of inevitable historical processes rather than the free actions of the participants. As we noted in Chapter 6, taking a 'hard' determinist line undermines all talk of human responsibility and accountability in the standard moral sense in which people are praised and blamed for their behaviour because it is their choice, effort or character which are at least important elements in the circumstances under scrutiny. If in a narrow sense people cannot control or act against their desires in the light of moral principles and are causally bound to do what they in fact do, then it makes no sense to blame or praise them for their conduct. For such reasons Marx seems no more inclined to blame capitalists than to praise proletarians: both are slaves to a process which rules their lives with an iron necessity. This may mean that when Marx denies that capitalist distribution is 'unjust' he intends to say not only that it is formally just within the system of capitalism, in that it is in accordance with the rules of the capitalist system, but also that it is meaningless to criticise this arrangement as materially unjust because it is an inevitable and historically necessary stage in human evolution. In moral terms, this means that capitalism is neither just nor unjust (see Miller, 1984).

Nevertheless, we have noted that this critique presupposes the labour theory of value according to which the value of a product is the quantity of labour that has gone into the making of it. This may involve the covert assertion that those who work to produce something are deserving of possessing, enjoying or disposing of it. There is a running assumption in the fierce rhetorical Marxian critique of capitalism that the exploitation of proletarians is wrong because they are the real creators of wealth. In the end, capitalists are seen to be superfluous parasites, even thieves, who contribute nothing of their own to the productive process and hence may be said to be undeserving of the rewards which they 'steal' from the workers. This fits easily enough into a critique of capitalism as unjust by the meritorian standards to which it makes ideological appeal but fails to achieve in practice. Since it makes perfect sense to say, in this context, that the proletarians deserve more and the bourgeoisie deserve less, we may see a meritorian view at work in the exposition of the shortcomings of capitalism.

Moreover, while Marxists agree that history is in the main a causally determined process, this is admitted to be – to an extent – a matter of degree, particularly in relation to the historical period in question. Specifically it is alleged that, with the demise of capitalism, which culminates in a highly determined series of cataclysms, the developing forms of socialist and then communist society are marked by the growing emergence of the freedom of men and women to control their own destiny and make the institutions of society fit their genuine needs and hence achieve real fulfilment. The determinist veto on meritorian justice would not therefore apply once communism is achieved.

There are further reasons why justice is not to the fore in the Marxian picture of the communist millennium, particularly the assumption that the achievements of communist society will be communal, not individual. It is assumed that production methods will be social in that they involve a large number of people working together with the tools of modern industry. In this situation, since no one can claim to be the sole producer, it becomes increasingly difficult to identify the contribution of each individual to the final product and so the idea of rewards being commensurate with input of particular persons seems inapplicable. The results of communal effort may seem, by definition, to exclude the possibility of distribution in accordance with individual merit. This is a view which is echoed in Rawls's critique of natural desert and features in the communitarian critique of liberal individualism.

Yet it is normal to conceive of the deserts of groups as well as individuals, particularly where there are democratic processes at work, and the complete rejection of the individualisation of production in socialist accounting is too sweeping to be compatible with other elements of Marxist theory. It cannot take in, for instance, Marx's endorsement of reward according to contribution which pertains in the transitional stages of socialist society, nor does it accord with the degree of individualism implied by the communist slogan, 'from each according to his ability, to each according to his needs', a principle which calls for the identification of what it is that the individual contributes as well as individualised assessment of the needs which have to be met by communist production and distribution. This putative principle of communist distribution requires further analysis if we are to see how it might relate to the tradition of meritorian justice on which Marx depends in making many of his assessments of the different types of society.

The centrality of 'need' in the normative theory of communism is open to many different interpretations. To emphasise needs can be seen as a form of ethical utilitarianism, primarily 'negative' utilitarianism, in that it may indicate the material lacks which cause suffering and suggest that resources be directed towards eliminating the sort of human suffering which Marx saw as reaching its climax in the last days of capitalism, but also 'positive' utilitarianism, in that the object of communist society could be to maximise human happiness. This approach does not fit easily, however, with Marx's denunciations of utilitarians like Jeremy Bentham. Marx, in the communitarian tradition, criticises both the individualistic theory of human nature espoused by the classical utilitarians and the ethical view that the satisfaction of any and all human desires is morally good.

Some compromise is possible here if we hold, in contrast to Benthamite utilitarians, that it is genuine happiness which results from real human fulfilment, and not simply the satisfaction of any desires, that Marx adopts as the criterion of value, his quarrel with Bentham being the latter's view that satisfying the wishes of men as they are in non-communist societies is productive of happiness. This line of thought leads into a more clearly non-utilitarian interpretation of Marx's concentration on need according to which it represents a teleological view of human nature of an almost Aristotelian type. *Homo sapiens,* as a species, exhibits its full potential only when it achieves a certain way of life which expresses its inner nature, an end which requires a development in the material conditions of life and corresponding social organisation that makes it possible for men and women to live together in harmony as creative and social beings. This teleological interpretation of the language of need in Marx's political philosophy draws heavily on his early writings with their themes of man as a 'species being' who is alienated from his own nature under the capitalist system. However, as an overall interpretation of Marxian ideas, this position rides rather uneasily with many of the things that Marx has to say about the plasticity of

human nature and its derivative status in relation to the variable
economic base of society.

Such issues cannot be settled by any evaluatively neutral analysis
of 'need'. Certainly needs are often contrasted with wants, and to
this extent appear non-utilitarian since utilitarians have characteristically sought maximum satisfaction of all wants, but the concept
of need is in itself so open-ended that it admits of almost any
practical deployment. Anything which can be said to be required
to achieve any objective can be regarded as a need, so that any
'want' can thereby be the basis for a need. There is no necessary
assumption that the objective for the attainment of which something is needed is morally good rather than evaluatively indifferent
or even bad. In consequence, those who use 'need' as a political
concept require to state and defend the goals which they covertly
espouse by the use of this logically incomplete terminology. Some
such goals – such as human survival – can, perhaps, be taken for
granted, and it is often 'basic' needs, that is, the requirements for
continued material existence, that are invoked by the political discourse of needs. Marx himself is clearly concerned with such basic
needs not only because their neglect generates great suffering but
also because it is the basis of his empirical theory of historical
materialism that the manner in which a society goes about satisfying
the material needs of its members determines everything else
about it.

Once we go beyond the idea of basic needs it is possible to
construct some hierarchy of needs which relate to the pursuit of
an infinite variety of possible human objectives. It is at this point
that it is possible to introduce a 'naturalistic' or natural law postulate to pick out certain goals as best suited to expressing human
nature. Plausible contenders for this status have included rationality, autonomy and moral capacity. In Marx's case the most likely
combination of 'natural' goals is a blend of creativity and sociabil-
ity. It seems misleading to present these values, however, as a form
of natural law theory, since Marx makes none of the characteristic
natural law epistemological claims to the effect that the ends of man
can be ascertained by rational insight or deduction from observation of normal human behaviour. Indeed the idea that communist
society is directed towards the satisfaction of human needs is an
open-ended principle that may well be compatible with a wide
variety of ideas about fulfilling human activities. This strand of
Marxism can be discerned in the theories of Sen and Nussbaum

who emphasise that equality (Sen, 1992) and human rights (Nussbaum, 1999) relate to the exercise of human capacities.

It can therefore be argued that the Marxian approach to justice is similar to Rawls's theory of justice with respect to the alleviation of basic needs. This, it is said, is in effect to benefit the least advantaged section of society. Certainly, in his reaction to the suffering caused by capitalism, Marx is moved primarily by the plight of those experiencing the greatest material deprivations. While such extreme suffering could not arise within the plenty of communist society, the analogous priority would be those whose personal characteristics make it most difficult to achieve a satisfying way of life.

It is doubtful, however, if the improvements which communism offers over capitalism with respect to the effective satisfaction of basic needs would be regarded by Marx as a matter of justice as distinct from liberty, community, self-realisation or plain humanity. In so far as prioritising basic needs implies an acceptance of the equal worth of all human beings and the suffering of each person counts equally, regardless of class or wealth, Marx's position has the ring of justice discourse about it, but such equality of worth could be said to underline other prescriptive principles, such as equal beneficence, or the equal maximisation of human potential.

At this stage in the analysis of socialist justice it is perhaps pointless to speculate on the extent to which Marx himself would regard the need principle as expressive of justice rather than some other ideal, but it is important to note that there is no built-in antithesis between need-satisfaction and meritorian justice. If, following Sadurski, we say that need-satisfaction is reserved for basic needs, then this leaves plenty of scope for meritorian distributions in non-basic matters. Justice is then relevant to the surplus that remains once scarcity has taken care of basic needs. What, presumably, is not allowed is to make the satisfaction of basic needs conditional on desert.

On the other hand, if the need principle is interpreted in a broad manner, so that it takes in what is required for a particular lifestyle, then this lifestyle can be delineated in such a way as to include the idea of treating people in accordance with their deserts. This is something which – it could be argued – is necessary for maintaining mutual respect and individual dignity within a society of responsible agents. A neo-Marxian account of justice may be unlikely to give such meritorian considerations the dominant role in the distribution of material goods, but its relevance to the distribution of more socialist values, such as creative opportunities and socially respons- ible tasks, to say nothing of the allocation of those important ingredients of social life – praise and blame – might well be deemed appropriate. It is not only a coherent but also in principle an attractive idea that human beings need to be treated as autonomous agents who are responsible for their actions and answerable for their conduct. Moreover, even basic needs are relevant to meritorian justice in that their satisfaction is often a necessary prerequisite for engaging in the sort of conduct which is the subject of meritorian assessment. We cannot live well unless we have the wherewithal to sustain our lives.

The issues here are not merely conceptual. Problems also arise from the difficulty we have in imagining what it would be like to live in an affluent and egalitarian society which does not depend on the positive sanctions of economic incentives or the negative sanctions of punishment to attain its objectives. In liberal theories of justice much effort goes into seeking to demonstrate that such sanctions are 'just' in that they are not only instrumentally necessary but also in some way 'deserved'. People must be bribed to work hard, but they also deserve rewards if they do work hard. In fully developed communism the incentive element drops out, but this does not imply that no recognition would be given to those who devote themselves to socially productive tasks. In the changed conditions of commun- ist society rewards may be unnecessary and those of high ability, who are required to give more to the communal effort, may not in any important sense 'deserve' their higher abilities, but in a society which has escaped from the domination of historical forces and is able freely to explore the fulfilment of human nature it is likely that evaluations of behaviour in terms of its moral worth would be not only better founded, but of continuing significance. Thus, socialist justice might have to do with non-monetary ways of recognising the worth of the different efforts made by individuals and groups towards the realisation of a socialist society in which the full satis- faction of genuine human needs is the corporate telos.

Such speculations are of more than purely theoretical interest. It is important for the evaluation of the socialist ideal to know whether a communist society would be organised around the maximisation of pleasure or devoted to the development of a form of life which emphasises responsible choice and critical evaluation of conduct in terms of values other than pleasure. Moreover, coming to terms with the significance of (meritorian) justice for communist society has implications for the way in which socialists react to the language of justice within non-socialist societies. There is a major difference between totally dismissing all justice talk as an intellectually confused form of ideology, on the one hand, and using it to undermine the particular claims that are made about justice under capitalism, on the other. If the latter approach is adopted it becomes possible to argue the shortcomings of capitalism without endorsing the nihilistic view that justice is inevitably a chimera and to go on to use the terminology which has been developed in pre-socialist societies to commend a possible future in which at least some aspects of the unrealised ideal of liberal ideology would come to fruition.

Socialist justice

The intellectual contortions which must be performed in order to bring out a meaningful contrast between liberal and socialist theories of justice have much to do with the fact that basic social and political concepts are closely intertwined with the complex sets of ideas and practices which constitute different social structures. Where radically dissimilar types of society are under consideration there can be no neat way of identifying the major contrasts in their political concepts. Thus simply to feed in 'needs' to the formula 'to each according to their *Xs*' cannot focus adequately on the move from liberal to socialist assumptions. Such a formula, particularly when $X =$ need, conjures up the picture of a vast allocative mechanism externally attached to an economic system which produces the goods to be distributed and imposes the burdens which the system and its political supports demand. According to this model, the role of justice is to superimpose a reallocation of benefits and burdens on an essentially aggregative productive system which is directed towards the efficient output of material goods.

This approach cannot adequately encapsulate the socialists' shift of emphasis towards the idea that all social enterprises be directed towards an existence 'in which the free development of each is the condition for the free development of all' (Marx and Engels, 1958, vol.2, p.54). This vision of communal endeavour directed towards the realisation of a fulfilling way of life for all members of society is claimed to transcend the sort of formula which is appropriate to the

allocation of scarce benefits and oppressive burdens between competitive and self-interested individuals. Bringing about varied and
fulfilling creative activities for all is not primarily a matter of
distributing money, 'manna', or even education and employment,
according to some mechanical equation. If justice has a role in this
model of society, then it will be at once less evident and more
central. Socialist justice has to do with more than the rectification
of injurious interpersonal behaviour, the struggle to make competitive economic systems more 'fair', and the provision of a safety
net for the sick, the old and the disabled. Rather it enters into
the organising principles of all social activities, which will be directed at the satisfaction of 'needs' in a sense broad enough to take in
all the creative and community aspirations of the fully developed
individual.

Within the liberal tradition from which socialist theory has
emerged it is more natural to present such a goal in terms of liberty
than in the language of justice or equality, for liberty, when conceived of in positive terms as involving the power to realise capacities as well as the absence of the constraints of oppressive laws and
social conventions, more readily captures the flavour of the contrast
between socialism and capitalism. Yet it is misleading to present this
as a contrast between liberty and justice, for it is assumed that the
genuine interests of all members of a socialist society will have equal
weight and it is denied that the tensions between these two norms,
which is manifested in liberal societies, will be a feature of socialist
ones.

There are clearly conceptual problems arising from the break-
down of the neat distinctions between aggregation and distribution
and between liberty and justice. What we are left with is too diffuse
and speculative to withstand detailed analytical criticism. And yet, if
we accept a version of the meritorian analysis of justice which traces
the roots of the liberal concern with justice to the idea of treating
individuals as responsible agents whose well-being matters equally,
and if we can free this notion from the accompanying individualistic
assumptions that people are responsible only to the extent that they
act by themselves rather than in concert with others, then it is
possible to point to meritorian as well as egalitarian elements in
the model of socialist society as the essence of socialist as well as
liberal justice. It is because a socialist society will be, amongst other
things, a community which encourages the fulfilment of the human
capacities for choice, autonomous action and purposeful creativity,

so that people are not only in command of their own environment but are in fact responsible for their social and individual existences, that it is illuminating to talk of a socialist society as a just society, although this may not be the principal thing that we might wish to say about it.

All this may seem rather by the way if we consider that the significance of Marxist theory has faded with the demise of Soviet communism. This ignores the fact that Soviet communism was only contingently related to Marxist theory and, indeed, need not be seen as in any way an instantiation of Marx's vision. Moreover, it is reasonable to consider drawing on the Marxist tradition for ideas of how to develop non-liberal theories of justice which express an egalitarian version of communitarianism. I have suggested that there are also meritorian ingredients in Marx which can be taken up and woven into some form of democratic socialism. We can certainly look to aspects of Marxian theory, such as the analysis of exploitation, to formulate critiques of liberal capitalist systems whose moral status remains under ongoing scrutiny, particularly in relation to the extensive and deep inequalities and unfairnesses between rich and poor within and between nations.

9 Justice as Empowerment: Young and Affirmative Action

Feminist views on justice have evolved in line with general developments in feminist political theory. From the nineteenth century onwards, liberal feminists have regarded justice as involving equal rights for women and men and their great achievement has been to gain acceptance for the claim that there is no good reason to exclude people from basic civil, political, social and economic rights on the basis of gender and, more recently, that political and economic arrangements which disproportionately disadvantage women are unacceptable. The liberal feminist's goal is equal rights – the same rights for men and women – so that gender is simply irrelevant in the distribution of benefits and burdens.

More radical feminists have gone on to question the content of the rights accepted as basic in a patriarchal or male-oriented society which they regard as biased towards male interests and concerns. The equal rights approach is insufficient if the rights in question are rights which protect primarily male interests. Feminists in general question, for instance, the exclusion of the 'private' world of family and employment from evaluation in terms of justice and equality. They also question the recurrent and characteristically liberal endeavour to separate 'the right' from 'the good', or deontological from consequentialist ethics, or norms from values, dichotomies which, in feminist theory, emerge in the context of the public and the private worlds, with men, drawing on an ideology of impersonal and neutral justice, dominating in the public sphere and patriarchal 'benevolence' prevailing in the so-called 'private' world of family, friendship and employment. These are major themes in contemporary theories of justice, the implications of which are still to be worked out (see Pateman, 1988).

Contemporary feminist thought has been extended to include a critique of the whole idea of rights, or indeed justice itself, as a normative foundation of a human society. The individualistic competitiveness of rights and the rule-dependency of justice are argued to exclude the spontaneous contextual caring and sharing of the private sphere which should, on this view, be extended to the public world and substitute caring for regulation. This cultural critique echoes socialist concerns about rights (see Campbell, 1983) and is to be found in communitarian analyses of the priority given to individual rights.

Further, postmodern feminists, turning the tables on their liberal forebears, are suspicious of all grand theories, particularly theories of justice, which, in their very theoretical nature, tend to exclude what is different about women and are in general insensitive to the differences between women of different races, classes and circumstances, swamping the contextualised concerns of all members of society in fine-sounding generalisations which are expressed in terms of normative measures that are unresponsive to multiple gender perspectives. In consequence there is a growing emphasis on the cultural and sometimes the genetic differences between men and women which are ignored in the pursuit of allegedly universal but actually male characteristics.

There are many themes which could be taken up and explored with respect to feminism and justice. Some of these relate to the suspicion of rule-governance which many feminists share with socialist theorists. There is, for instance, the famous thesis of Carol Gilligan that there is a major psychological divide between the 'justice perspective, often equated with male reasoning' which places emphasis on rules and rights, and the more feminine caring perspective in which 'relationships become the figure, defining self and others' and what matters is sustaining good relationships, not establishing whose rights have been violated (see Gilligan, 1987, pp.33–5; and Noddings, 1984).

Feminist themes are also pertinent to the doubts which we have cast on the claim that justice is unquestionably the overriding consideration, even if only in the public domain. Indeed the radical feminist emphasis on the priority of caring can be seen as an endorsement of the thesis that humanity should often trump justice, rather than vice versa (see Held, 1995).

I have chosen to concentrate on the work of Iris Marion Young, one of a limited number of contemporary feminists who do not wish to repudiate the discourse of justice and seek to reclaim it for themselves, not because they wish to retreat into unreconstructed liberal feminism, but because they see in the traditional dialogue elements which can be developed to good effect in the furtherance of feminist causes. Carol Smart (1989) is a pioneer in this regard. Another feminist who retains the discourse of justice, Claudia Carol, goes so far as to endorse the role of desert in a conception of justice which is pertinent to gender injustice since 'fairness in friendship does require responsiveness to pesonal desert and worthiness' (Held, 1995, p.82).

Young takes the position that 'issues of gender and sexuality should be analyzed as issues of justice', for, 'as the primary political virtue, justice should be central to feminist moral theory and politics' (Young, 1997, pp.95–7). In her important book, *Justice and the Politics of Difference* (1990), Young fastens on to the fact that the discourse of justice is in large part a discourse of injustice, of wrong, and of unacceptable harms. Distinctively, she urges that

> 'instead of focussing on distribution, a conception of justice should begin with the concept of domination and oppression. Such a shift brings out issues of decision-making, division of labor, and culture that bear on social justice but are often ignored in philosophical discussions. It also exhibits the importance of social group differences in structuring social relations and oppression; typically, philosophical theories of justice have operated with a social ontology that has no room for the concept of social groups. I argue that while others are oppressed, social justice requires explicitly acknowledging and attending to those groups in order to undermine their oppression.' (1990, p.4)

This chapter focuses on the issues of power and group oppression as they are raised by Young, not as a grand theory, but as neglected themes.

A feminist reconstruction of justice

It is a refreshing feature of Young's book that it breaks with what can reasonably be seen as the male-dominated approach to justice and reaffirms some neglected aspects of the discourse of justice which have evident bearing on disadvantaged and marginalised groups. She offers a perspective which provides a firm grounding for strong affirmative action and revives what was formerly a conservative and corporatist idea of group representation as a novel democratic means of reducing injustice as oppression.

In her preliminary analysis of justice, Young declines to be dictated to by standard conceptual claims about justice and, in a pragmatic way characteristic of many contemporary feminists, seeks to draw on the power of the language of justice to stir moral indignation and provoke social criticism (1990, p.35). In this regard, she is open to using any methodology which will assist this task.

More particularly, she rejects the thesis that distribution of benefits and burdens is the be-all and end-all of justice. Redistribution does feature in her total scheme, but as a subordinate element in an approach which highlights liberty over distributional equality by emphasising the active, doing aspects of human experience over the passive, consumer-oriented possessive view: 'Social justice means the elimination of institutionalized domination and oppression' (1990, p.15). This viewpoint is largely excluded by distributive theories which 'tend to focus on material goods and in relation to nonmaterial goods renders them static' (1990, p.16). Further, there are some values, such as self-respect, which are fundamental to justice and yet which cannot be concieved of as things which can be distributed fairly. Indeed, rights themselves are difficult to think of as possessions that can be distributed, for rights are ultimately a matter of correct interpersonal relationships, which lay down how people may interact with each other, rather than things to be divided up equally and shared around. To this extent Young goes along with Nozick's critique of end-state theory, according to which the objective of justice is to establish and reestablish a certain pattern of distribution (see p.64). This means that 'Distributive issues are certainly important but the scope of justice extends beyond them to include the political as such, that is all aspects of institutional organization insofar as they are potentially subject to collective decision' (1990, p.9). In particular, she argues that the dominant distributive paradigm does not fit such matters as child custody disputes and issues concerning the family, reproduction and sexuality (1997, p.97).

All this is, however, a matter of enlarging rather than narrowing current conceptions of justice. She seeks to retain the liberal insight that individual freedom matters and accepts that this means endorsing a pluralism of values which permits individuals to pursue their own ideas of the good life, but this does not mean that these ideals of the good life are not intimately involved with justice. Justice concerns establishing institutional arrangements which allow the legitimate expression of these conceptions of the good life, in line with the moral tradition of the ancient Greek philosophers: 'Social justice concerns the degree to which a society contains and supports the institutional context necessary for the realization of these values' (1990, p.36). This is very much in line with the communitarian critique of liberalism's concentration on justice or 'the right' as opposed to values or 'the good', except that Young seeks to incorporate these values into the judgements which have to be made in evaluating cultural arrangements, and thus includes both the right and the good in her conception of justice.

This institutional context, it turns out, is essentially a democratic one in which those affected by social norms have the opportunity and capacity to affect the outcome, provided that the democratic process is directed towards liberation from oppression and domination: 'I have proposed an enabling conception of justice. Justice should refer not only to distribution, but also to the institutional conditions necessary for the development and exercise of individual capacities and collective communication and cooperation' (1990, p.39).

This is clearly a very broad interpretation of justice. Indeed, Young claims that 'the concept of justice is coextensive with the political' in that 'when people say a rule or practice or cultural meaning is wrong and should be changed, they are usually making claims about social justice' (1990, p.9). In effect this means that any 'good reason' is relevant to issues of justice (1990, p.216). However, justice is restricted to the critique of institutional arrangements, particularly with respect to their role in empowering human agents.

Moreover, justice is definitively grounded in a particular type of critical reflection which arises from 'hearing a cry of suffering or distress or feeling distressed oneself' (1990, p.6). This reflection presupposes the centrality of human desires and the experience of disappointment when these are frustrated. The negativity of these basic human experiences gives rise to the immanent critique of the social situations from which they arise. Contextualising her position further, Young points to social movements of the 1960s and 1970s in the United States whose consciousness is not reflected in the philosophical theories of justice which currently dominate (see 1990, p.7).

Key elements of this consciousness include the neglect of social and gender differences involved in current oppression and domination, the hidden partiality of the language of impartiality and equal rights, the social significance of groups as distinct from individuals, and awareness that it is social structures and institutions more than individual evil intent that produces the injustices which characterise much modern life.

We have seen that liberal feminists stress human similarities as the basis for claims to equal treatment. In common with other radical feminists, Young stresses human differences as the basis for claims to equal outcomes. The divide between those who stress sameness and those who emphasise difference has given rise to major debates within feminism as to the comparative significance of similarity and difference. Some emphasise that inequality arises from assuming differences between genders when there are none which are relevant to social justice. Others point out that treating people as if they are the same when their situations are quite different is also damaging and unfair. Young repeatedly emphasises the problem of difference: 'This book seeks to show how a denial of difference contributes to social group oppression and to argue for a politics that recognizes rather than suppresses difference' (1990, p.10). She is particularly wary of the idea of 'impartiality' which suggests that 'all moral situations should be treated in accordance with the same rules'. It is this outlook, she thinks, which enables those exercising political and administrative power – principally men – to generalise from their own experiences and to neglect those that are foreign to them.

The same problem of suppressed difference crops up in a number of guises. The idea of merit, for instance, assumes that there can be criteria for distributing jobs and other benefits in a way which is culturally neutral. The idea of community also serves to suppress the awareness that 'communities' are made up of groups whose situations are starkly different. She is therefore suspicious of communitarianism to the extent that it emphasises the 'logic of identity and excludes difference', preferring the idea of the city to that of the community because it has 'an openness to unassimilated otherness' (1990, p.227).

The emphasis here is on differences between groups rather than simply between individuals. Indeed the notion of the group is central to Young's approach to the causes of oppression which are ignored in liberal individualism. Her definition of a group refers to

people with similar ways of life and experiences which form the
basis for an associational relationship:

> 'A social group is a collective of persons differentiated from at
> least one other group by cultural forms, practices, or ways of life.
> Members of a group have a special affinity with each other
> because of their similar experiences of a ways of life, which
> prompts them to associate with one another more than with
> those not identified with the group.' (1990, p.43)

This is very different from an 'aggregate' which is simply the total
of those persons who have a similar characteristic. Such similarities are important for group formation, but the phenomenon which
primarily characterises a group is the shared experiences which
generate a felt affinity and lead to cooperative association and a
sense of common identity. Such groups have a permanence
and significance quite distinct from interest groups and ideological
political groups which she sees as transient aggregations of individuals.

This analysis is in line with the general communitarian critique of
individualism which, it is claimed, ignores the fact that even an
individual's personal identity is tied in with their social relationships
so that the idea of individuals as such creating social organisations
is simply inconceivable. The experience of being an individual
emerges from certain types of social relationship. This means that
Young can attribute a distinct and independent ontology or existence to groups and make them the focus of her approach to justice.
This in turn, enables her to stress differences between individuals in
terms of group differences, and to pave the way for making a
positive valuation of group differences: 'Social justice ... requires
not the melting away of differences, but institutions that promote
reproduction of an aspect of group differences without oppression'
(1990, p.47).

Young's collectivist analysis of social structure highlights her
point that most injustice does not arise from the intentions of any
individual or aggregate of individuals to oppress or dominate
others. These outcomes arise from social arrangements which transcend the intentions and control of individual persons. This is not a
universal claim, since there have been and are intentionally committed atrocities in human history, but it is a fact about her own
society where

'the disadvantage and injustice some people suffer not because a tyrannical power coerces them, but because of the everyday practices of well-intentioned liberal society... the vast and deep injustices some people suffer as a consequence of often unconscious assumptions and reactions of well-meaning people in ordinary interactions, media cultural stereotypes, and structural features of bureacratic and market mechanisms – in short the normal circumstances of everyday life.' (1990, p.41)

Young's commitment to difference and to cultural specificity are part of her antipathy to framing a general theory of justice. Theorising she regards as a form of oppressive activity to be avoided. This is a characteristic postmodern position whose feminist guise is a rejection of theorising as an essentially male activity. In Young's words, 'I do not construct a theory of justice. A theory of justice typically derives fundamental principles of justice that apply to all or most societies, whatever their concrete configuration and social relations, from a few general premises about the nature of human beings, the nature of societies, the nature of reason' (1990, p.4). Her complaint against theories of justice is that they oversimplify and assume a position of judging societies from an external point of view which is comprehensive, self-standing and produces a unified and timeless set of unchallengeable principles.

In fact, not all theories exhibit these characteristics, but Young has in mind those approaches, said to be characteristic of Enlightenment theories, which do lay claim to a rationality which defies social context. This applies to those social theories which seek to turn the study of society into a science, such as Posner's economic analysis, and also to those which claim knowledge of eternal moral truths, as the early Rawls may be interpreted. Rawls's approach is 'theoretical' because it seeks to build on moral intuitions which transcend our particular circumstances. Young seeks to be nontheoretical in that her objective is to articulate the experience of oppression, not to make acontextual generalisations about it. Her approach is not to look for a priori insights into universal moral truth but to listen to the pleas and claims of other people, for 'The call to "be just" is always situated in concrete social, and political practices that precede and exceed the philosopher' (1990, p.5).

Young is here articulating the position of an acceptable type of theory, critical theory, which takes its starting-point from a value-laded commitment to a particular social experience in order to find within it the basis for a transformative response which makes that situation more acceptable. This is a process which is highly intellectual but not separated from emotion. It requires conceptual clarification, but not an appeal to timeless or objective conceptual essences:

> 'Rejecting theory does not entail eschewing rational discourse about justice. Some modes of reflection, analysis, and argument aim not at building a systematic theory, but at clarifying the meanings of concepts and issues, describing and explaining social relations, and articulating and defending ideals and principles. Reflective discourse about justice makes arguments, but these are not intended as definitive demonstrations. They are addressed to others and await their response, in a situated political dialog. In this book I engage in such situated analysis and arguments in the mode of critical theory.' (1990, p.6)

In the case of justice, critical theory means responding to suffering as experienced by others or oneself and drawing on these experiences to understand the situations from which they arise and formulate proposals for radical change. Grand theories get in the way of this process which is better carried on by political dialogue than by philosophical reflection. The defect of theorising, in the sense in which it is criticised, is that its outcome is too abstract to be of any real use to those whose suffering is at stake and tends to bypass the factors in the particular social situations which require to be tackled and changed.

Oppression and Domination

The context-dependent approach of Young's critical theory does not exclude some pragmatic and tentative universal claims. Thus, human beings, she claims, are better conceived of as doers rather than passive receivers, which gives rise to the most important values in any conception of the good life that can be expressed in two simple propositions: '(1) developing and exercising one's own capacities and expressing one's experiences, and (2) participating in determining one's actions and conditions of one's action'. These, she says, are 'universal values, in the sense that they imply the equal moral worth of all persons, and thus justice requires their promotion for everyone. To these two general values correspond two social conditions that define justice: oppression, the institutional constraint on self-development, and domination, the institutional constrain on self-determination' (1990, p.37). These universals are presented as extrapolations drawn from the experiences of particular oppressed social groups, such as 'socialists, radical feminists, American Indian activists, gay and lesbian activists'(1990, p.39) and other oppressed groups, all of whom share the assumption that 'the basic equality of life situation for all persons is a moral value; that there are deep injustices in our society that can be rectified only by basic institutional changes' (1990, p.14).

This 'enabling conception of justice'(1990, p.39) breaks down into two aspects of empowerment which are responses to the twin evils of oppression and domination, the central types of constraint that inhibit equal life situations.

Oppression relates to the inability to fulfil and express human capacities, which, in her society at least, she imputes to the unintended consequences of specific social structures. The common element in all forms of oppression is that it involves 'some inhibition of [people's] ability to develop and exercise their capacities and express their needs, thoughts and feelings' (1990, p.40). Domination is the structural exclusion of people from a role in deciding how to conduct their own lives. Injustice is where domination leads to oppression. This is why justice is not fundamentally about distribution since domination is a form of relationship rather than a quantifiable good that can be shared around equally (see 1990, p.32). Both oppression and domination are most forcefully illustrated in racism and sexism.

Oppression is divided into five different types or categories: 'exploitation, marginalization, powerlessness, cultural imperialism, and violence' (1990, pp. 42f). Exploitation takes up the Marxist conception of the systematic transfer of the output of those who work to other social groups who have not shared in that labour. The illustrations she uses are not the male-centred class divisions analysed by Marx himself, but the situation of women whose work is expropriated by men who would not be able to achieve their material and social goals without the ongoing support of women's work. This is oppressive not so much because of the maldistribution that results, but because of the structural coercion involved in the situation from which exploitation arises (see 1990, p.49). This may not be something for which individual men are to be blamed, since they generally have no choice but to rely on women's work to survive in a society which is structured as it is, but it is 'oppression' in the sense which applies in modern liberal democracies.

Marginalisation is that feature of contemporary societies whereby those groups for whom the economy has no useful role are simply put to one side and forgotten. Those people whom the system has no use for, or chooses not to involve in mainstream economic and social life, find themselves in the position of having no real chance to develop their capacities and express themselves. This applies to those who are unemployed or homeless, or who suffer from a mental illness.

Powerlessness, on the other hand, applies also to those who are in employment, but whose work experience is a crushing negation of their freedom to be themselves and develop their abilities. Thus, in most work situations the majority of people lack any genuine autonomy. They have no chance to be creative and engage in activities which generate respect. Ordinary non-professional employees are without authority, without a sense of self-signific-ance, and overall have no real decision-making power. This too gives rise to a sense of oppression and a conviction that the system is unjust.

Politically, powerlessness is manifest in the situation where government policy is settled by the congruence of pressure groups to the exclusion of those who are principally affected by the decisions in question. The interest group pluralism described by current political science and regarded as typical of liberal democracies is something which works to the exclusion of citizen participation in the interests of powerful groups. Similarly, the legal process becomes the domain of specialist groups and unresponsive to the needs of those who are unable to utilise its services.

Cultural imperialism refers to the ideological function of culture which presents the ruling group's view of the world as if it were the sole view and excludes from that world-view the perspective and experience of other groups, which are thereby made to feel as if they were quite 'other', even non-existent or invisible, in their own society (see 1990, p.59). Finally, the violence which contributes to oppression is the use of force in ways which humiliate and terrify its victims. Beyond the horror of the actual physical attacks and injuries there is a deeply oppressive aspect of the unprovoked attacks and commonplace use and threat of domestic violence which serve to undermine self-respect and inhibit the capacities for self-expression.

None of these sources of oppression are removed by a more equitable taxation system or a reallocation of distributable goods. All of them call for structural changes which individuals alone cannot achieve. Hence the dissatisfaction which leads to insurgent political movements and the general disillusionment with the nature of modern social and economic life.

At the core of Young's critique of modern systems is a penetrating analysis of the rhetoric of impartiality which is used to settle disputes in ways that do not address the underlying structural problems of oppression and domination. She articulates her position in relation to that stream of feminist thought which tends to reject justice and rights altogether. Young notes:

'A growing body of feminist-inspired theory has challenged the paradigm of moral reasoning as defined in the discourse of justice and rights. In this paradigm moral reasoning consists in adopting an impartial and impersonal point of view on a situation, detached from any particular interests at stake, weighing all interests equally, and arriving at a conclusion which conforms to general principles of justice and rights impartially applied to the case at hand.' (1990, p.96)

This powerful feminist theme is represented most famously by Carol Gilligan's contrast between male children's concern for rules, rights and justice and female children's greater preoccupation with cooperation and sharing (Gilligan, 1982), which has been developed into a full-scale oppostion of an 'ethic of rights' and 'an ethic of caring' or an 'ethics of responsibility' (Blum, 1980; Noddings, 1984) that draws on communitarian socialist suspicion of rule-based relationships, principally because they dehumanise the natural and spontaneous cooperative conduct which features in genuine egalitarian communities and do not fit the personal relationships which call for engagement and commitment, as in family, friendship and close community situations. Further, the ethics of rights inevitably solidify the unjust relationships characteristic of oppressive societies.

Young herself adopts a position nearer to that of Friedman (1987) and Okin (1989), who distance themselves from any straight opposition of justice and care, with the continuing assumption of two spheres, a private one for caring and a public one for justice. Young concentrates instead on a sweeping attack on impartiality as the basis for moral thinking in any sphere.

This critique of impartiality centres on her defence of difference, for

> 'the ideal of impartiality in moral theory expresses the logic of identity that seeks to reduce difference to unity. The stance of detachment and dispassion that supposedly produces impartiality is attained only by abstracting from the particularities of situation, feeling, affiliation, and point of view. These particularities still operate, however, in the actual context of the action.' (1990, p.97)

Superficially, this critique can be countered by seeing that the rules used in impartial judgement are more complex rules, which take into account the differences which are suppressed by very general and abstract principles. It may be argued that no rules can be specific enough to cover the particular situation of each oppressed person, but it can still be maintained that many situations could be improved by making general principles somewhat more specific in identifying, for instance, women, blacks, black women, American Indian women. Indeed, it would seem that the collectivities which meet Young's definition of a social group could form the basis of such classificatory rules.

However, this leaves untouched the deeper claim that the ideal of impartiality encourages certain unacceptable dichotomies. One is between the private sphere, which historically is women's territory, and the public sphere, reserved for men. This is unacceptable when oppression is as much a feature of the private as of the public world. Another unacceptable dichotomy is that between feeling (private and feminine) and reason (public and male). On philosophical grounds it can be shown that this opposition is untenable, not only because reason is driven by feeling and feelings are affected by reasoning, but because the two cannot be uncoupled in practical reasoning. On political grounds it is equally suspect because of the prioritising of 'reason' over 'feeling'. This applies also to the higher status of what is 'universal' over what is 'particular', an assumption which downgrades genuine concern for individuals and particulars.

These points are developed by Young in relation to the theme of 'identity' as explored in postmodern philosophy (see Irigaray, 1985) which opposes the reduction of diversity to unity through a single comprehensive formula by demonstrating that all judgements of identity presuppose at the same time the identification of differences. Young summarises their position lucidly:

> 'Difference, as I understand it, names both the play of concrete events and the shifting differentiation on which signification depends. Any identifiable something presupposes a something else against which it stands as a background, from which it is differentiated. Understood as different entities, events, meanings are neither identical nor opposed. They can be likened to in certain respects, but similarity is never sameness and the similar can be noticed only through difference. Difference, however, is not absolute otherness, a complete absence of relationship or shared attributes.' (1990, p.98)

This highly abstract philosophical analysis is used to identity a frame of mind or mode of thinking which seeks to isolate distinct elements of the world in order to control it, with the unfortunate consequences that those things which are left out are rejected and ignored as 'other', leading to misleading dichotomies between essences and accidents, good and bad, normative and deviant (see 1990, p.99), for instance, institutionalised 'marriage' privileges certain types of relationship (such as heterosexual ones) over other (1990, p.106).

The upshot of this analysis for moral reasoning is that we should abandon the so-called impartial point of view in which we seek to detach ourselves from our own situation and the multitude of particularities that in fact make up our own selves in the mistaken view that the moral is the universal. In particular, we should abandon the idea that the moral reasoner, without feeling, attachments or viewpoint, should apply the same universal principles to all persons as an undifferentiated unity. The weakness of universal impartiality in ethics as 'the moral point of view' is first that in so far as we do succeed in getting near to such a point of view, we lose the capacity to make any decisions of right or wrong, good or bad. A thoroughly detached person is an empty person, more amoral than moral. This, critics allege, is how Rawls's original position under the veil of ignorance turns out: empty and unknowable.

Another associated weakness of impartiality is that it inevitably leads to the rejection of what are in fact highly relevant differences between individuals and groups. Rawls may say that his individuals, or, as we have seen, his one individual in the original position, know all about the differences that pertain between actual persons in actual societies; nevertheless, these are not the factors that dictate his judgements as may be seen in the highly general maxims that emerge from his model. The 'view from everywhere' turns out to be 'the view from nowhere'.

The practical effects of the pursuit of impartiality is the neglect of oppressed groups whose views are excluded or marginalised in the processes by which universal laws are formulated. The no doubt unrealisable ideal of complete impartiality reinforces and sustains oppression and domination, because what actually happens is that the viewpoint of partial groups comes to be viewed as the universal viewpoint, and *their* world becomes *the* world. This may be seen as a failure to be sufficiently impartial, but the analysis shows that, morally, impartiality is bound to be a failure because it abstracts from the sight and sound of the particular oppressions from which morality stems.

Nowhere is this seen more clearly than in the idea that there can be a system of rights that represents an impartial or neutral point of view within the framework of which people can pursue their private visions of the good life. The rigid dichotomy between the right and the good as the foundation of the phoney idea of a neutral state represents the tangible and unacceptable outcome of the mistaken faith in impartiality as a moral guide. It follows that, if justice is to be a moral concept it cannot be opposed to caring: 'As a virtue, justice cannot stand opposed to personal need, feeling and desire, but names the institutional conditions that enable people to meet their needs and express their desires' (1990, p.121).

Young's alternative to impartiality is justice: justice first in relation to oppression and its structural causes, and justice in relation to domination and its political manifestations. In moving from the consideration of oppression to domination the focus moves to politics, in particular to democratic politics of a sort which involves everyone, particularly oppressed groups, in working out a new structure for an empowered society. The vision is of a politics of dialogue in which individual needs and interests are all on the table to be considered and taken account of in a manner which is fair and responsive.

Here Young draws on the civic republican tradition in which participation in politics was a duty of the individual to engage in dialogue about what constitutes the common or public good. She accepts the idea involved here of a communicative ethics according to which moral rationality is 'understood as communicative inter-action... dialogic, the product of the interaction of a plurality of subjects under conditions of equal power that do not suppress the interests of any', a notion very much akin to that of Jürgen Habermas.

However, the civil republican model is very much a male model which confines and excludes women, together with the affective, desiring, bodily-oriented aspects of life with which women were identified. 'Impartial civilized reason characterizes the virtue of republican man who rises above passion and desire... Modern normative reason and its political expression is the idea of the civic republic... attain unity and coherence through the expulsion and confinement of everything that would threaten to invade the polity with differentiation' (1990, p.111). It is by broadening this dialogue to take in the particular, the affective and the neglected differences that the ideal of civil republicanism can be brought in to provide the means for a political system which overcomes domination.

The drive to feminise politics leads Young to advocate special representation for oppressed groups as the only way to ensure a fair outcome of such dialogue. This is because she is not entirely trustful of dialogic processes which smack of the disciplined and unemo-tional attributes of the 'impartial' male and are open to the manip-ulation of dominant groups which can better utilise the capacities of speech and persuasion as they can other resources. She is also wary of talk of dialogue which presupposes underlying agreements. She therefore prefers a more communicative model of democracy in which differences are recognised as real and permanent, as well as one which is free of all elements of domination. To this end, the realities of group oppression require that there should be group representation in such a system so 'constructing a protection-of-interests' (1993, p.123) by ensuring that the interests of these 'others' are not ignored in the determination of a fair outcome: 'I propose a system of representation for oppressed and disadvan-taged social groups as a means of addressing the problems of quantitatively fair democracy' (1993, p.135). This is intended to enhance the sort of non-domination which is both central to her analysis of justice and at the core of her conception of democracy, themes which I consider further in the context of Habermas's pro-cedural account of justice and democracy.

Affirmative action and the myth of merit

The title of this section is that of Chapter 7 of *Justice and the Politics of Difference* which has the most specific application of her theory of justice. It is in the context of affirmative action programmes, which seek to give priority in employment to black or female persons so that as groups they are better represented in the work-force, that her emphasis on the importance of thinking in terms of social groups comes most clearly to the fore.

In Young's analysis affirmative action programmes challenge both the primacy of the principle of non-discrimination and the individualism which are central to liberal theories of equality. Host-ility to affirmative action derives, she believes, from an overly individualistic view of societies in association with the distributive model of justice which ignores the position of oppressed groups.

Young's critique of liberal equality of opportunity, which is based entirely on non-discrimination, is to tackle the concept of merit which is used in the liberal view of distributive justice in employ-ment, namely that some positions are more important than others and should be paid more than others, and that individuals should compete for these positions on the basis of their qualities as an individual which, on non-discrimination principles, excludes such factors as race and gender which are irrelevant to the capacity to perform the jobs in question.

Young's position is not so much to question the idea of merit as such as to question its applicability to employment. She questions the assumption that it is possible to test employment skills accord-ing to evaluatively neutral standards which identify who is most meritorious amongst candidates for particular positions, for 'most criteria of evaluation used in our society, including educational credentials and standardized testing, have normative and cultural content'. 'Since impartial, value-neutral, scientific measures of merit do not exist, I argue that a major issue of justice must be who decides what are appropriate qualifications for a given position, how they will be assessed, and whether particular individuals have them' (1990, p.193).

In practice, Young maintains, the principle of merit works out just the same as traditional hierarchies:

> 'A class of powerful people establishes normative criteria, some
> of which have the function of affirming its power and enforcing

the organized system that makes it possible. To occupy positions within the hierarchy they choose persons who have certain status credentials (instead of coming from the "right" family they went to the "right" school) and persons who by nature or training exhibit the preferred behavioral and temperamental characteristics.' (1990, p.212)

Turning on its head the argument of Rawls that differentially rewarded jobs are justified if they are open on conditions of fair equality of opportunity, Young argues that if there cannot be appointment on the basis of merit, the hierarchy of jobs cannot be legitimated. In its place, justice requires that we have a range of jobs which are similar to professional ones in that they permit individuals to develop and express their capacities, thus addressing the issues of exploitation, powerlessness and cultural imperialism. Here again, a democratic structure is seen as a possible remedy for injustice.

Young contrasts her approach to that which justified affirmative action as a means of recompensing past injury through exclusion from employment on grounds of race or gender. This, she points out, addresses a relatively small range of examples and is exceptionally difficult to implement. A better argument is that affirmative action counters ongoing discriminatory attitudes in the system of appointments and promotion. This is a matter of acting in a discriminatory way by preferring 'worse qualified' blacks and women on the grounds that there is actual discrimination in deciding who is better qualified. In theory, this means that affirmative action can be phased out as the principle of non-discrimination is more recognised and applied in practice.

All this, Young claims, assumes that discrimination is the problem, but this is not the case. Discrimination matters only because of the oppression associated with it: 'Taking a principle of equal treatment, or non-discrimination, as an absolute or primary principle of justice assumes...an ideal of equality as sameness...the elimination of transcendence of group differences' and is therefore unacceptably 'assimilationist' (1990, p.195). On her model of group equality what we should strive for is an equal presence of groups in all institutional positions, something which will always require an element of differential treatment. Affirmative action serves the cause of eliminating oppression, not fulfilling some abstract and unrealisable principle of individual equality.

This also fits into Young's theme that injustice is more structural than intentional. Non-discrimination on the liberal model is primarily aimed at intentional or at least conscious biases on the part of those involved in positions of power. As it is often difficult to prove that there is such bias in particular cases, anti-discrimination law may not require proof of deliberate bias, but point to a pattern of decisions which lead to outcomes that disproportionately impact on the welfare of particular groups. Thus affirmative action programmes may set targets for employing people in a way which has the end-state of mirroring the race or gender proportions in employment with those which pertain in the community at large. However, as long as these programmes are seen simply as a way of getting at conscious discrimination, they still overlook the deeper causes of inequality in the oppression of particular social groups, the facts which make it impossible for them to compete on equal terms with those situated in more favoured groups. The discrimination approach, by focusing on the perpetrator rather then the victim, fails to address the root issue.

This then takes us back to the theme of ideology, for the liberal model of discrimination appears to be affirming a universal equality while in effect serving to reinforce hierarchy by drawing attention away from the causes of oppression. Non-discrimination should not, therefore, be seen as an end in itself but as a possible means to greater justice. It is a rather ineffective means in oppressive societies unless it involves strong and continuing affirmative action to maintain acceptable group representation in employment as well as in politics. The problem with the merit system is more who makes the decisions than what decisions are made.

In working out the democratic mechanism for arriving at acceptable decisions in the area of employment, Young makes it clear that participation in the decision-making has to be based on working out what is fair as well as what is acceptable to all:

> 'As I understand it, fairness in such decisions include the following: (1) Criteria for qualifications should be explicit and public, along with the values and purposes they serve. (2) Criteria should not exclude any social groups from consideration from positions, either explicitly or implicitly. (3) All candidates for positions should be given consideration according to formal procedures which are publicly announced. (4) People with particular group affinities, social positions, or personal attributes may be

preferred, but only to undermine oppression or compensate for disadvantage, and never to reinforce privilege.' (1990, p.212)

This analysis of the nature and purpose of affirmative action programmes neatly captures the core elements of Young's theory of justice, bringing in the economic and social analysis of oppression as the experience which fuels the real-life discourse of justice, and the essentially political notion of domination which points to the solution to injustice lying in a system of communicative democracy in which groups have a constitutionally recognised role.

Interestingly, her critique of distributive justice does not entail abandoning at least some of the core ideals of liberal justice. There remains an affirmation of equal worth, in her case based on the notion of human beings as creative agents who suffer through the denial of self-expression. Even the significance of merit remains in those areas where it can be given acceptable rationales and implementation. She accepts that there can be good reasons for differential pay which include 'rewarding hard work and extra effort, compensating the sacrifice that may be involved in acquiring specialized skills, providing incentives to perform otherwise less desirable work, and rewarding better than average productivity'. Indeed she assumes a meritorian approach to criticise 'the huge differentials typical in American society' (1990, p.216).

Apart from the evident problems which would arise in the institutionalising of social group political representation (see Phillips, 1993, pp.99ff.) (which groups, on what basis and with what powers?), the shifting emphasis in the analysis of justice from content to decision-making raises complex problems for both justice and democracy. What happens, for instance, if a properly constituted communicative democracy comes out with structures which do not match the ideas of fairness and justice which are used to justify the democratic constitution in the first place. How can we know that such democratic systems would adopt the enabling conception of democracy? Some of the answers, no doubt, lie in the fact that it is that conception of justice that legitimises communicative democracy, but it is more than just a fanciful possibility that those who participate in such a system would have very different conceptions of what constitutes oppression, domination, fairness and 'good reasons'. In these circumstances Young is bold to hang on to both a substantive conception of justice in terms of oppression and domination and a procedural mechanism for putting it into effect. In the next chapter, I consider a more purely procedural theory which goes beyond the association of justice and democracy to something more like an assimilation of justice into democracy. In so doing it is in danger of losing the substantive bite provided by those feminist theories of oppression which are rooted in the adverse experiences of actual social groups.

10 Justice and Democracy: Habermas and the Promise of Politics

Most contemporary liberal theorists of justice attempt to derive substantive principles of justice from some combination of debate, consent, information and impartiality. In many respects the early Rawls is the boldest of these since he seeks to bring together a decision-making model for institutionalising informed and impartial consent with a separate claim that what comes out of this model are principles which we can independently evaluate as sound and acceptable standards of justice. Drawing on both sources of moral insight he seeks to make them mutually reinforcing by drawing them together through a process of critical reflection aimed at 'reflective equilibrium' (see p.99). Having exposed himself on both these fronts – procedural and substantive – Rawls has attracted a barrage of criticism which has led him to retreat into a more secure but less daring position from which he holds himself out as doing no more than providing a path to a pragmatic political consensus in certain types of liberal society. Similar fates have befallen the less ambitious approach of Dworkin and the more simplistic theories of Nozick and Posner.

In contrast, Jürgen Habermas appears less daring in that he seeks to establish only the procedural path to justice. In his case, this involves actual ongoing dialogue rather than the purely counterfactual and often fanciful hypotheses of other theorists He derives from his analysis of actual social interactions as experienced by those involved in honest dialogue what he calls an 'ideal speech situation' involving conditions of freedom and equality that generates 'communicative rationality'. He does not go on to test this path by reference to moral critique of what is to be found at its destination. That would be to prejudge the outcome of actual deliberative dialogue. In this respect his is a theory which Rawls would call 'pure procedural justice', where everything depends on the procedure and there is no independent access to knowledge of the outcome.

Nevertheless, Habermas's position is potentially more powerful than the later Rawls's both in its claims to have achieved some philosophical grounding for his epistemic path to knowledge of justice and with respect to its applicability to real-life processes of social communication in contrast to the exercise of reflection by an imaginative and super-intelligent individual which is at the core of Rawls's more individualistic approach. Moreover, Habermas's method is, in general, less a priori in that he relies to a significant extent on the social theory which is drawn from the study of existing societies at particular stages of their development. In this he goes beyond the idea of 'neutral dialogue' over the distribution of power (see Ackerman, 1980), an approach covered in the first edition of this book which in other respects is a good and accessible introduction to the ideas propounded in greater detail and complexity by Habermas.

Again in contradistinction to the later Rawls, Habermas retains the claim that he has identified a method that enables communities to transcend their own culture and gain a perspective on those universal rights and duties which he equates with 'morality', the universal norms of justice, as opposed to 'ethics', that is, the values or goods of individuals or groups expressed in their self-understanding. Moreover, he is willing to argue that some existing political societies approximate closely enough to the ideal speech situations which generate moral truth to acquire moral and political legitimacy. In all this there is a strain of liberal universalism reminiscent of the early Rawls.

Habermas's model of deliberative democracy is that of a procedure which establishes legitimate claims to govern in the name of justice. It contains communitarian elements which root normative validity in the social life from whence political dialogue takes its origins. Habermas is accepting of the 'facticity' of social interaction, in much the same way as Dworkin incorporates in his rights schema the legal history of the jurisdiction in question, thus promising an attractive combination of liberal and communitarian traditions. Although Habermas seeks to distinguish his approach from those communitarians who argue that the language of justice cannot transcend the cultural context in which it operates, much of the force of his argument against 'philosophers of justice', like Rawls, is that they posit an unreal and acontextual ideal which is not sufficiently related either to what he calls the 'life world' of everyday existence or to the real world of actual political systems.

Habermas's vision of interactive dialogue differs from the model of restrained conversation put forward in Ackerman (1980) in that it aims to produce a measure of agreement on shared norms rather than a mere aggregate of self-interested preferences, thus bringing with it ideas of solidarity, loyalty, mutual respect and shared social understanding, all of which characterise the communitarian response to Rawls. An exciting and challenging thing about Habermas's approach is this combination of the philosophical impetus to moral rightness and the sociological focus on social cohesion. He maintains that the norms of justice which emerge from those communities which have progressed to a stage of rational communicative deliberation have an objectivity which transcends the cultural and political relativism in which communitarianism is based, thus offering what many people find a most attractive coalescence of competing traditions.

For all its procedural emphasis, Habermas's analysis of communicative rationality embodies some unexpectedly substantive ingredients which characterise the ideas of justice which we would expect to emerge from such dialogue, such as a commitment to political liberty and social equality. This is because equal and fair participation in the sort of dialogue that manifests communicative rationality presupposes a significant measure of social and economic equality. This happy coincidence of procedural and substantive virtues raises doubts about the initial moral neutrality of the theory that are similar to those which critics have raised against Rawls's original position. But any circularity which there may be in Habermas's elaborate theory is mediated by complex and wide-ranging sociological and philosophical analyses which merit careful study.

In this account of Habermas's theory of justice, I conclude by focusing on the way in which he draws on his analysis of justice to provide both justification and limitations for the judicial review of legislative action, that is, the power of the courts to override democratically enacted law. This is because there would appear to be a potential contradiction inherent in Habermas's combination of radical participatory democracy and judicial veto which undercuts his claim to have established a purely procedural theory of justice that subordinates the consideration of substantive principles of justice to the elaboration of a politicised version of his theory of discourse ethics. In so far as justice is constitutionalised in a system of judicial review of legislation it is in effect removed from the normal procedures of deliberative democracy.

Habermas's position on constitutional justice is unexpected in the light of his commitment to deliberative processes which involve all those affected by political decisions which are binding on them. His position on constitutional rights seems to depend on key ingredients of Rawls's liberal schema, such as the prioritising distinction between the right and the good. This may be seen in Habermas's contrast between 'morality', including justice, which has an objectivity which transcends the 'ethics' of normal social interactions, and his insistence that at least some law-making is about establishing norms of a deontological sort that are quite distinct from the evaluations we make in selecting certain lifestyles. In this respect the flavour of Habermas's recent work is distinctly liberal and certainly more universalistic than the later Rawls. Arguably, however, his general theory has potentially more radical democratic and egalitarian implications than his current constitutional theory displays.

The theory of social interaction

Habermas's work is voluminous and developing, and my account is unashamedly selective. His writings are deeply scholarly and a full appreciation of its nuances requires great knowledge of mainstream European social theory together with Anglo-American social and political philosophy. Indeed, sometimes his writing appears so eclectic that it is difficult to pin down his own distinctive contribution to contemporary political thought. My exposition draws, in the main, on *Knowledge and Human Interests* (1971), *The Theory of Communicative Action* (1984 and 1987), and his more recent *Between Fact and Norms* (1996a).

The importance of *Knowledge and Human Interests* is that it makes clear that Habermas is committed to a social theory which takes an insider or participant understanding of society rather than a detached scientific approach based entirely on external observation and generalisation. In his terminology, he prefers the historical–hermeneutical or interpretive method to the nomological or scientific law method in the study of society. In fact, his position is based more on the view that there is no such thing as purely objective or detached observer's knowledge, even of the natural world. It is in this context that he maintains that all knowledge is sought and obtained in the pursuit of certain human interests or concerns. In this he is primarily critical of philosophical positivism, according to which all knowledge is derived from science and all science is, at base, dependent on empirical generalisations which are testable by sensory observation. The interests which are served by natural science are, in Habermas's analysis, technical or manipulative. Science is directed towards the control of nature in the service of human objectives for 'theories of the empirical sciences contain information about reality from the point of view of technical control everywhere and at all times under specifiable conditions' (1971, p.162; see also p.309). For this reason empirical science is particularly useful in economic activity and Habermas, like Marx, has no problem in accepting its use in this domain, for the reliable predictions which they generate can be used to great practical effect. However, it is a mistake to think that empirical science is sufficient to solve human problems: 'the positivist self-understanding of the *nomological* sciences lends countenance to the substitution of technology for enlightened action. It directs the utilization of that scientific information from an illusory viewpoint, namely that the practical mastery of history can be reduced to technical control of objectified processes' (1971, p.316).

Habermas acknowledges that the methods of empirical science can be utilised in the study of society as well as nature, and that they may be helpful in the instrumental pursuit of social change, but he has three fundamental objections to the dominance of this approach in social studies. The first objection is that human beings can understand and then act to falsify social scientific generalisations about their conduct. In consequence, empirical social science is not as technically effective as natural science. The second is that it is impossible to have real insight into the nature of human existence without understanding it from an insider or participant point of view. The interactions of human beings are crucially dependent on their awareness of each other and the normative social environment in which their interactions take place. This is the hermeneutical approach adopted by many nineteenth-century historians and theologians and partially incorporated into social theory by Max Weber, whose exposition of *verstehen* (interpretive understanding) is enormously influential in the European tradition of social theory on which Habermas builds.

The third objection to the exclusive use of empirical methodologies in the social sciences is that positivist social science can be used to dominate human beings by giving them to believe that they have no choice but to conform to the laws of social science. Adopting a purely nomological, or empirical law, approach to human society is a misguided and immoral effort to manipulate and control people by denying them the capacity for autonomy, something to which Habermas ascribes great value. Positivistic social science is a form of ideology which manipulates through the false consciousness of its subjects. In contrast, the knowledge which emerges from such hermeneutical or interpretive social studies is practical, not theoretical, and is morally preferable in its recognition of human freedom. In this, Habermas carries on Marx's vision of emancipating humanity from enslavement to allegedly necessary scientific laws to the point where human beings can make their own history. However, contra Marx, this is not to be achieved by violent revolution, but by critical 'self-reflection' which 'releases the subject from dependence on hypostatized powers' (1971, p.310), although, as in Marx, the prospects of emancipation are related to social developments not in the control of the individual.

Like many Enlightenment theorists, Habermas fastens on language as the distinctive human capacity which enables us to appreciate the nature of human society. In Volume 2 of *The Theory of Communicative Action*, he develops this theme into a general theory which serves as the basis for his commitment to human emancipation through critical self-reflection. In his methodology, Habermas may be said to combine the philosophical methods of Immanuel Kant with the social theoretical approach of Max Weber. From the philosophical perspective his work utilises a version of transcendental deduction, a method used by Kant to uncover the presuppositions of certain unavoidable assumptions of everyday experience in order to establish a priori truths from which can be derived moral and epistemological claims. Thus, some of Kant's transcendental deductions lead him to assert the a priori nature of space and time as indispensable presuppositions of all our sensory experience. The same sort of reasoning establishes a necessary connection between moral choice and freedom of the will.

In a similar vein, Habermas claims that we cannot engage in reasoned argument about what we do and say without adopting commitments to sincerity, truth and rightness. Starting from our experience of engaging in genuine debate, Habermas draws out the assumptions of such linguistic activity and identifies them as necessary preconditions of linguistic social interaction. Although these presuppositions are the necessary framework of language-based social interaction they are not fully instantiated in actual interactions and are to that extent counter-factual. This means that the unavoidable assumptions of such linguistic exchanges can be used to identify the criteria for determining how we ought to go about attaining truth and justice. The bottom line of his analysis is that dialogue which embodies these characteristics of what he calls an 'ideal speech situation' is a sufficient requirement, not simply for successful communication, but for justification or legitimation of what is contained in that dialogue.

Understanding of the interactive dialogue from which these presuppositions are drawn takes Habermas deep into the study of language as a social practice and to the work of the great European social theorists such as Emile Durkheim, Max Weber and the Frankfurt School of which Habermas himself is a member. Following the analyses of Weber, he distinguishes two forms of social practice: the instrumental orientation of labour and the social interaction of persons. Labour involves all the connotations of Marx's analysis of productive engagement with nature, involving distinctive techniques that generate correspondingly distinctive social structures. This constitutes the economic or material domain of human life and coincides with his ideals of instrumental rationality. Interaction, on the other hand, has to do with the ways in which human societies and political systems develop and utilise rules to create forms of life that meet their interests as a community of persons. This broadly coincides with the social domain, which is the prime focus of his attention, although he draws on both instrumental and communicative rationality to establish the presuppositions from which his social and political theory of justice emerges.

Habermas uses social theory not simply to describe social communication but also to reconstruct it in a way which draws out and purifies its basic elements. Habermas adopts Max Weber's technique of articulating an 'ideal type' that brings together what are regarded as significant elements in historical phenomena from which extrapolations are made that can then be used as the basis for both understanding societies and making empirical generalisations about social phenomena. In particular, he uses his ideal type of communication as a basis for both describing and criticising actual social practices, an approach which leads to an ideal type of 'communicative rationality', an empirically and phenomenologic-ally based normative ideal grounded in the concept of an 'ideal speech situation' in which people strive to reach agreement about truth and justice in conditions which are uncoerced and in which participation is equally open to all. This 'ideal speech situation' and the associated idea of communicative rationality encapsulate Habermas's decisive assumptions about significant social phenom-ena in much the same way that Rawls projects his moral view into his 'original position', the main difference being that Habermas makes the claim that his ideal type is an emerging characteristic of modern societies associated, in particular, with the role of law in pluralistic post-capitalist democracies.

Habermas's striking thesis is that striving for agreement or con-sensus in an ideal speech situation focuses on the pursuit of know-ledge and legitimacy. This does not mean that these norms are identified with mere social agreement, for when people participate in such dialogue they are necessarily committed to a mutual search for objective truth and justice. This search for knowledge requires a commitment to establishing agreement in a manner which tran-scends mere shared belief. In genuine dialogue, truth is assumed to be more than inter-subjective agreement, and yet, although knowl-edge is not constituted by agreement, its attainment requires pursuit of agreement.

The ideal speech situation is most easily grasped if we think of a detached intellectual discussion about a disputed scientific theory, in which the appeal is always made to evidence and reason and never to the personal interests of prior dogmatic beliefs of those involved. The same principles apply to all claims and counter-claims as to the propriety of action-guiding beliefs and norms. In this respect, epistemology is not morally neutral. Communicative rationality is an enterprise which presupposes both freedom and justice, at least in so far as this involves equal participation in the dialogue. There is thus a close and necessary link between the intellectual and the moral aspects of discourse. Justice comes into the matter both as a requirement of communicative rationality in general, for dialogue presupposes the equality of the participants, and as one of the objectives to which communicative rationality is addressed, for instance, when seeking to justify legitimate social and economic inequalities. Truth and justice are thereby united as indis-pensable presuppositions of dialogue.

It is the combined methodology of transcendental deduction and ideal types which offers a way out of both philosophical abstraction and the relativism of simply accepting a community's culture, thus giving Habermas the basis for making socially grounded universal claims about justice. Since both procedures appear to involve elements of selectivity, Habermas's approach invites scepticism. In examining further the assumptions of discourse which are crucial in Habermas's methods, we must have a close eye on exactly what it is that allows Habermas to claim that his theory of justice is founded on an examination of actual linguistic social interactions and at the same time to come out with recommendations as to how societies can become more democratic and hence more just.

The presuppositions of communicative action

Following up the insights of linguistic philosophers into speech as a form of action, which can be traced to Wittgenstein's account of language as rooted in specific ways of life, Habermas explores the idea that talking is a type of action. To engage in dialogue is a performance with a certain content and purpose. Using the 'speech act' theory of John Searle, Habermas arrives at a view of communicative action as a communal alternative to the modern ideal of practical reason as the subjective capacity of the individual to determine what is in his own interests. This social communication is infused with what Habermas calls 'the linguistic telos of mutual understanding' which 'forms an ensemble of conditions that both enable and limit' (1996a, p.4).

The instrumental rationality, which we have seen is characteristic of labour, involves action that aims at the individual's own personal objectives. Habermas identifies, for instance, as a subclass of instrumental action the 'strategic' activity of influencing other people in order to achieve personal objectives, as in establishing a relationship for domination or manipulation of the other persons. Even in the supposedly individualistic model of instrumental reason individuals have beliefs about the material world in the light of which they make their personal choices. Given the existence of linguistic capacity, these beliefs can be subject to challenges which call for a response. From this emerges the idea of making claims about the world which are 'criticisable' and may or may not have 'validity' depending on whether they can be sustained. Essentially, these are claims to truth, which must be supported by giving reasons, and are valid if they can be agreed by all rational persons. Out of this comes a 'communicative rationality', that transcends instrumental reasons and seeks a mutual understanding and sharing of outlooks on a basis other than self-interest. In this way communicative rationality establishes the basis of genuine rather than merely strategic social cooperation.

Much depends here on what it is to be 'rational' in communicative discourse. This Habermas approaches through the analysis of the assumptions we bring to debates that we are conscious of in our everyday interactions. In communicative action which is, by definition, free from any attempt to persuade by non-rational or deceptive means, participants in dialogue must make certain suppositions, such as that linguistic expressions have identical meanings for different users, for only thus can the content of a thought be independent of the individual's experience and without it no communication is possible. Similarly it must be assumed that the same term keeps its same meaning in its different expressions. Further, we must assume that individual participants take responsibility for their views as being their own. If we engage in genuine dialogue then we must assume that all the participants are committed equally to reaching agreement, that they are committed to accepting only valid claims and that they are ready to accept the practical consequences of agreement. This amounts to the claim that the basic use of statements (that form of expression which may be true or false) requires a commitment to their truth or falsity. These are existential commitments within dialogue which cannot be bracketed off just for the sake of argument. To use Habermas's own example, to say 'this ball is red' is to assert that there is a ball which is red and not simply to present the idea of a red ball, and this is an assertion which we must act upon and be prepared to defend with reasons if challenged.

The transcendental deduction involved in this analysis is the same for 'rightness', or evaluative justification, as it is for truth. In debate on rights and duties we cannot but make validity claims about rightness. Moreover, the search for justice is as much a cooperative matter as the search for truth, for 'every speech act involves the raising of criticisable validity claims aimed at intersubjective recognition' (Habermas, 1996a, p.18). Normative dialogue assumes a commitment to reaching an understanding which constitutes agreement. This is so even for the most underdeveloped communication, for all communication must be potentially validated through citing reasons first to those who are being addressed and then to a wider audience of the total 'interpretative community'. These commitments are as necessary for normative as for descriptive discourse.

The commitment to accepting only valid claims breaks down into the mutual assumptions of those involved that they are: (1) telling the truth, (2) being personally sincere in seeking uncoerced agreement and (3) believing in the normative rightness of their claims. All these commitments presuppose that the process is non-coercive in that it is influenced only by the validity of claims undertaken in the search for a mutual understanding. This is understood to be in a context of individuals sharing a common language and seeking to coordinate their actions and reaching understandings to this end. In other words we are looking at the conditions of social integration through a process of reaching a common view of the world and of the norms we are committed to following.

At the same time, communication could not take place unless we shared a common 'life world', as Habermas calls the customary patterns of conduct in everyday life. This life world, Habermas contends, already contains vast realms of consensus. We may not understand how there can be such stable interpersonal structure for thoughts, but we can work out these important presuppositions of the reality of successful dialogue as we experience it, make them explicit and encourage their institutionalisation.

For Habermas, discourse has a logic, or inner structure, to which not all actual discourse conforms to, but which does apply in valid discourse, that is, discourse which is free, open and rational in the sense that arguments are not accepted as a result of manipulation or coercion or self-interest. This applies in relation to both facts and norms. Truth is what can be legitimately asserted and what can be legitimately asserted is the result of valid dialogue in which we instantiate the presupposition that the discourse is aimed at truth or rightness. In this, his position is a development of the classical liberal thesis of John Stuart Mill (1863) that such certainty as we can achieve is the outcome of subjecting our beliefs to sustained criticism.

It follows, for Habermas, that 'only those norms can claim to be valid that meet (or could meet) with the approval of all affected by them in their capacity as participants in a practical discourse' (1990, p.66). He accepts that his ideal speech situation is counter-factual, in that it does not (completely) exist. It is in this sense more like a Kantian 'regulative ideal' which informs the process rather than

anything that is fully realised in practice. Nevertheless, the ideal
speech situation can be grasped from an examination of what it is to
argue on the basis of reason rather than force or self-interest. The
ideal speech situation can be viewed as a reconstruction of what
might have occurred, and actual situations are to be assessed by
considering whether they could have been the result of such processes. In this respect, Habermas presents us with a form of 'conjectural history', a method developed in the Scottish Enlightenment
as a mode of historical explanation and used by Nozick as a style of
justification (see p.65). These hypothetical possibilities are, however, less important than the claim that we cannot consistently
and without contradiction take part in communication with other
people unless we endorse the assumptions which he finds at work in
non-manipulative social intercourse.

As far as the mode of argument used in communicative rationality goes, Habermas's method can be viewed as a form of the
Kantian procedure for testing maxims of conduct by seeing whether
they can be endorsed as applicable to all similar situations and
persons, an ideal of universalisation which enables us to speak of
autonomous individuals each legislating for themselves. For Kant,
as ultimately for Rawls, this is a decision procedure which can be
carried out by a single person. For Habermas it is unalterably an
interpersonal process, a socialised and socially situated version of
these more individualistic theorists. This is at the core of his conception of the universal principles of justice (1996a, pp.66, 283).
This means that the basic principles of communicative rationality
require that all those who may be affected by the adoption of a
norm must have an equal and uncoerced opportunity to participate
in the discourse by which it is adopted. Kantian universalisability,
which is classically formulated in the test of whether or not the
individual can consistently endorse a maxim of action as 'universal
law', that is, as applying to every person in similar circumstances
including that individual him- or herself, is thus transformed into a
democratic social process in which everyone affected by a decision
must endorse the consequences.

Habermas is within the tradition of Hegel and Marx in seeking to
identify a developing rationality in human society. Knowledge and
justice are not individual achievements but are embodied in a social
development that can be examined in the evolution of public
opinion in a rather special sense in which a 'public sphere' is
identified with dialogue directed at agreement about public

goods and social values, rather than a process of pure bargaining between self-interested individuals. In this context Habermas talks of 'discursive will-formation' as the product of an interactive process of uncoerced equal and open debate on matters of general interest.

Habermas contends that we do engage in such public dialogue and that when we reflect on what we do when we try to reach rational agreement on matters of public concern, we can unearth the inherent drive towards a social interaction which is free of domination and force and in which all social relations have to be legitimated by an appeal to rational consensus involving all those affected rather than to threats of force or claims to superior individual authority. Of course, actual dialogue is full of domination and distortion engendered by the interests of those involved. Real arguments are largely strategic discourse and therefore purely self-referential, in that each individual is concerned purely with their own interests and treats others as means towards their own particular ends. This is excluded from the ideal speech situation but is a feature of actual debate, although it does becomes acceptable within discourse ethics when the bargaining is conducted fairly and is directed towards a just or legitimate outcome.

The process of critical self-reflection emerges at a stage in society at which there is genuine public debate leading to a degree of emancipation from the deficiencies of actual discourse. This may be compared with the way in which Marx sees the evolution of economic systems ultimately as undermining the false consciousness that explains why oppressed classes accept the ideological structures of the ruling classes. Reflection on the experience of dialogue leads to a gradual unmasking of epistemological false consciousness. At this stage Habermas encourages the prospect of a progressive approach to undistorted knowledge which produces at least a measure of certainty, a social achievement that is intrinsically linked to the telos of responsible autonomy that is involved in the ideal speech situation.

In looking at this argument in more detail we have to be aware of the way in which the method of transcendental deduction is undermined if extraneous or unnecessary normative assumptions are introduced, for these then do the real work in the process by which prescriptive conclusions emerge from apparently factual premises. This is particularly the case where the initial analysis takes the form of creating Weberian ideal types through an insider's analysis of social experience from which extrapolations are then drawn for the purpose of discovering truth and justice.

In Habermas's scheme, there does appear to be an illicit favouring of some form of speech acts (such as truth-telling and justice-seeking speech undertaken in good faith and sincerity) over others (such as self-interested persuasion and deceit) which would appear to require a natural law-style identification of a distinctive 'telos' or God-given purpose for speech, namely the pursuit of honest agreement. The claim that this telos is immanent in actual discourse may depend ultimately on showing that other purposes are dependent on the pursuit of truth and rightness in that, if the primary logic of discourse were not oriented towards agreement on the basis of truth and right, the other uses of language could not get off the ground. It may be, for instance, that we cannot successfully tell lies unless we normally tell the truth, but, we should note, this does not mean that a sincere communal effort to arrive at truth and justice by reference to publicly challengable reasons is a sufficient method for obtaining these objectives.

Habermasian justice

Habermas's general position on justice is relatively clear. Justice concerns the deontological, not the teleological, aspects of discourse. He identifies justice with 'morality' (in his rather restrictive use of the term) as covering universal norms that transcend those individual and group preferences that concern values, matters about which we can only have personal and group priorities. The articulation of values includes the working out of individual and group identities and self-awareness which lead us to formulations of ideals of this or that way of life, which communitarians place at the centre of their conceptions of justice. For Habermas, 'justice is not one value among others' but 'a predicate of the validity of the universal normative sentences that express general moral norms'. Justice is always, therefore an abstract concept to do with equality in the Kantian sense, for a valid norm of justice 'must survive a universalization test that examines what is equally good for all'(1996a, p.153). Yet, while 'justice questions concern the claims contested in interpersonal conflicts', this does make it a matter of mere distributive justice. Indeed justice is rooted in equal freedom and 'injustice means primarily the constraint of freedom and the violation of human dignity' (1996a, p.418). However, he does insist that a fair distribution of good is a feature which follows from 'the self-organization of a community of free and equal citizens', for 'the just distribution of social benefits is simply what *results* from the universalistic character of a law intended to guarantee the freedom and integrity of each' (ibid.).

There is nothing particularly original in the idea that 'a norm is just only if all can will that it be obeyed by each in comparative situations' and that 'whether we should accept a program . . . depends on whether the corresponding practice is *equally* good for *all*' (1996a, p.161). However, these points are no more than a background for Habermas's own contribution to the theory of justice, which relates to his arresting blend of social and normative theory. Attempts to produce concrete principles of justice from abstract principle, Kantian or otherwise, are seen as inadequate because they are purely philosophical theories of justice and are not grounded in theories of actual social processes. So, while he sees much to commend and adopt in Rawls's theory, such an approach is acceptable only as part of an enterprise which balances the normativity of philosophical approaches to justice with realistic sociological theory that dwells on what he calls the 'facticity' of social processes. This he finds in the classic modern theories of society, Emile Durkheim, Max Weber and Talcott Parsons, who enable us to view societies as structures to be understood both from the viewpoint of the external observing scientist and through the self-understanding of its members.

More specifically Habermas sees justice as relating to law as a subsystem of society which has particularly to do with the function of social interaction. Law is in modern society a social mechanism which is required to provide established expectations as the basis for social cooperation, a function which was previously performed by religion. This is particularly true of post-capitalist society which is marked by an irreducible plurality of values, lifestyles and opinions and the absence of the traditional sources of cohesion, a fact which renders consensus more difficult to attain, and which requires more of law in this regard.

Law fulfils its crucial cohesive role through providing a mandatory framework within which people can pursue their diverse objectives. Conformity is achieved in part by force since the diversity is such that it is necessary to use some coercion to achieve conformity. Yet producing social solidarity is not a function that can be adequately performed unless there is a general acceptance of its validity through a general sense of its moral acceptability. Justice as a normative ideal is thus crucial in producing the established patterns of life which generate legitimate expectation of order and limits on individual and group diversity, which are necessary even in a multicultural society. Factual stability based on a mix of coercion and consensus combines to produce the conditions for valid common morality beliefs and their pragmatic implementation through laws appropriate to the particular situation of each society. Justice is part of the normative self-understanding of law. It is 'the moral content of modern legal orders' (1996a, p.43).

Arguing along Weberian lines, Habermas takes law to involve legitimate coercion. Justice comes in as an element of that legitimacy which is related to the deontological imperatives centring on the rights of citizens affected by coercive sanctions. As we come to concretise the abstract principles of justice in relation to actual law, the universal principles of justice become bound up with the norms on which social solidarity is based.

Here there emerges a close tie between justice and social cohesion. Habermas's view of social integration is that it is dependent on a consensus on the norms which govern strategic interactions. Force in itself is never enough, but there must be agreement on what force can be used to impose. These basic agreements are represented in a system of rights that permits coercion to be used in protecting the bases of social integration. This system is not itself the outcome of strategic bargaining, rather it emerges from a direct concern for proper social relationships.

The upshot is that justice is attained and developed not through the speculations of philosophers or other external critics but as an outcome of a dialogue whose conditions include the assumption that there is such a thing as universal justice. Justice is a presupposition of ideal communicative action, a process which aims at an outcome that can be adopted by all as legitimate. It is therefore a process which is mediated through social reality and found in the political consciousness of a public of citizens which combines the perspectives of all those involved. In this respect Habermas resembles those eighteenth-century theorists, such as Adam Smith, who saw an interactive process of sympathetic imagination as an essential part of a process which results in agreement of feeling and opinion through what we would now call empathy as well as mutual self-interest.

All this cannot be achieved in the abstract and requires an actual system of law. This is because law must be a set of norms which meets the legal positivist model of societal facts which have to be acknowledged, obeyed and applied, as well as fulfilling the necessary standards of legitimacy, in order to function as the basis for the legitimate expectations on which social life depends. Hence the rule of law is necessarily connected with democratic dialogue and justice is part of the validity conditions of democracy.

In *Between Facts and Norms*, Habermas articulates this conception of justice through the social ideals which he sees as underpinning the process through which basic rights are framed, interpreted and applied. These ideals are social constructs which provide the paradigms that affect pivotal judicial decisions. In developing this conception he adopts a historical approach, contrasting the nineteenth-century liberal ideal of private autonomy protected by a neutral framework of law embodying formal equality and private rights with the twentieth-century ideal of the social welfare state, in which the state uses law as an instrument for promoting the general welfare. This social welfare conception of justice triumphed over the individualistic market paradigm as a means of providing more substantive equality of opportunity and hence actual freedom, only to weaken the private autonomy of the previous liberal paradigm by making the paternalistic state the source of the material prerequisites of fair competition, thus provoking a fresh search for a new paradigm of law and justice.

Habermas believes that he can discern this new ideal in the proceduralist paradigm of law according to which

> 'the vacant places of the economic man or welfare-client are occupied by a public of citizens who participate in political communication in order to articulate their wants and needs, to give voice to their violated interests, and, above all, to clarify and settle contested standards and criteria according to which equals are treated equally and unequals unequally.' (Habermas, 1996b, p.777)

Habermas views this model as a compromise between those republican models which have a pure idea of democratic dialogue which focuses entirely on the public good rather than working out what will satisfy the articulated preferences of individuals and groups and the market model of democracy which acts as no more than an aggregation of personal preferences and demands.

   In fact this new paradigm, in which public and private autonomy are mutually sustaining, is far more than just another historical stage. It represents real progress towards an ideal of autonomy that transcends any particular period of society. In a vision which matches that of Rousseau, when he sought to explain how individuals can cast off the chains of their current oppressive social relationships and regain the essence of their primeval liberty while still living within civil society, Habermas finds that the proceduralist paradigm renders not only compatible, but mutually necessary and supportive, the partial ideals of private autonomy and welfare security. The only way in which citizens can retain their private autonomy with the material benefits that are necessary to make real use of the otherwise purely legal freedoms is by becoming the originators of the laws on which their society operates. This means that private autonomy (individual economic self-determination) and public autonomy (group political self-determination) must go hand in hand in that each is conditional on the realisation of the other, a relationship of mutual dependency. The open discourse of the public arena would not exist without the background experiences of private autonomy within civil society, while justice and freedom in private relations can only be secured by a discourse process which emerges from an authentic public sphere in which the conditions of communicative rationality are secured:

> 'After the formal guarantee of private autonomy has proved insufficient, and after social intervention through the law threatens the very private autonomy it means to restore, the only solution consists in thematizing the connection between the forms of communication that simultaneously guarantee private and public autonomy in the very conditions from which they emerge.' (Habermas, 1996b, p.777)

It is thus clear that Habermas's conception of justice involves a degree of actual social and economic equality, but it matters crucially that this substantive equality is reached by the enactment of positive law after a fair and open procedure. Further, the precise articulation of what this actual equality involves is a genuinely open and debatable question that cannot be known prior to the outcome of an actual democratic dialogue which is already marked by sufficient measure of actual equality to make it free and equal: 'Only the affected persons themselves can clarify the "relevant aspects" – the standards and criteria – that define equality and inequality for a given matter', for

> 'no regulation, however sensitive to context, can adequately concretize the equal right to an autonomous private life, unless it simultaneously strengthens the effectiveness of the equal rights to exercise political autonomy, that is, the right to participate in form of political communication that provide the sole arenas in which citizens can clarify the relevant aspects that define equal status.' (Habermas, 1996a, p.784)

For all the abstraction and open-endedness of this position, it conjures up a remarkable incorporation of substantive justice within the preconditions of procedural democracy that appears to offer some hope of reconciling fundamental divergencies between liberal individualism, communitarian consensus, the egalitarianism of the socialist tradition and a vision of democratic politics which rises above the dominance of oppressive majorities and the narrow self-interest of market-style politics.

Critical comments

The easy critique of Habermas's conception of justice is to say that he adds to the familiar criteria of consent, impartiality and information the requirement of honesty and the commitment to reaching agreement based on good reasons and that this does not go far enough to give us confidence that the outcome of deliberation, however rooted in a context of a historically particular group at a particular stage of historical development, will bring us closer to knowledge of what is right and just. In this respect, his moral theory is both formal and empty (see Pettit, 1982).

It is not enough to say, in reply, that non-coerced agreement is worthwhile in itself, so that every effort must be made to achieve voluntary and informed social consensus, whatever it is that is agreed upon. The value of consensus, other things being equal, is not in question in any mainstream conception of substantive

political values. Moreover, since commitment to non-coercive
dialogue is a presupposition of the theory, it cannot be hailed as a
product of the theory, however desirable reasoned consensus may
be. Habermas must provide additional and independent arguments
for the epistemic value of the outcome of communicative rationality
in democratic decision-making. In fact, of course, he does not
present democracy as a means to reach political consensus for its
own sake but as legitimating certain claims as to what constitutes
just social order. Reasoned agreement is a test of rightness, not
simply an end in itself, but something which produces a proper
balance between private autonomy and public self-determination
which gives content to the ideals of truth and justice in pluralistic
societies.

This is the philosophical nub of his theory, and his argument is
open to serious criticism which emerges in a variety of guises. There
are, for instance, difficulties surrounding (1) the effectiveness of
deliberative democracy in generating agreement, (2) the nature of
the alleged interdependence of private and public autonomy and (3)
the gap between a commitment to reasoned debate among all persons affected by a decision on the basis of equal participation and
the objective worth of the outcome beyond its utility in generating
voluntary agreement. Concentrating on the third issue, we may
accept that the conditions he places on discourse do remove features
which cast doubt on the acceptability of the outcome of many actual
deliberations. Threats, manipulation and emotive appeals undoubtedly reduce confidence in the moral significance of acquiescence or
agreement. Yet, this does not establish that the factors which
remain at work in deliberative processes are capable of generating
insight into moral truths. Agreement may be reached at a very high
level of abstraction about human equality and dignity but this does
not carry over into a means of generating agreement about what
these abstract concepts mean in terms of specific rules and practices.
At this more concrete level we have no positive reason to believe
reasoned unanimity will emerge amongst well-informed people who
together sincerely search for the right answer.

Habermas, in the liberal tradition, seeks to reduce the problem of
continuing disagreement by excluding evaluations of competing
preferences and confining justice to a matter of abstract deontological norms expressing the principles of equal freedom and dignity.
As we have seen, this is ultimately an indefensible distinction. Once
we put to one side empirical disagreements about the likely

consequences of different types of conduct, the values which we use to assess those consequences present moral imperatives as powerful and insistent as any abstract statement of rights. Indeed it is not possible to appreciate, for instance, the deontological force of the right to life without an evaluation of what is worthwhile in human life any more than we can understand the importance of freedom of speech without an awareness of its role in promoting human self-development.

Habermas accepts that any principles of justice must address the question of what constitutes equality and what is permissible in terms of relevant differences when we seek to apply the maxim of treating equals equally. In such matters our evaluations of ways of life and preferred ultimate life objectives are inseparable from judgements of relevant differences and commitments to non-negotiable norms of the sort we associate with deontological morality. These philosophical doubts make it difficult for us to share the confidence of Habermas that such disagreements on justice as persist are the result of imperfection in the actual discourse of real societies, rather than a manifestation of moral disagreement which is not amenable to consensual reasoning in areas in which there are no knock-down arguments to be had.

It may be objected that this is rather an old-fashioned way of putting the matter, in that there is no place in a postmodern culture for talk of what is objectively right or wrong in terms of justice or any other moral–political ideal, or even in terms of what is descriptively true and false of the world. Habermas, after all, speaks of criticising validity claims, not reaching objective knowledge of truth and justice. However, he must himself be committed to a conception of objectivity at least as powerful as that presupposed in genuine dialogue. What, then, is it that participants in the dialogue are committed to achieving? Are they really seeking knowledge of truth and justice or are they much more concerned with reaching a working accommodation with those whose agreement they need both in matters of shared technical instrumentality and concerning norms for managing non-economic social relationships. From the internal, hermeneutical, interpretive point of view, do dialogue participants seek to determine what is just in some sense beyond being able to offer reasons for what they believe in which might convince an impartial discussant? That is a matter on which different hermeneutical interpretations could be offered and defended. The most helpful answer, for understanding Habermas, is to say that discussants share a belief in objective justice as a regulative ideal, that is, as an ideal which directs how they approach the matter of disagreement about justice, but cannot and do not make any claims about their superior knowledge of what that ideal contains. This means that it is legitimate to raise the question of whether Habermas has made out his case that communicative rationality can deliver what it assumes to be possible. Further, it is hard to see that he can rule out the possibility that deliberative democracy may come to recognise the moral authority of sources beyond its own operations. Indeed, as we shall see, he appears to take precisely this line with respect to judicial review of legislation.

All this still leaves open the question of what the debate is about in substantive terms. An ideal of justice must be more than a commitment to whatever is required for free, equal and reasonable discourse, since this discourse is set up with a purpose, namely reaching agreement as to what is just. To reach such substantive agreement discussants must agree on more than the procedural matter of what constitutes an ideal political speech situation. At this point Habermas can offer a socialised form of the Kantian principle of universalisability, but, as a theory of justice, this is seriously incomplete if it cannot identify the sort of factors which are fundamental to the question of whether or not it is just or unjust to universalise a particular maxim of action. His procedural approach offers no guidance as between the relative importance of ever-present tension between the promotion of happiness, the minimisation of pain, the response to merit and demerit and the affirmation of equal human worth. Thus, even if we accept his theory we have to draw on some conception of substantive justice for the purposes of engaging in the dialogue.

Putting these substantive matters to one side, the question remains as to what should be done in real polities where the requisite equalities of freedom, resources and linguistic capacity do not obtain? This is the familiar problem about how to legitimise democracies in which there is insufficient knowledge, economic opportunity for political involvement or educational capacities to have any faith that the outcome of elections represents a real and authentic choice of the voters. Given that there is some point at which the situation of ideal speech no longer applies so that the outcome of the less than ideal discourse is no test of normative validity, how are we to identify that point and what are we to do once we decide that it does not exist?

Constitutional consequences

Habermas cannot assess the significance of constitutive failures in actual discourse ethics by looking at the outcome of the deliberations in question, since we do not know in advance what these should be. In practice, he leans on the substantial social analysis, which he takes on through the European corpus of social theory, to make the assumption that something reasonably approximate to the ideal speech situation obtains in many countries of the contemporary world. Yet this is clearly something which is patchy and incomplete, and, even where it does obtain, it cannot be said to have produced agreement on fundamental norms of justice.

At this point it is interesting to note that position he takes on constitutional justice, that is, those matters of right and wrong which are taken out of the normal democratic process of parties, elections and legislative decision after open public discussion and given over to courts, particularly constitutional courts, to articulate and administer. Constitutional justice might well be taken to represent the results of communicative rationality in modern societies. Yet if there is an identifiable corpus of basic rights and if they really are the outcome of a deliberative process in which everyone affected is able to participate, then there would appear to be no need to take these matters outside the scope of electoral politics, for they would scarcely be in any danger. Indeed, if legitimate agreement is the result of communicative rationality involving all those affected, their validity would seem to depend on an ongoing democratic consensus. On the face of it, an exciting thing about discourse democracy is that it can in theory dispense with the external controls which are necessary to contain tyrannical majorities and popularly elected dictators. Given the requisite public debate and democratic will formation, there should be no need for the checks and balances of traditional liberal constitutions or the power of courts to review legislation in the light of a list of constitutional rights which are designed to prevent uninformed and perhaps evil-minded majorities perpetrating injustice on individuals and minority groups. On the other hand, if we are in a situation of less than ideal speech, then it is hard to see how we can be in a position to identify the fundamental rights which require judicial protection against the democratic deficits of existing electorally-based politics.

Habermas may take one of at least two constitutional lines when faced with ideal speech deficits. He may retain constitutional rights as checks on temporary democratic lapses that result in oppression and injustice. Or he can take the line that judicial review applies only to those rights which are part of the preconditions of the democratic process, on the grounds that if the ideal speech situation is fostered then the failures in justice arising from democratic legislation will be self-corrected through the democratic system. In practice this second line may not differ too greatly from the first if the preconditions of discourse democracy involve substantial economic and social equality, but both face the problem of disagreement about the essential prerequisites of procedural democracy.

The dilemma facing Habermas here is acute. He is committed to the validation of social norms through the agreement of all those concerned, and he gives a central role to law in modern society as the mechanism whereby a pluralist society attains a framework which can obtain a working consensus and claim to be just. His system requires the 'legally institutionalized practice of civic self-determination' (1996a, p.169). Moreover, he realises that overturning legislation in terms of content is itself a sort of legislative process (1996a, p.262). He is, therefore, suitably cautious about welcoming the judicial review of democratically endorsed legislation and contemplates the alternative of legislatures subjecting their own decisions to scrutiny in the light of abstract justice, noting that 'this method of internalizing self-reflection on its own decisions would have the advantage of inducing legislators to keep the normative content of constitutional principles in mind from the very start of their deliberations' (1996a, p.241). And yet, by admitting into the political process as legitimate and indeed essential the demands which arise from private autonomy, albeit in the context of the pursuit of fair bargains, and placing higher than realisable standards on the quality of public debate, he does have qualms about simply accepting the outcome of actual democratic politics. Further, his communitarian leanings towards respecting the outcome of historical processes lead him towards giving special status to the general principles of well-established legal systems.

Ultimately he does in fact accept the need for the allocation of considerable power to constitutional courts in relation to what he calls 'abstract judicial review'. He does this, not primarily on the grounds which would appear to fit in best with his general approach, namely that courts can maintain the preconditions of good democratic procedures. He does give careful consideration to what John Hart Ely calls the 'representation-reinforcing' view of the

US Constitution, which confines judicial review to protecting such matters as freedom of speech and equality of political franchise that have a direct bearing on the democractic legitimacy of the political process (Ely, 1980). The standard criticism of Ely's theory is that it does not cover many of the rights in the Constitution, many of which have only a tangential relationship to democratic decision-making. This point applies less forcefully to Habermas in that he puts more than the liberal American presuppositions into what is requisite for a properly functioning democracy and includes the actual rather than the formal right to participate in the democratic dialogue on an equal basis, which has major economic and social implications. Such a wide-ranging review of democratic presuppositions would have the result of taking a large range of education and economic issues out of the power of legislatures and vesting them in courts which would have the duty of forming a polity into a free and equal dialogic community. This must certainly run counter to the vision of a participant democracy that itself is seeking to articulate and instantiate precisely what they believe to be involved in a just social order. Habermas is aware that there is no theoretical or principled way to limit powers of judicial review on the representation-reinforcing view, and backs off from giving full support to this tactic, despite the fact that it would fit neatly with his conception of procedural democracy.

If Habermas were to take the radical path of making it a purely democratic rather than judicial function to articulate the specifics of what is just, then this would not undermine his model of a politicised version of the ideal speech situation, since democratic assemblies would certainly have the duty of reaching a consensus on the specific articulation of what is to count as freedom and equality in political decision-making. Participant deliberative democracy would require an extension of the focus of justice beyond procedure and beyond the formalities of the universalisability principle to a more direct and concrete engagement with less abstract principles of justice. At that point there would be need for a substantive debate, at the level of more detailed principles which Rawls and others have sought to articulate, and an engagement with the more traditional issues of the relationship between justice, desert and responsibility on the one hand and, on the other hand, the equally forceful claims of humanity, the reduction of suffering, the promotion of happiness and the fair distribution of the means thereto, with which we started this book.

In the event, Habermas retreats into the position that the courts have the capacity for superior insight and legitimate influence in the identification and enforcement of basic deontological rights asserted in highly general terms, so, in his view, helping to maintain the balance between autonomy and welfare which he sees as crucial to his third way in modern politics (see 1996a, chapter 6). Constitutional courts, he concludes, should act as tutors of the democratic process, with the task of reviewing the delicate balance between private and public rights in a manner which fosters their mutually reinforcing complementarity and contributes to the democratic system by preserving the compromise between the claims of liberal private autonomy and the functions of the administrative welfare state. This makes it possible for him to endorse a less value-oriented version of German constitutional law.

In making this move Habermas draws on the Dworkinian apparatus of fundamental deontological rights rooted in equal concern and respect, thereby retreating from his criticism of the philosophers of justice who bypass the real world of political dialogue and seemingly downgrading the welfare state element in his third way. This retreat is as dramatic and, perhaps, as disappointing as Rawls's reinterpretation of his early theory of justice, for it goes back on the commitment to decision-making processes that potentially involve obtaining the reasoned agreement of all those affected by the decision. Both revisions may be regarded as manifestations of the philosophical weaknesses of their basic positions, in the case of Rawls through an overconfidence in the epistemic power of impartiality and in the case of Habermas a mistaken reliance on the dubious distinction between deontological and teleological morality. Nevertheless, his theory of deliberative democracy and the associated norms of constitutional justice do allow for the possibility that, as a democratic process approximate to the politicised version of the ideal speech situation, it will be possible to contemplate a participatory dialogic democracy that can be trusted to sustain its own prerequisites.

Full circle

In Habermas we have a theory of justice which is formal in that it is primarily addressed to the question 'what is justice?' rather than to the question of 'what is just?' Habermas's major contribution is to fill out his formal answer in terms of what may be called a social epistemology, a way in which political communities can arrive at justified agreement as to what is just. Even so, as a theory of justice, this is disappointingly empty and it is no wonder that those who are motivated by struggles against oppression find Habermas's approach rather too rationalist and lacking in content (Young, 1997, p.7). While the desire to avoid begging questions as to what will be the outcome of political dialogue (albeit supervised by judicial authorities) is laudable from the democratic point of view, it is rather timid and uninformative for those seeking guidance about the substance of the debate. If we wish to undertake a Habermasian dialogue on justice we will need to draw on other sources for intimations of which criteria are relevant to the determination of the rights and duties which are to be adopted in our societies. In this sense, the procedural theory of justice, as essentially to do with democratic mechanisms and ideals, takes us back full circle to the identification of those evils which we identify as unjust and those aspirations to which the discourse of justice seems apposite.

For these purposes, the more ambitious theory of the early Rawls is to be preferred in so far as it provides us with both an epistemological methodology and an indication of what, in broad terms, acceptable principles of justice might be. It may be that the attractions of Rawls's substantive conclusions, particularly the maximin principle, have worn rather better than his methodology, which claims much more than it can deliver and arbitrarily biases us towards certain sorts of liberal outcomes. Nevertheless, the early Rawlsian approach does focus on the sort of substantive questions in which our consciousness of justice (and even more of injustice) are rooted. It is not surprising, therefore, that some of the most salient theoretical discussions of justice are those which directly address more substantive issues, such as mass starvation, unemployment, environmental selfishness, child abuse and political oppression (see Sen, 1992; Singer, 1993; Young, 1997; and Nussbaum, 1999).

11   Justice in Eclipse?

It is not the primary purpose of this book to commend any particular conclusions as to the concept and content of justice but rather to present a picture of some of the options available to those who have an interest in political theories of justice. However, it is hoped that readers will seek to develop their own views so that they may better articulate and enter into the political choices which fall to be made in contemporary democracies. It is on this basis that I have developed the theory of 'equal worth and unequal worthiness' as the key ingredients of a concept of justice which sees justice as a particular moral focus on political issues. If we wish to identify the specific forms of good and evil which best exemplify justice and injustice in their specific meanings, our analysis should be, I suggest, that the distinctive discourse of justice presupposes the ideal of basic human equality, what I call the 'prior equality' of equal human worth, complemented by the practical recognition of differential deserts on the part of responsible agents, so that justified inequalities are based on unequal worthiness. My favoured interpretation of this concept of justice involves a qualified egalitarianism according to which all inequalities in the distribution of benefits and burdens must be justified. Justice contributes rationales for differential desert to decision-making about the best all-things-considered outcomes alongside other relevant and overlapping but nevertheless distinctive ideals, such as autonomy, the general welfare, humanity and community.

In highlighting the distinctive elements of equality and desert in those examples of contemporary justice discourse which utilise a reasonably specific and particular sense of 'justice', the meritorian approach brings a coherence to the variety of distinctive uses of the language of justice in a way which identifies its peculiar contribution to the range of social and political values. In doing so it is illuminating and clarificatory. It is particularly powerful in identifying an important aspect of what it is that is wrong about certain oppressive and unfair situations and why it is that social and political life should be arranged to eliminate or ameliorate them.

We have seen that this does not make justice the inevitably dominant normative claim upon us, either politically or individually. A theory of justice should, amongst other things, put justice in its place, and one way of doing this is pointing out that utility, for instance, need not always give normative way to justice and more particularly that humanity, or the commitment to the alleviation of suffering, deserved or undeserved, is as much claim to political priority as obtaining distributions of benefits and burdens which accurately match the equal worth and unequal worthiness of those involved.

By way of summary and conclusion this chapter illustrates this meritorian approach in relation to law, economics and democracy, and speculates on the future of justice as a key political concept in the light of the increasing global significance of the discourse and institutions of human rights.

Justice in law

Nowhere is a desert or meritorian analysis of justice more pertinent than in relation to criminal law. The intentional infliction of pain, suffering and deprivation by an institution of the state is difficult to sustain in the face of the evident inhumanity of such a system without some reference to the ill deserts of those who are punished. Justified punishment requires that people are punished only for what they choose to do in the context of clear notice that penalties will be visited on such conduct. Hence the importance of having clear, explicit and promulgated rules which are applied in all relevant cases, which we have identified as the key ingredient of formal justice.

Justice requires also that there be an impartial and thorough inquiry into whether or not the person accused actually did the acts in question and that the prohibitions or requirements of the criminal law are justified in that there are good reasons for their existence. In other words, the person to be punished must be shown to have voluntarily broken a democratically justified official behavioural norm. The conscious perpetration of publicly recognised harm is the core of criminality and a prerequisite of justified punishment. If a person is punished without proof of the occurrence of such conduct this is a paradigm example of legal injustice. Anything less is unfair and unjust. These basic principles are an evident recognition of the key role of responsibility and desert in the discourse of justice.

Such an account will be accused of being too partisan to count as a morally neutral analysis of the justice paradigm. Retributive theories of criminal justice which make punishment in accordance with desert the be-all and end-all of the system are generally regarded as extreme and indefensible. Punishment merely for the sake of giving people their just deserts seems not only barbaric but also impossible, given how difficult it is to know how far people are responsible for their conduct in the sense of actually being able to control their actions. Criminal law, it is argued, should only exist to prevent harm and promote benefit and never used as a form of moral account-keeping in which wickedness is balanced with appropriate amounts of pain.

However, once it is clear that the meritorian analysis of justice claims no monopoly of moral relevance, the debate takes on an altogether more balanced form. The reduction of harm, for instance, can be given the major role in the determination of the proper content of substantive criminal law, for the theory outlined above requires only that the prohibitions and requirements of criminal law be justified, not that these justifications themselves be couched in terms of justice. The relevance of justice to criminal law is not to counter utilitarian reasons for having criminal law but in requiring that only those means of enforcing criminal law which are compatible with treating human beings as of equal worth and unequal worthiness are permissible. Justice comes in to require that the punishments associated with criminal law be enforced only where people have the opportunity to know in advance what the law requires and the capacity to conform to that law, and have actually committed the offence in question. Otherwise the punishment is undeserved.

Further, justice requires that no punishment be disproportionate to the harm caused by the offence, something which, as is discussed in Chapter 6, utilitarian approaches to crime overlook when, for instance, they license imposing high penalties for those minor offences which are difficult to detect and therefore hard to deter without severe penalties. Such proportionality makes no sense without reference to underlying ideas about the moral seriousness and therefore the degree of ill desert which the criminal acts in question characteristically exhibit.

Yet we know that, in practice, desert does not act as an overriding veto on the operations of the criminal law, a sphere in which 'rough' or approximate justice is inevitable. That this is usually a matter of regret acknowledges the powerful moral imperatives behind having a system of criminal law which combats harmful conduct and promotes social utility even at the cost of some injustice. Political decisions about the detailed content and operation of criminal law quite properly take into consideration the social utility of deterring harmful behaviours, the inhumanity of inflicting severe and institutionalised punishments, the benefits which flow from reforming criminals, as well as the need to take justice into account by ensuring that unmerited punishments are not imposed. In the balancing of these various factors, justice is simply one very important but not necessarily overriding factor. It may be worth noting that meritorian justice is a factor which in practice comes in more on the side of leniency than severity, for any informed study of the actual operations of criminal law reveals that those who are convicted and sentenced are more often vulnerable and inadequate people deserving of help than they are evil and wicked persons deserving of punishment.

Civil (that is non-criminal) law governing, for instance, contractual relations and providing remedies through compensation for harms perpetrated by the negligent conduct of others do not include the requirement that those found liable of breach of contract or negligence actually intended to breach their legal duties, something which is generally a necessary condition of criminal guilt. However, this does not mean that considerations of desert are not at work in these areas of law. Underlying principles of civil law in general require that those who are found liable and are required to compensate others for any resulting injury or damage could and ought to have foreseen the consequences of their conduct. Commutative and corrective justice have regard to the morality of promise-keeping and the duty to take care as well as the provision of a set of agreed rules and standards for resolving disputes in an efficient manner. The principles to which I have referred in relation to criminal law – utility, humanity, truth and justice – all apply in the sphere of civil law, albeit with different contents and different weights.

In the development of these arguments recourse may usefully be had to the theories of justice discussed in this book. Our exploration of the limitations of Richard Posner's utilitarian theory of criminal justice can readily be supplemented by, for instance, the desert theory of Wojciech Sadurski or the critical approaches of Marx or Young, all of which have direct relevance to criminal law. Similarly Dworkin's principle of equal concern and respect has immediate implications for the assessment of existing civil law, as have the cruder simplicities of Nozick's entitlement theory and the more diffuse contractual approach of Rawls. Further, the interpretation, comparison and modification of these theories can usefully be undertaken from a meritorian perspective.

Yet, all theories of justice, particularly those which offer guidance as to why formal justice is important and which types of situation are substantively just, are inherently controversial and serve more to identify points of disagreement than to promote political consensus. The political inconclusiveness of the resulting reflections on justice underlines the need to supplement these relatively substantive theories of justice with procedural recommendations which indicate how we might go about arriving at working agreements in actual political systems. Here we may contrast Dworkin's court-centred approach to the practical epistemology of justice with Habermas's scheme for a democratic dialogue, which echoes Rawls's more fanciful hypothetical social contract in an 'original position'. These procedural or democratic approaches may themselves be regarded as based on considerations of justice, at least to the extent that they are seen as ways in which citizens take and share responsibility for the rules they impose on themselves and others. However, as I argue in Chapter 10, such procedural considerations need to be supplemented by guidance as to the content of the institutionalised debate, something which requires continuing analysis of the moral substance of justice that can be tested in dialogue against our considered intuitions as to what is fair and just in criminal and civil law.

Justice in the economy

Similar points arise in considering the import of theories of justice for political economy, that aspect of economics which seeks to go beyond a concern with increasing gross national productivity and takes into account the distribution of wealth and the impact of economic arrangements in terms of fundamental political values, such as autonomy, humanity and justice.

The simple division of values, with either general utility or autonomy rights reigning in the economic sphere and, say, humanity
and/or justice in other aspects of society, breaks down as soon as
distributive arrangements are assessed in terms other than their
impact on the totality of wealth generated by economic activity.
The basic entitlement approach of Nozick is the closest approximation we have to a theory which excludes distributive considerations
from politics and we have seen how flimsy its fundamental postulates turn out to be. Nozick leaves the problem of the suffering of
those who lose out in the entitlement competition to the private
endeavours of charitable individuals and organisations. To give the
state the task of relieving extreme suffering is tantamount to theft
on Nozick's scheme because it requires citizens to hand over their
properly acquired wealth so that it may be redistributed to those in
need.

Justifying such state intervention is often seen as a matter of
justice overriding property rights or individual autonomy and this
makes sense if we regard the sufferings of the poor as unmerited and
the wealth of the comparatively well off as greater than they
deserve. Yet the imperative of relieving suffering must surely arise
in relation to the undeserving as well as the deserving poor and it
may be argued that even deserved wealth ought to be deployed to
relieve human misery. For these reasons redistribution which centres on what Rawls identifies as the worst-off group in society is
better conceptualised as a matter of humanity rather than justice. It
may be this insight which encourages Nozick to regard the alleviation of poverty as a private rather than a public duty. In either
case, however, such rationales for the relief of poverty leave largely
unaffected the operations of the economic system itself. Relief of
poverty is an economically external matter which supplements
rather than governs economic activity.

Justice enters more directly into the economic sphere where the
labour and rewards of different economic activities are themselves
criticised as unfair or undeserved. It is at this point that the major
divergencies of contemporary politics emerge with 'economic
rationalism' taking the line that such considerations are irrelevant
in the economic sphere and other political players, such as social
democrats, accepting that politics can and should regulate economic activity in the interests of values other than respecting certain
basic entitlements or autonomy rights or maximising national
wealth.

We have seen that the liberal theory of John Rawls makes just such a move by insisting that, whatever inequalities there may be between offices and employments, these should be open to competition in terms of fair equality of opportunity in a way which goes beyond the utilitarian requirement that there should be competition for office and employment to the point that this is a cost-efficient way to get properly qualified people into economically useful roles.

Precisely why such real equality of opportunity is important for Rawls is not clear. He simply declares that it is something that we would insist upon, in the original position, when we choose the terms of our social compact. However, genuine equality of opportunity, which takes into account the provision of the educational and material prerequisites of developing the skills, knowledge and personality which fit people for employment, can be conceptualised as a prerequisite of a natural (or 'moral') desert approach which rewards people making admirable choices and hard work. Rawls himself rejects 'natural' desert on the grounds that individuals can take no personal credit for the upbringing and genetic endowment that make it possible for them to meet such criteria. Nevertheless, putting to one side the utilitarian reasons for employing and promoting those who perform best as being a relevant moral justification for equality of opportunity but one which is unconnected with an acceptable ideal of justice, the appeal to justice in the context of equality of opportunity does seem to presuppose that it makes sense to praise and reward people for seeking to make themselves able to perform the tasks which society deems important, just as it makes sense to punish people who deliberately break the rules of acceptable conduct in their community.

The question for a theory of justice is to determine precisely what constitutes fair equality of opportunity and in particular how far this should take into account the disparate genetic, educational and economic backgrounds which contribute to the development of those capacities which are required by the offices and employments in question. Many theories of justice go some way down the path to requiring that certain factors, such as gender, race and social class, should not count in selection processes, and these theories have been put into practice through anti-discrimination legislation, but it is not so clear which positive characteristics render candidates for employment meritorious, as our discussion of Sadurski's approach to economic distribution brings out.

It is evident that no economy can function effectively if jobs are allocated, and perhaps even designed, on the basis of moral desert, relating to worthy choices and sustained effort alone, rather than merit in the sense of actual capacity to perform well. It follows that justice cannot be the overriding objective of employment allocation and we must either be content with a very limited input of justice to economic competition or look to other mechanisms, such as progressive taxation and redistribution through a welfare state on the basis of identified needs, as a crude way of redressing the inevitable injustices of the an economic sphere in which raw talent counts more than personal commitment. Hence a prime implication of justice in an amorally competitive society must be in the sphere of progressive taxation and redistribution in accordance with individual needs. Such remedial considerations add to the imperatives of humanity which call directly for the relief of suffering, giving a political role to justice which calls for sustained articulation and theoretical development. In this context, the Marxist critique of capitalism as systematically exploitative and therefore, in our terms, unjust does not provide a realistic picture of an alternative economic system. Rawls, by making an initial assumption in favour of equality, succeeds in retaining, in his maximin principle, a strong measure of welfare redistribution in conjunction with a regime of equal basic liberties. However, his focus on improving the lot of the worst-off group in society is too restrictive and his rationale for ignoring relativities between other groups is inadequate. Sadurski provides a morally more satisfying approach to undeserved inequalities by reintroducing the significance of desert, but it is hard to see how to incorporate this value in a system which depends on incentives and rewards luck more than industry. Indeed, it is possible to argue that the utilitarian benefits of liberal democratic systems and global free trade are such that they outweigh, in moral and well as political terms, the moral intuition that only merited inequalities are justified. This may mean replacing a general concern for justice with a more limited focus on humanity as the principle which justifies the relief of suffering without respect to merit and a purely utilitarian conception of equality of opportunity.

On the other hand, it is doubtful whether any economic system can be segregated from the impact of the deep presupposition of equal human worth which the discourse of justice embodies. In this case we can look for reactions against the inequalities and unfairnesses of libertarian capitalism which reaffirm the relevance of justice and other political ideals for the operation of economic systems. This need not take the form of a reaffirmation of state-centred welfare provision, indeed it is likely to involve rejecting the assumption that justice is an external supplement to the functioning of economies, and replacing the idea of the social democratic welfare state with a programme in which justice informs the very substance of economic life itself.

Justice and democracy

Currently there is something of a decline in theorising justice as a specific political virtue. At the moment, critics and supporters of liberal capitalism turn more naturally to the discourses of community or, more commonly, human rights. This may reflect the fact that the discourse of justice is tied in to theories of the nation state, particularly the concept of a welfare state, forms of political organisation which are said to be of declining significance in a world of global markets and entrepreneurial capitalism. It may also be due to a general postmodern disinclination to indulge in the types of grand theory and ambitious social schemes with which justice is often associated, or, again, the move away from the discourse of justice may also reflect a disenchantment with the operations of representative democracy.

The decline of justice as the preferred moral language of politics may account for the fact that many of the currently influential theories of justice, such as Habermas's deliberative model, are in effect theories of democracy in that they suggest ways in which we should reach temporary agreements on how to live together in the common polity of a globalising world and perhaps rekindle some citizen enthusiasm for democracy without proffering any strong advice as to what it is that we should agree about.

Of course, such theories of democracy are partly founded on justice in that they presuppose the significance of equal political rights and the participation of everyone in a dialogue in which the better arguments prevail. This line of thought is enhanced by considering that deliberative theories of democracy are recommended as improvements over the orthodox accounts of democracy which are more utilitarian in flavour, stressing the importance of voting, speech and pressure group activity as means for the protection of the interests of those involved, particularly the interests of the majority of political participants against powerful minorities. Dissatisfaction with theories of democracy which stress the purely instrumental role of the democratic process in translating the wishes of the majority of individuals or groups into a political outcome which benefits the majority of citizens has given rise to the alternative or supplementary view that democracy is a process of debate and contestation in which conflicting manifestos elaborating a vision of the common good are subject to scrutiny and moral choice.

We have seen that considerable doubt must arise over claims that open debate or neutral dialogue can resolve fundamental issues of value disagreement. There is no available method by which we may approach objective certainty even about the content of fundamental rights. This is a major difficulty for those who look to such a system of rights as the basis providing some relief to those permanent minorities whose preferences are systematically devalued by majoritarian institutions. The increasingly standard mechanism for safeguarding minorities in an electoral democracy is the device of entrenched constitutional rights. This is the system presupposed by Nozick, Dworkin and Rawls, all of whom take for granted the propriety of a system of government in which certain matters, listed within a bill or covenant or charter of rights, are beyond the power of elected legislatures to change or override. This domestic system of government can be traced to the work of John Locke whose theory of natural rights forms the philosophical background for the 'self-evident' rights of life, liberty and property enshrined in the US and many subsequent constitutions. It has now become reinforced and supplemented by the system of international human rights deriving from the foundation of the United Nations in 1945 and the proclamation of the Declaration of Human Rights in 1946. The implementation of US-style constitutions complete with bills of rights in post-communist Europe and the increasing willingness of states to recognise the propriety of intervention in the domestic affairs of other states when issues of human rights are at stake have helped to make the discourse of fundamental human rights the dominant vehicle for progressive political programmes which used to be justified by reference to justice. The rise of human rights has come to eclipse the significance of justice.

The idea that justice is a matter of treating people in accordance with their rights, perhaps primarily their human rights, has been considered in some detail in Chapter 3, and found wanting in respect to its epistemological foundations. Both Nozick's attempt to deduce so much from the self-evident proprietary right of the individual over their own body and Dworkin's efforts to find a principle of equal concern and respect through the interpretation of existing laws which can then be deployed to articulate a set of fundamental rights which are immune from democratic control were found to be unavailing. Rawls's scheme also comes up against the inherent controversiality of determining which rights are to be accepted as fundamental, how they are to be understood, and in what circumstances they must give way to other rights or the general interest.

There is no doubt, however, that there is a profound attraction to any scheme which seeks to identify rights and to provide protection for them, if necessary in courts of law, no matter what the the consequences, in contradistinction to a system of government which is geared to enforcing distributive patterns. At a time when governments are retreating from a direct commitment to social justice, citizens may well look to courts as better protectors of their interests than the discredited domain of politics and politicians.

It is, however, ironic, that a concentration on human rights should be conjoined with the development of a system of articulating and developing these rights from which the mass of people are excluded. On any approach which gives a central role to autonomy in politics, the right to self-determination with respect to formulating the rules which are enforced as law must be regarded as basic. Yet the success of human rights rhetoric is such that more and more crucial issues of domestic and international law, such as criminal process and punishment (including capital punishment), reproductive rights (including abortion), and economic policy (particularly free trade and intellectual property rights) are decided by courts and not by elected assemblies. Indeed, given the increasing extension of human rights to cover all areas of economic and social life, it is foreseeable that every political issue will be subject to judicial oversight in a manner which nullifies the right of peoples to live under laws of their own making.

As this global tendency to embrace the idea of human rights in conjunction with the replacement of the power of elected politicians with that of judicial officers and international organisations develops further, the theoretical problems of human rights will become more evident. Disagreement about their content, their weight, their priority over each other and over the forceful moral demands of utility and humanity will render more questionable both the alleged self-evidence of these rights and the capacity of judges to articulate their content at the level of specificity at which they have to be applied in practice.

Moreover, as it comes to be appreciated that corporations as well as individuals are ascribed fundamental rights and that the humanitarian concerns of human rights pressure groups are quite distinct from the more ideological rights of free trade and intellectual property, the constitutionalising of human rights will raise more and more questions about their epistemological and moral foundations. This is likely to turn attention back to those theories of justice which help us to think through, as part of the democratic process, precisely which legal rights we wish to adopt in the light of the complex considerations to which these theories refer. Justice, along with other basic political values such as autonomy, humanity and utility, will then reemerge from its temporary eclipse to shed light on the process of choosing which positive rights we wish to ascribe to all human beings and which rights, if any, we wish to have defined and specified by courts rather than democratic assemblies.

It is one of the virtues of viewing justice as distinctively concerned with the assumption of prior equality, together with the central role of desert in justifying inequalities, that the respect for the moral capacity of human beings which is implicit in this theory can serve as a basis for a commitment to democratic process as the expression of moral autonomy (in addition to any role it may have in promoting general welfare). As the political disadvantages of settling political disagreements through court-centred disputes about the proper content of officially defined 'human rights' become apparent, we may look again to electoral politics to articulate the substance of our political choices, leaving courts to concentrate on the important formalities of adjudication we associate with formal justice. The discourse of substantive justice can then be expected to emerge from the shadow of institutionalised human rights to reclaim its former role as the prime moral discourse of the democratic process.

Guide to Further Reading

For a general introduction to the topic of justice, covering the first two chapters of this book, it is best to begin with Rawls's masterly A *Theory of Justice* (1971), which is dealt with in Chapter 5. This may be supplemented by David Miller, *Social Justice* (1976) and Alan Ryan (ed.), *Justice* (1993). Other excellent introductions include Arthur and Shaw (1978), Pettit (1980), Sterba (1986), Walzer (1983), and Honoré (1970). For a wider context see Raphael (1970), Sen (1970), Weale (1983) and Wolff (1996). For more advanced methodological analyses see Cornell *et al.* (1992) and Barry (1995). For the communitarian and liberal background see Mulhall and Swift (1996). Kymlica (1992) has extensive relevant materials.

For the discussion of rights in Chapter 3, see Waldron (1984), Feinberg (1970b) and Campbell (1983). The best introduction to Nozick is Wolff (1991). See also Lessnoff (1999), chapter 11. For critical essays, try Paul *et al.* (1982) and Cohen (1978). For Hayek, see Kukathas (1990).

For Chapter 4, Dworkin's most accessible book is *Law's Empire* (1986). For a sympathetic introduction, try Guest (1992). For a collection of critical essays, see Hunt (1991). Cohen (1984) contains a range of commentaries on the work of Dworkin and deals with the issue of discrimination, for which see also Goldman (1979).

Commentaries on Rawls are legion, but, for Chapter 5, see particularly Barry (1973), Daniels (1975), Wolff (1977), Blocker and Smith (1980), Lessnoff (1986), Raz (1982), Kukathas and Pettit (1990) and Mulhall and Swift (1996). For welfare issues consult Weale (1983) and Plant *et al.* (1980). For Rawls's later work see Arneson (1989).

For Chapter 6, the background to the economic analysis of law is well covered in Burrows and Veljanovski (1981). Posner's own works are very readable: see particularly Posner (1977). General critiques of Posner are to be found in Baker (1975) and Coleman (1984 and 1988). For the application of EAL to criminal law see Becker (1968). An excellent collection on utilitarianism is Glover (1990).

For Chapter 7, 'desert' is analysed in Kleinig (1971), Feinberg (1970a) and Garcia (1980). The justice as desert approach is criticised in Goodin (1985). For Rawls on desert, see Slote (1973). Issues of remuneration are considered in Dick (1975) and Sher (1979). The balancing theory of justice occurs in Ake (1975) and there is a similar thesis on the reciprocity theory of criminal law in Murphy (1979).

In relation to Chapter 8, the dispute about Marxian justice is dealt with in Cohen *et al.* (1980), Buchanan (1982) and Wood (1983). For a more general discussion of socialism and justice, see Campbell (1983), Lukes (1985) and Elster (1985).

For Chapter 9, from the impressive literature on gender and justice, see Gilligan (1982), Noddings (1984) and Held (1995). Of Young's own work the most important is Young (1990). For a similar and more general approach see Smart (1989) and also Phillips (1993). An extensive body of relevant material is available in Olsen (1995).

For Chapter 10, in addition to Habermas (1996), which is quite heavy going, see Ackerman (1989), Raffel (1992), Deflem (1996) and Lessnoff (1999).

Bibliography

Ackerman, B. A. (1980) *Social Justice in the Liberal State* (New Haven, Cann.: Yale University Press).
—— (1983) 'On Getting What We Don't Deserve', *Society, Philosophy and Politics*, vol.1, pp.60–70.
—— (1989) 'Why Dialogue?', *Journal of Philosophy*, vol.86, pp.5–22.
Acton, H. B. (ed.) (1973) *The Philosophy of Punishment* (London: Macmillan).
Ake, C. (1975) 'Justice as Equality', *Philosophy and Public Affairs,* vol.5, pp.69–90.
Arneson, R. (1989) 'Symposium on the Later Writings of John Rawls: Introduction', *Ethics*, vol.99, pp.695–720.
Arrow, K. (1984) *Social Choice and Justice* (Oxford: Blackwell).
Arthur, J. and W. H. Shaw (1978) (eds) *Justice and Economic Distribution* (Englewood Cliffs, NJ: Prentice-Hall).
Baker, C. E. (1975) 'The Ideology of the Economic Analysis of Law', *Philosophy and Public Affairs,* vol.5, pp.3–48.
Barry, B. (1973) *The Liberal Theory of Justice* (Oxford: Clarendon Press).
—— (1995) *Justice as Impartiality* (Oxford: Clarendon Press).
——, B. R. Barber, J. S. Fishkin and R. C. Flathman (1983) 'Symposium on Justice', *Ethics,* vol.93, pp. 328–90
Becker, G. S. (1968) 'Crime and Punishment: An Economic Approach', *Journal of Political Economy,* vol.76, pp. 169–217.
Bertram, C. (1988) 'A Critique of John Roemer's General Theory of Exploitation', *Political Studies*, vol.36, pp.123–30.
Blocker, H. G. and E. H. Smith (eds) (1980) *John Rawls' Theory of Social Justice* (Athens: Ohio University Press).
Blum, L. (1980) *Friendship, Altruism and Morality* (London: Routledge & Kegan Paul).
Buchanan, A. E. (1979) 'Exploitation, Alienation and Injustice', *Canadian Journal of Philosophy*, vol.IX, pp.121–31.
—— (1982) *Marx and Justice* (London: Methuen).
—— (1989) 'Assessing the Communitarian Critique of Liberalism', *Ethics*, vol.99, pp.852–82.
Burrows, P. and C. G. Veljanovski (1981) *The Economic Approach to Law* (London: Butterworths).
Campbell, T. D. (1973) 'Formal Justice and Rule Change', *Analysis,* vol.33, pp.113–18.

—— (1974) 'Humanity before Justice', *British Journal of Political Science,* vol.4, pp.1–16.

—— (1983) *The Left and Rights* (London: Routledge & Kegan Paul).

——, D. Goldberg, S. McLean and T. Mullen (1986) *Human Rights: From Rhetoric to Reality* (Oxford: Blackwell).

Carney, S. (1991) 'Sandel's Critique of the Primacy of Justice', *British Journal of Political Studies,* vol.21, pp.511–21.

Carr, C. L. (1981) 'The Concept of Formal Justice', *Philosophical Studies,* vol.39, pp.211–26.

Coase, R. H. (1960) 'The Problem of Social Cost', *Journal of Legal Studies,* vol.3, pp.1–26.

Cohen, G. A. (1978) 'Robert Nozick and Wilt Chamberlain: How Patterns Preserve Liberty', in J. Arthur and W. A. Shaw (eds), *Justice and Economic Distribution* (Englewood Cliffs, NJ: Prentice-Hall).

—— (1995) *Self-Ownership, Freedom and Equality* (Cambridge: Cambridge University Press).

Cohen, M. (1984) *Ronald Dworkin and Contemporary Jurisprudence* (London: Gerald Duckworth).

——, T. Nagel and T. Scanlon (eds) (1980) *Marx, Justice and History* (Princeton, NJ: Princeton University Press).

Coleman, J. (1984) 'Economics and the Law: A Critical Review of the Foundations of the Economic Approach to Law', *Ethics,* vol.94, pp.649–79

—— (1988) *Morals, Markets and the Law* (Cambridge: Cambridge University Press).

Cornell, D., M. Rosenfeld and D. G. Carlson (eds) (1992) *Deconstruction and the Possibility of Justice* (New York: Routledge).

Daniels, N. (1975) *Reading Rawls* (Oxford: Blackwell).

Deflem, M. (ed.) (1996) *Habermas, Modernity and Law* (London: Sage Publications).

Dick, J. C. (1975) 'How to Justify a Distribution of Earnings in *Philosophy and Public Affair,* vol 4, pp.248–72

Duff, R. A. (1986) *Trials and Punishments* (Cambridge: Cambridge University Press).

Dworkin, R. M. (1978) *Taking Rights Seriously* (2nd impression) (London: Gerald Duckworth).

—— (1981) 'What is Equality?', *Philosophy and Public Affairs,* vol.10, pp.185–246.

—— (1985) *A Matter of Principle* (Cambridge, Mass.: Harvard University Press).

—— (1986) *Law's Empire* (London: Fontana).

—— (1990a) 'Foundations of Liberal Equality', *Tanner Lectures on Human Values,* vol. XI, pp.3–119.

—— (1990b) *A Bill of Rights for Britain: Why British Liberty Needs Protecting* (London: Chatto).

—— (1996) *Freedom's Law: The Moral Reading of the American Constitution* (Oxford: Oxford University Press).

Elster, J. (1985) *Making Sense of Marx* (Cambridge: Cambridge University Press).

——(1992) *Local Justice* (Cambridge: Cambridge University Press).
Ely, J. H. (1980) *Democracy and Distrust* (Cambridge, Mass.: Harvard University Press).
Feinberg, J. (1970a) *Doing and Deserving* (Princeton, NJ.: Princeton University Press).
——(1970b) 'The Nature and Value of Rights', *Journal of Value Inquiry*, vol.4, pp.243–57.
——(1973) *Social Philosophy* (Englewood Cliffs, NJ: Prentice-Hall).
Finnis, J. (1980) *Natural Law and Natural Rights* (Oxford: Clarendon Press).
Fishkin, J. (1983) *Justice, Equal Opportunity and the Family* (New Haven, Conn.: Yale University Press).
Fried, C. (1981) *Contract as Promise* (Cambridge, Mass.: Harvard University Press).
——(1985) 'Distributive Justice', *Social Philosophy and Policy*, vol.1.
Friedrich, C. J. and J. W. Chapman (eds) (1983) *Justice: Nomos VI* (New York: Atherton Press).
Fuller, L. L. (1969) *The Morality of Law*, revised edn (New Haven, Conn.: Yale University Press).
Galston, W. A. (1980) *Justice and The Human Good* (Chicago, IL.: University of Chicago Press).
Garcia, L. A. (1980) 'Two Concepts of Desert', *Law and Philosophy*, vol.5, pp.219–35.
Gauthier, D. (1974) 'Justice and Natural Endowments', *Social Theory and Practice*, vol.3.
Geras, N. (1988) 'On Marxism and Justice', *New Left Review*, vol.150; pp.47–89.
——(1989) 'The Controversy about Marx and Justice', in A. Callinicos (ed.), *Marxist Theory* (Oxford: Oxford University Press).
Gewirth, A. (1978) *Reason and Morality* (Chicago, IL.: Chicago University Press).
Gibbard, A. (1991) 'Constructing Justice', *Philosophy and Public Affairs*, vol.20; pp.101–33.
Gilbert, A. (1982) 'An Ambiguity in Marx's and Engels' Account of Justice and Equality', *American Political Science Review*, vol.76.
Gilligan, C. (1982) *In a Different Voice* (Cambridge, Mass.: Harvard University Press).
——(1987) 'Moral Orientation and Moral Development', in E. F. Kittay, and D. T. Meyers (eds), *Women and Moral Theory* (Totowa, NJ: Rowman & Littlefield).
Glover, J. (1990) *Utilitarianism and Its Critics* (London: Collier Macmillan).
Goldman, A. H. (1979) *Justice and Reverse Discrimination* (Princeton, NJ: Princeton University Press).
Goodin, R. E. (1985) 'Negating Positive Desert Claims', *Political Theory*, vol.13, pp.575–98.
Guest, S. (1992) *Ronald Dworkin* (Edinburgh: Edinburgh University Press).
Gutman, A. (1985) *Liberal Equality* (Cambridge: Cambridge University Press).
——(1985) 'Communitarian Critics of Liberalism', *Philosophy and Public Affairs*, vol.14, pp.308–22.

Habermas, J. (1971) *Knowledge and Human Interests* (Boston: Beacon Press).
—— (1984) *The Theory of Communicative Action*, vol.I (Boston: Beacon Press).
—— (1987) *The Theory of Communicative Action*, vol.II (Boston: Beacon Press).
—— (1989) 'Justice and Solidarity', *The Philosophical Forum*, vol.21, pp.32–53.
—— (1990) *Moral Consciousness and Human Action* (Cambridge, Mass.: MIT Press).
—— (1996a) *Between Facts and Norms* (Cambridge: Polity Press).
—— (1996b) 'Paradigms of Law', *Cardozo Law Review*, vol.17, pp.771–84.
Hart, H. L. A. (1961) *The Concept of Law* (Oxford: Oxford University Press).
—— (1973) 'Bentham on Legal Rights', in A. W. B. Simpson (ed.), *Oxford Essays in Jurisprudence* (Oxford: Clarendon Press).
Hayek, F. A. (1976) *The Mirage of Justice* (London: Routledge & Kegan Paul).
Held, V. (ed.) (1995) *Justice and Care: Essential Readings in Feminist Ethics* (Boulder, Colo: Westview Press).
Heller, A. (1986) *Beyond Justice* (Oxford: Blackwell).
Honoré, A. M. (1970) 'Social Justice', in R. S. Summers (ed.), *Essays in Legal Philosophy* (Oxford: Basil Blackwell).
Hume, D. (1739) *A Treatise of Human Nature* (London: John Noon).
Hunt, A. (1991) *Reading Dworkin Critically* (New York: Oxford University Press).
Irigaray (1985) *Speculum of the other woman* (Ithaca, NY.: Cornell University Press)
Jackson, M. W. (1986) *Matters of Justice* (London: Croom Helm).
Katzner, L. I. (1971) 'Presumptive and Non-Presumptive Principles of Formal Justice', in *Ethics*, vol.81, pp. 253–58.
Keans, D. (1983) 'A theory of Justice – and Love: Rawls on the Family', *Politics*, vol.18, pp.36–42.
Kleinig, J. (1971) 'The Concept of Desert', *American Philosophical Quarterly*, vol.8.
Kukathas, C. (1990) *Hayek and Modern Liberalism* (Oxford: Clarendon Press).
—— and P. Pettit (1990) *Rawls's A Theory of Justice and Its Critics* (Oxford: Polity Press).
Kymlicka, W. (1989) *Liberalism, Community and Culture* (Oxford: Clarendon Press).
—— (ed.) (1992) Justice in Political Philosophy, vols 1 and 2 (Aldershot: Elgar).
Lessnoff, M. (1986) *Social Contract* (London: Macmillan).
—— (1999) *Political Philosophers of the Twentieth Century* (Oxford: Blackwell).
Lucas, J. R. (1980) *On Justice* (Oxford: Clarendon Press).
Lukes, S. (1983) 'Justice and Rights', in A. Ryan (ed.), *Justice* (Oxford: Oxford University Press).

—— (1985) *Marxism and Morality* (Oxford: Oxford University Press).
Lyons, D. (1965) *Forms and Limits of Utilitarianism* (Oxford: Clarendon Press).
MacCormick, D. N. (1977) 'Rights in Legislation', in P. M. S. Hacker and J. Raz (eds), *Law, Morality and Society* (Oxford: Clarendon Press).
MacIntyre, A. (1981) *After Virtue* (London: Duckworth).
—— (1988) *Whose Justice? Which Rationality?* (London: Duckworth).
MacKinnon, C. (1989) *Toward a Feminist Theory of the State* (Cambridge, Mass.: Harvard University Press).
Macpherson, C. B. (1977) *The Life and Times of Liberal Democracy* (Oxford: Oxford University Press).
Marx, K. and F. Engels (1958) *Selected Works*, 2 vols (London: Lawrence & Wishart).
Mill, J. S. (1863) 'Utilitarianism', in J. S. Mill (1910) *Utilitarianism, Liberty, Representative Government* (London: J. M. Dent).
Miller, D. (1976) *Social Justice* (Oxford: Clarendon Press).
—— (1992) 'Survey Article: Distributive Justice: What People Think', *Ethics* vol.102, pp.555–93.
—— and M. Walzer (eds) (1995) *Pluralism, Justice and Equality* (Oxford: Oxford University Press).
Miller, R. (1984) *Analyzing Marx* (New Haven, Conn.: Princeton University Press).
Mulhall, S. and A. Swift (1996) *Liberals and Communitarians*, 2nd edn (Oxford: Blackwell).
Murphy, J. (1979) *Retribution, Justice and Therapy* (Boston, Mass.: D. Reidel).
Nagel, T. (1991) *Equality and Partiality* (Oxford: Oxford University Press).
Nielsen, K. (1979) 'Radical Egalitarian Justice: Justice as Equality', *Social Theory and Practice*, vol.5.
Noddings, N. (1984) *Caring: A Feminine Approach to Ethics and Moral Education* (Berkeley: University of California Press).
Nozick, R. (1974) *Anarchy, State and Utopia* (Oxford: Blackwell).
—— (1989) *The Examined Life: Philosopical Meditations* (New York: Simon & Schuster).
Nussbaum, M. (1999) *Sex and Social Justice* (New York: Oxford University Press).
O'Connor, F. (1977) 'Justice, Desert and Rawls', *Philosophical Studies,* vol.25.
Okin, S. (1987) 'Justice and Gender', *Philosophy and Public Affairs*, vol.16, pp.42–72.
—— (1989) *Justice, Gender and the Family* (New York: Basic Books).
Olsen, F. (1995) *Feminist Legal Theory* (Aldershot: Dartmouth).
O'Neill, O. (1996) *Towards Justice and Virtue* (Cambridge: Cambridge University Press).
O'Neill, S. (1997) *Impartiality in Context: Grounding Justice in a Pluralist World* (Albany: State University of New York).
Pateman, C. (1998) *The Sexual Contract* (Palo Alto, Calif.: Stanford University Press).

Paul, J. (ed.) (1982) *Reading Nozick* (Oxford: Blackwell).
Pennock, J. R. and J. W. Chapman (1982) *Ethics, Economics and the Law: Nomos* XXIV (New York: New York University Press).
Perelman, C. (1963) *The Idea of Justice and the Problem of Argument* (London: Routledge & Kegan Paul)
Pettit, P. (1980) *Judging Justice* (London: Routledge & Kegan Paul).
—— (1982) 'Habermas on Truth and Justice', in G. H. R. Parkinson (ed.), *Marx and Marxisms* (Cambridge: Cambridge University Press).
Phillips, A. (1993) *Democracy and Difference* (Philadelphia Pennsylvania: Pennsylvania University Press).
Plant, R., H. Lesser and P. Taylor-Gooby (1980) *Political Philosophy and Social Welfare* (London: Routledge & Kegan Paul).
Pogge, T. (1989) *Realizing Rawls* (Ithaca, NY: Cornell University Press).
Posner, R. A. (1977) *Economic Analysis of Law,* 2nd edn (Boston, Mass.: Little, Brown).
—— (1979) 'Utilitarianism, Economics and Legal Theory', *Journal of Legal Studies*, vol.8, pp.453–76.
—— (1981) *The Economics of Justice* (Cambridge, Mass.: Harvard University Press).
—— (1985) *The Federal Courts, Crisis and Reform* (Cambridge, Mass.: Harvard University Press).
—— (1990) *Problems of Jurisprudence* (Cambridge, Mass.: Harvard University Press).
—— (1995) *Overcoming Law* (Cambridge, Mass.: Harvard University Press).
Raffel, S. (1992) *Habermas, Lyotard and the Concept of Justice* (Basingstoke: Macmillan).
Raphael, D. D. (1970) *Problems of Political Philosophy* (London: Pall Mall).
—— (1980) *Justice and Liberty* (London: The Athlone Press).
Rawls, J. (1971) *A Theory of Justice* (Oxford: Oxford University Press).
—— (1980) 'Kantian Constructivism in Moral Theory', *Journal of Philosophy*, vol.77, pp.515–34.
—— (1993) *Political Liberalism* (New York: Columbia University Press).
Raz, J. (1975) *Practical Reason and Norms* (London: Hutchinson).
—— (1982) 'The Claims of Reflective Equilibrium', *Inquiry*, vol.25, pp.307–30
—— (1990) 'Facing Diversity: The Case of Epistemic Abstinence', *Philosophy and Public Affairs*, vol.19, pp.3–46.
Rescher, N. (1966) *Distributive Justice* (Indianapolis: Bobbs-Merrill).
Roemer, J. (1982) *A General Theory of Exploitation and Class* (Cambridge, Mass.: Harvard University Press).
—— (1989) *Free to Force* (Cambridge, Mass.: Harvard University Press).
Rorty, R. (1985) 'Postmodern Bourgeois Liberalism', in R. Hollinger (ed.), *Hermeneutics and Praxis* (Notre Dame, Hyndiana: University of Notre Dame Press).
Ryan, A. (ed.) (1993) *Justice* (Oxford: Oxford University Press).
Sadurski, W. (1985) *Giving Desert its Due: Social Justice and Legal Theory* (Dordrecht: Reidel).

Sandel, M. J. (1982) *Liberalism and the Limits of Justice* (New York: Cambridge University Press).

Sen, A. K. (1970) *Collective Choice and Social Welfare* (San Francisco: Holden-Day).

—— (1992) *Inequality Reexamined* (New York: Russell Sage Foundation).

Sher, G. (1979) 'Effort, Ability and Personal Desert', *Philosophy and Public Affairs*, vol.8, pp.361–76.

—— (1997) *Beyond Neutrality: Perfectionism and Politics* (Cambridge: Cambridge University Press).

Sidgwick, H. (1901) *The Methods of Ethics*, 6th edn (London: Macmillan).

Singer, P. (1993) *Practical Ethics* (Cambridge: Cambridge University Press)

Slote, M. A. (1973) 'Desert, Consent and Justice', *Philosophy and Public Affairs*, vol.2, pp.323–47

Smart, C. (1989) *The Power of Law* (London: Routledge).

Sterba, J. P. (1974) 'Justice as Desert', *Social Theory and Practice,* vol.3.

—— (1986), Recent work on Alternative conceptions of justice'. American Philosophical, ILL Quarterly, vol.23, pp.1–22.

Sunstein, C. (ed.) (1990) *Feminism and Political Theory* (Chicago, IL: Chicago University Press).

Taylor, C. (1985) *Philosophical Papers* (Cambridge: Cambridge University Press).

Tronto, J. C. (1989) 'Women and Caring: What Can Feminists Learn about Morality from Caring?', in A. Jagger and R. S. Bordo (eds), *Gender/ Body/Knowledge* (Newark, NJ: Rutgers University Press).

van der Veen, R. and van Parijs, P. (1985) 'Entitlement Theories of Justice: From Nozick to Roemer and Beyond', *Economics and Philosophy*, vol.1, pp.69–81.

Veljanovski, C. J. (1982) *The New Law and Economics* (Oxford: Centre for Socio-Legal Studies).

Waldron, J. (1984) *Theories of Rights* (Oxford: Oxford University Press).

—— (1988) *The Right to Private Property* (Oxford: Clarendon Press).

Walzer, M. (1983) *Spheres of Justice* (Oxford: Martin Robertson).

—— (1990) 'The Communitarian Critique of Liberalism', *Political Theory*, vol.18, pp.6–23.

Warnke, G. (1992) *Justice and Interpretation* (Cambridge: Polity Press).

Weale, A. (1983) *Political Theory and Social Policy* (London: Macmillan).

Wolgast, E. (1987) *The Grammar of Justice* (Ithaca, NY: Cornell University Press).

Wolff, J. (1991) *Robert Nozick: Property, Justice and the Minimal State* (Cambridge: Polity Press).

—— (1996) *An Introduction to Political Philosophy* (Oxford: Oxford University Press).

Wolff, R. P. (1977) *Understanding Rawls* (New Haven, Conn.: Princeton University Press).

Wood, A. W. (1983) *Karl Marx* (London: Routledge & Kegan Paul).

Young, I. M. (1990) *Justice and the Politics of Difference* (New Haven, Conn.: Princeton University Press).

—— (1993) 'Justice and Communicative Democracy', in R. S. Gottlieb (ed.), *Radical Philosophy* (Philadelphia: Temple Press).

—— (1997) *Intersecting Voices: Dilemmas of Gender, Political Philosophy and Policy* (New Haven, Conn.: Princeton University Press).

Zaitchik, A. (1977) 'On Deserving to Deserve', *Philosophy and Public Affairs*, vol.6, pp.370–88

Index